CONSTRUCTED ECOSYSTEMS

IDEAS AND SUBSYSTEMS IN THE WORK OF KEN YEANG

KEN YEANG
SHIREEN JAHNKASSIM
HUMAEDAH ROSLY
ROBERT POWELL

APPLIED RESEARCH +DESIGN PUBLISHING

CONSTRUCTED ECOSYSTEMS

IDEAS AND SUBSYSTEMS IN THE WORK OF KEN YEANG

KEN YEANG

SHIREEN JAHNKASSIM

HUMAEDAH ROSLY

ROBERT POWELL

APPLIED RESEARCH
+DESIGN
PUBLISHING

ESSAYS

IDEAS AND SUBSYSTEMS

CONTENTS

DEVELOPING SUBSYSTEMS: EVOLUTIONARY TRAJECTORY

Ken Yeang's work over the last four decades follows an evolutionary trajectory starting from his early doctoral research through investigative work in his professional life as an architect, during which he continued to research, write, teach, design and build. This full range of discursive activities enables him to carry out a cross-pollinated in-house programme – a version of industry R&D. A better description of his process of work, where there is continuous development of ideas and subsystems, might be RD&D or Research, Design and Development. The outcome of this process is a number of innovative subsystems found in his built work.

In the process of implementing his abstract ecological theories and ideas originating from his early doctoral dissertation, Yeang has been forced by necessity to devise devices for built work. Some date from the early 1980s, others are more recent. These contribute to an inventory of components dedicated to ecologically-driven architecture and masterplans. They form part of Yeang's contribution, albeit at the micro level of subsystems, to architectural discourse in the 21st century.

The 'Double Roof' was first used by Yeang in a house designed in 1984. The aptly named Roof-Roof House in Kuala Lumpur, Malaysia, has become an icon of green design, studied over its thirty-year life by numerous academics and architectural students who have used it as a primer for their own research.

'Mixed-Mode Cooling' was also used in the Roof-Roof House. Yeang's use of mixed-mode cooling is a hybrid approach that combines natural ventilation and low-energy mechanical systems, including air-distribution mechanisms. The basic mixed-mode strategy is to encourage natural ventilation when the outside temperature is conducive, and, in periods when the external temperature is not favourable, to change over to a mechanically assisted ventilation system. In 1992, mixed-mode cooling would be employed in the Menara Mesiniaga and subsequently in most of his other projects, including the National Library of Singapore in 2005 and the Solaris project in Singapore in 2010.

The effectiveness of a mixed-mode design is dependent on benign interaction between the interior of a built form and exterior ambient forces. Mixed-mode built forms usually have greater transparency and complexity because they admit and control ambient energy sources. The development of a mixed mode in a built form is dependent on the cost-effective exploitation of ambient energy sources without incurring any penalties in terms of discomfort.

Design strategies usually associated with these buildings include the use of solar gain in temperate climates for winter warmth, natural lighting, and ventilation. Mixed-mode use aims to create as natural of an internal environment as possible, while building occupants have control over their environment and thermal comfort via opening windows

ROBERT POWELL

ABOVE
Plaza of Nations

and drawing blinds. In a competition entry for Sheffield Children's Hospital in 2012, Yeang employed both passive heating and passive cooling in the three-storey entrance atrium; a built example of mixed-mode design in a temperate climate is the Morgan Stanley Clinical Buildings at Great Ormond Street Hospital (GOSH), built in London in 2011. Examples of other mixed-mode systems include ceiling fans, demister fans, double facades, and Trombe walls.

Yeang also experimented with 'Evaporative Cooling' in the design of the Roof-Roof House, where a swimming pool is located upwind of the principal habitable areas. This subsystem would later find its way into other projects, including the design of the Mumbai Glassworks Tower (2012), where a resident's private swimming pool is located in the northwest corner of the tower at podium roof level so that the wind blowing from the west/northwest provides evaporative cooling to residential apartments.

The concept of 'Green Ecoinfrastructure' is central to many of Yeang's projects, from the 1998 EDITT Tower in Singapore and the 1998 BATC Tower in Germany to those currently underway. Green ecoinfrastructure is essentially a network of interconnected natural areas and open spaces within a site that links to surrounding vegetation and habitats. That framework provides water management through drainage infrastructure that manages rainfall and run-off to bioswales, retention ponds, and permeable surfaces. In 2001, green ecoinfrastructure formed the basis of the West Kowloon Waterfront in, Hong Kong, and again in the 2007 Plaza of Nations project in Vancouver, Canada. Green ecoinfrastructure is also central to the 2008 Zorlu Ecocity project in Istanbul and the 2008 SOMA Masterplan in Bangalore. In 2010, the masterplan for the Gyeong-Gi Complex in Seoul, South Korea, commenced with an examination of the green ecoinfrastructure, similar to the Solaris project in Singapore in 2010 and the L Tower in Kuala Lumpur in 2013.

Yeang's 'Green Wall' is essentially a continuation of green ecoinfrastructure into the vertical plane and establishes a continuous habitat on the façade of a building, thereby enhancing its ecological performance and contributing to the site's biodiversity. This green armature is especially conducive to populations of butterflies and species of small birds. Green walls reduce solar gain and, by extension, building energy costs, but principally they provide ecological continuity.

The concept of the green wall was first explored by Yeang in his 1985 design for the IBM Plaza in Kuala Lumpur that incorporated stepped planter boxes. It was also employed in a competition entry for the Tokyo-Nara Tower in Nagoya in 2003. Later, it would be

used by Yeang in another competition entry for Zorlu Ecocity in 2008 and for the Plaza of Nations complex in Vancouver that same year. In built form it is most visibly demonstrated in the DiGi Technical Operations Centre in Selangor and is incorporated in the design of the Mumbai Glassworks Tower.

Yet another subsystem, 'Skycourts', entered Yeang's architectural vocabulary in 1992 with the design of the iconic Menara Mesiniaga and would appear in quick succession in the 1993 MBF Tower and Menara UMNO, completed in 1997. Skycourts provide the users of tall buildings with direct access to a naturally ventilated external environment. More importantly, they act as thermal buffers and reduce the ambient temperature of buildings.

Skycourts were later employed for the Tokyo-Nara Tower in 2003, the National Library of Singapore in 2005 and the Zorlu Ecocity in 2008. In the 31-storey Mumbai Glassworks Tower, two-storey-high skycourts are provided for every apartment in addition to six communal skycourts. These 'outdoor rooms' provide space for cultivation of herbs such as coriander, mint, jasmine, fenugreek, and red pepper; these edible plants assist in meeting bio-diversity targets. Skycourts also were a key ingredient in the design of a 2008 project for Jabi Lake Gardens, a mixed-use development in Nigeria.

The 'Linear Park-in-the-sky' device was first explored by Yeang in his 1998 EDITT Tower and next appeared in his 2003 design for the Tokyo-Nara Tower. Its built form emerged from the 2005 Mewah Oils HQ in Selangor and again, most spectacularly, in the 1.5-kilometre-long ascending landscaped ramp designed for Solaris in Singapore and completed in 2010. A linear park-in-the-sky was a key element of the 2010 design for the Geong-Gi Complex in Seoul.

Down-draft Cooling is an experimental system based on precedence from hot, dry climates of the Middle East that was used in a competition entry for Sheffield Children's Hospital in 2012. Down-draft cooling employs a 'wind chimney' and is the focus of research currently being carried out by a team at IIUM to verify its effectiveness in tropical climates.

Another device, the 'Raincheck Wall', was developed and used in the Solaris project in 2010, and a 'Double-Layer Façade' is being implemented in an office and retail complex currently under construction in the Malaysian Federal Capital of Putrajaya.

Many architects and regulatory authorities assume that green design simply means compliance with an accreditation system such as LEED or BREEAM or designing carbon-neutral architecture. But there remains much more to be investigated and invented before a totally green built system or architecture can be achieved.

The components and subsystems presented here illustrate ways in which ecological architecture could advance technically by the implementation of subsystems that articulate and enhance 'passive-mode' bioclimatic low-energy design or subsystems that foster ecological integration between organic constituents such as landscape and the human-made, mostly inorganic built environment.

Other devices and subsystems not presented here include Light Tubes (S Tower, Malaysia), Light Shelves (National Library of Singapore and Sheffield Children's Hospital), Rainwater Harvesting (Madinat Al-Arab, Dubai), Constructed Habitats (Bedok Apartments, Singapore), Wind Scoops (TTDI Phase 6D, Kuala Lumpur), and Multi-Seasonal Solar Shading Systems (MARG Tower, Switzerland).

Worldwide, sustainable design has advanced significantly over the last 5 to 10 years, so much so that now almost every architect lays claim to utilizing sustainable or green design. What differentiates the work of Yeang is its ecology-driven ethos. By being ecology-based it is more environmentally holistic, including consideration of both the organic constituents and the inorganic constituents of the environment acting as a whole. Many architects give only token consideration to organic constituents; the focus of such architects is on technical compliance. But Yeang's contention is that ecoarchitecture needs to fully embrace the natural world and to design buildings as 'living systems'.

Green design today is still in its adolescent phase, and there is considerable work to be done with respect to theoretical development, technical development, architectural integration and aesthetic development. The intention of this publication is to illustrate the need for such developmental work, and presented here are some of the subsystems and devices adopted or in the course of development by Yeang as a part of global green design discourse.

FACING PAGE
Plaza IBM (1984–87)

ABOVE
Roof-Roof House (1985)

THE ECO-ARCHITECTURE OF HAMZAH AND YEANG: STRADDLING DESIGN AND PERFORMANCE

Centuries ago, Vitruvius's three virtues of architecture, Firmitas, Utilitas, and Venustas, (strength, unity, and beauty) gave architects and builders the essential principles and fundamentals for design. Today, with the growing spectre of environmental devastation and global climate change, the timeless principles of Vitruvius must evolve into principles founded upon the virtues of quantifiable performance including reducing the use of non-renewable energy, minimizing of carbon emissions, and conservation of natural resources. Such criteria must eventually translate into the expressive field of architectural language and grammar. Similar to the Classical 'orders'; which in Classicism are defined as the underlying method and principle of beauty of the Antiquities; there must be a new set of 'orders' of architecture. The columns, shaft, capital, pediment and the entablature had made up a language that reflected the fundamentals, ideas and principles of Classicism. Similarly, ideas and criteria must now be reworked into a new palette of expression, a new language and grammar of architecture; one that expresses sustainability at its core.

As the world marches on into the 21st century, on the one hand, technology has never been more gleaming or attractive. Yet at the same time an era has begun where human-generated impairment of the natural world is unprecedented and threatens a discontinuation of humanity's standard of living. Buildings today consume approximately 50% of the electricity produced in the world. Whether commercial, institutional or residential, buildings and structures are responsible for approximately 30% of greenhouse gas emissions.

At the dawn of the 20th century, the world stood at a similar precipice – waiting with heightened expectations towards a new ethic grounded in a social agenda. The ethics and ideals of Modernism would give rise to a new aesthetic in architecture. After witnessing the destruction fraught by the two World Wars, architectural ideals converged onto functionalism and built upon the belief of the triumph of rationality over eclecticism – a philosophy championed by the Modern Masters. In both theory and practice, they brought forth the underlying principles of a movement with the intention of placing architecture on a rational and mathematical footing in order to render it as a part of 'truth'. Modernism was derived from such a rational basis of design but fused with a social agenda. These grew from the ashes of two World Wars into an acceptable spatial and constructional ethic which gave form to an aesthetic predisposition – in order to rebuild a 'new world' on a massive scale for a growing population.

Today, sustainable architecture must similarly leap from an ethic to an aesthetic. Architectural metaphors must now become 'operational' metaphors. Symbolic functionalism must be replaced by an ecological functionalism. As climate change looms over the

BELOW
Environmental Performance Analysis for the TTDI Residence

SHIREEN JAHNKASSIM

world today, an eco-ethic must become the dominating force influencing world economies and population lifestyles. This new ecological movement must give rise to an eco-aesthetic: one that must re-invigorate the now seemingly defunct fundamentals of Modernism. Looking at the recent architecture of many rapidly growing regions, we find a depressing gap between the march of modernization and the memory of vernacular traditions. This gap is a recurring urban phenomenon. Lessons learnt intuitively in traditional architecture seem to have been forgotten, while imported alien forms and construction methods are embraced and constructed at a rapid rate.

It is at this multifarious yet dichotomous juncture that stands the contribution of the constructed ecosystems of Ken Yeang. The architecture of Ken Yeang, with its own didactic premises and aesthetic propositions, stands at this precipice and junction; and represents one of the ways forward. It shares the ethic of eco-activism found outside of architecture. It seeks a solution through the expressive medium of architecture. Not only does it serve the environment by mediating it through practical action built on sustainable plans and solutions, but it also contributes to consolidating a new ethic. It seeks to transform idealistic and abstract visions for a sustainable future into ground-breaking outcomes. The resultant innovations, though experimental in some cases, contribute even from a small extent, to the reconstitution of the natural environment. Such endeavours are crucial not only to a socio-economic development but will congeal into an eventual global impact. They represent a consistent, cumulative and collective effort to improve the lives of people through both performance and representation. It is but one part of a global movement towards a new hope and a sustainable future.

Yeang, in the development of his bioclimatic theories, has not only presented visions but spurred innovation in his own work but in the work of many others. This work has evolved into its own architectural language: It contains a set of premises for design, which could potentially become part of the new 'order' for an environmentally responsive language and vocabulary. As with similar endeavours that start out as pioneering and avant-gardist efforts, they have become part of the continuum of global movements for green architecture, taking a route not unlike that of other avant-gardist movements of modernity that dominated the early years of the 20th century.

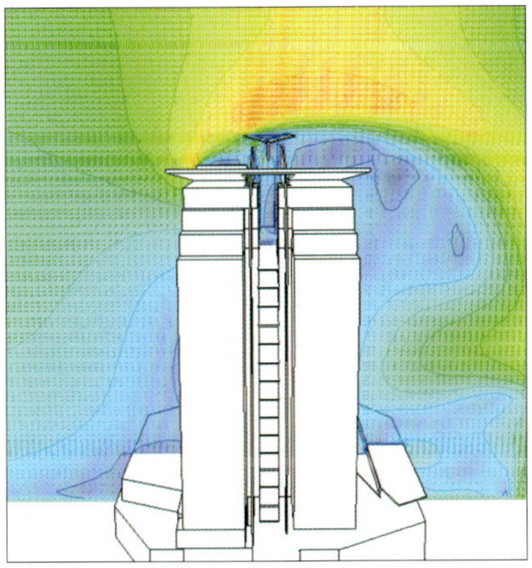

To articulate a consequent form, language and syntax, the new eco-architecture must be founded upon an ecological ethic that ultimately seeks a carbon-neutral ideal. Its architecture and its features must be re-aligned with the fields of the environmental, biological and ecological sciences. It must be founded upon new modes of architectural enquiry and critique based on environmental and scientific criteria and precepts. To revolutionize architecture, a new treatise of design must be formulated based on the urgency of climate change. Low carbon buildings must inevitably relate to, and selectively use, the forces of the surrounding climate, and subsequently be an almost seamless and benign bridge to the natural environment.

The beneficial use of ambient environmental factors (such as wind, daylight, sunlight, landscape, etc.) must be brought into the realm of the optimisation of 3-dimensional form and masterplans. At TRHY, this has been a practice undertaken through a continuous development process. The process responds to an analytical cycle. By adopting environmentally appropriate forms and optimizing their features and components, not only is the extent of environmental impact reduced, but design 'performs' both as a function and a symbol. Form becomes a statement of environmental sustainability. These cannot come about through gratuitous features. Analysis – whether through manual or computational methods – needs to be integrated with the designing. This translates into a process in contrast with conventional design. Analytical outcomes in the form of computerised simulations and manual calculations, must drive and inform design decisions at all stages. Such empirical outcomes and calculations become the basis and the drive behind the expression of built form.

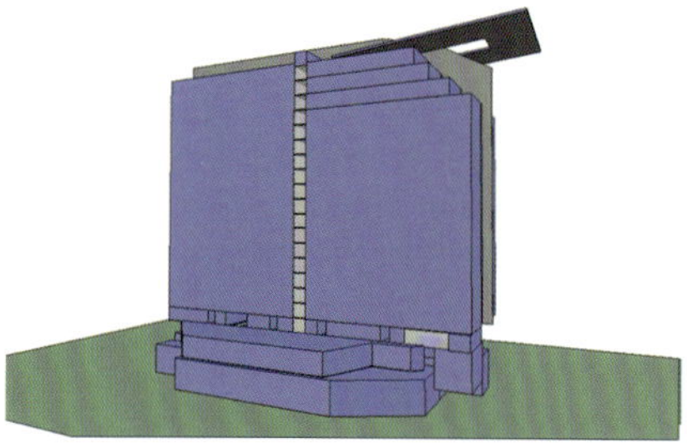

Yeang's ideas, systems and devices, such as solar shading, skycourts, vertical landscaping, ecocells, wind shafts, wind walls and other passive cooling techniques, are outcomes of a new pathway. Integral as parts of an aesthetic and a grammar, the subsystems must be empirically assessed at all times to ensure compliance with rigorous standards. This is achieved by being continuously tested, experimented on, and fine-tuned to maximise their performance in relation to ambient climatic conditions. Bioclimatic design requires that built form, its assemblies and its features be 'adjusted' to any region's climatic parameters. For example, the challenges of a tropical climate arise from an intense and generally singular type of climate regime (as compared to multiple seasons in other regions). As urbanisation explodes and expands in tropical countries, the equatorial climate's lack of extreme seasonal variability, the prevalence of low winds and the presence of high wet-bulb temperatures and humidity can drive architectural outcomes. This is in opposition to current buildings which function as mindless 'boxes' and with the use of high-energy consuming solutions.

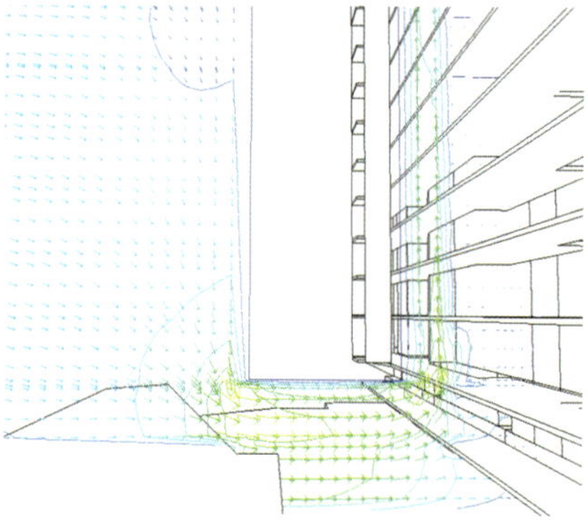

A carbon-neutral ethic implies a passive-mode or a low-energy strategy. This inevitably implies that both architecture and climatically-varied structures have to adapt to more climatically-varied environments. This ultimately must render a more forgiving acceptance by building users due to such fluctuations. A passive-mode building requires its occupants to be more adaptive and tolerant towards comfort conditions – compared to the high level of built environment. Such a consistent 'full-mode' mechanically controlled internal environment (such as in a fully air-conditioned space or a fully heated space in temperate zones) often produce 'bland' boxes. In most cases, to have a zero-carbon or carbon-neutral built form, necessitates an avoidance of a full-mode system of energy dependence in creating comfort conditions and such a stance or 'position' in design will give rise into its own formal expression.

It is important to note that despite the careful synchronisation of built form with the climate and ecology of its locality, the passive-mode design approach cannot compete with the full-mode approach in terms of the reliable provision of comfort and fulfilment of human expectations at all times. In many cases, they do not consistently operate at 100%. Climatically, Yeang's mixed-mode approach is intended for those opportune days in the year when wind forces sufficiently achieve an enhanced comfort condition as well as for compensation when wind forces are insufficient. This must consistently be coupled with the necessary control of solar gain. Features such as the combination of double walls and shading are crucial whenever natural ventilation is utilized. The negative impact of solar heat gain should not be allowed to overwhelm the positive benefits of airflow.

Ideas and devices in built form relate to the derivation of the 'tectonics' of a sustainable architecture. As postulated by Kenneth Frampton in Studies in Tectonic Culture: The Poetics of Construction in Nineteenth and Twentieth Century Architecture (Cambridge: MIT Press, 2001), where the architecture must avoid the 'culture of consumption' and coalesce into a more sustainable, constructionally varied language. To some extent, a more layered interpretation of the components of a built form (such as its walls, roofs, floors, double roof, landscape, and vertical shading) is needed. To generate a rich and expressive aesthetic instead of a dumb and sealed glass 'box', sustainable design must express and differentiate itself aesthetically from the current stock of buildings. Yeang's double roof, double walls and vertical shading not only operatively achieve the requisite thermal protection, but are intended to create the differentiated language of a 'shadowed' and 'layered' tectonic. While one can achieve the requisite minimum OTTV values, U value and shading coefficient values using a single piece of high-performance glass, the contention here is that these standards must generate their own expression. The environmental ethic must give rise to its own forms and tectonic systems. These become the physical and visual expressions of that ethic.

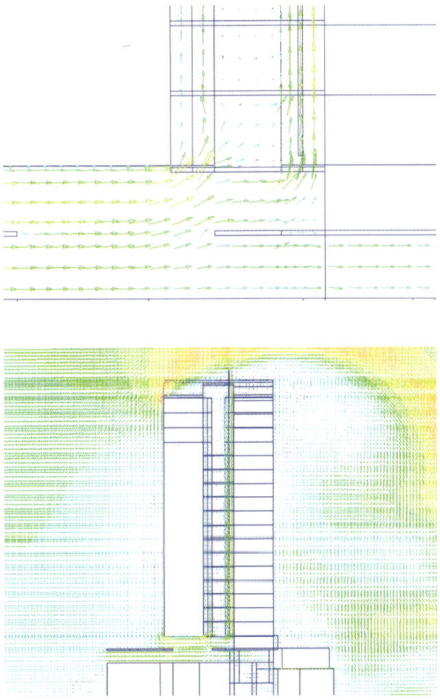

Environmental Performance Analysis for the TTDI Residence

Yeang's architecture to this day, is one that potentially bridges this gap. It is possible to be contemporary, utilising technological advances, yet rooted in durable traditional linkages to the climate of a place. 'Bringing in the climate to recall ancient wisdoms' is not only an ideal but a living dynamism reinterpreted in contemporary ways. Researchers in sustainability have come to conclude that sustainable design often involves bringing back earlier architectural wisdoms and principles. The ancients did not 'seal' dwellers out of his or her environment. They did not create the spatial disjuncture that we see in many urban built forms of today. There is always that respectful and recurrent link to nature. Through evolved built forms, they pay homage and obeisance to the living forces and 'soul' of the natural environment.

In this new eco-aesthetics forms, occupants, particularly urban dwellers, including those of the tropics, must adjust their standards and expectations of comfort. They must 're-ac-climatise' to natural settings. Through re-acclimatisation, the expectations of thermal comfort will be lowered and human beings will become re-accustomed to the more subtle dynamics of indoor environmental conditions and more acceptable of the variability of external conditions. Part of the problem of excessive air-conditioning in cities is the acclimatisation of dwellers to the consistently sealed, dry, cool air. This has come about with the onset of urbanisation and modernization. People have become accustomed to a consist-ently constant temperature throughout the day. They work and live in air-conditioned spaces, drive in air-conditioned cars, and shop in air-conditioned retail centres. With this, comes increased health issues, such as the rising trend of obesity, as well as the overall reduced health of urban dwellers. All are part and parcel of the outcome of these urban trends and lifestyles. It is reflective of the disjuncture of man and his natural environment.

There must be a reversion to the natural and the environmental. Yet, we cannot turn back the clock and revert in totality to the traditional ways. We need 'new', modern ways that achieve the same goal. We need to allow for the climatic elements to complement the technology of central heating and cooling. The successful environmental performance of novel bioclimatic subsystems depends on external climatic elements, yet these vary throughout the day and the year. Users need to welcome such variability. The aim is to achieve adaptive comfort, not shun the climate. Occupants cannot expect consistent internal environmental regimes. They must be aware that to be connected to a low-carbon future means to be to reconditioned to accept a more climate-responsive way of life. Accepting the variability of the climate and the variable ways one can use passive sustainable buildings implies that not all the passive devices and subsystems can function fully or as effectively as intended.

Passive 'bioclimatic design' can be traced to the roots of bioclimatic regionalism, advocated in the 1960s by the likes of Victor and Aladar Olgyay and Baruch Givoni, and later advanced by practitioners such as Dean Hawkes, Alan Short and Fielden Clegg. Since the advent of computerized methods and calculations, such computational processes have become inevitable parts of sustainable design. Bioclimatic architecture is a process that optimizes the ambient energies of a locality and attempts to synchronise climate with occupant comfort. In intense climates, this represents a challenging design task and goal.

Yeang's experiments in ecological subsystems are phases towards this goal. They ultimately refer to a continuing agenda to integrate climate with built form. The challenge seems to be, at its most acute, in the tropics. This is where prevailing heat and humidity conflicts with the constant achievement of thermal comfort. The use of analytical tools, such as solar sun path trajectory, daylight analysis, and computational fluid dynamics, must ensure the validity of their output, which needs to be affirmed through on-site monitored data. There must be a drive towards a continuous programme in the pursuit of innovation. There must be constant experimentation with an aim to complete the explorative process, which must end with the continuous post-occupancy analysis of these devices and subsystems for future improvements. At times, these studies reveal other unintended and unexpected benefits. Yeang's linear parks and vegetated skycourts have been found to have psychological benefits for building occupants and users – for example, the view and proximity of greenery afforded at the higher levels of a high-rise built form.

An example of this cycle: 'innovative idea, integrated design process, climatic and site context analysis, simulation, construction, post-occupancy analysis' is Yeang's down-draft wind shaft feature in a recent Malaysian residential project. In other climates, such down-draft features are part and parcel of catching 'windier and clearer' air high up in the urban environment. In Malaysia, this was found to cause overwhelming wind influx during storms, whereas during periods of still air sudden wind movements did not cause enough internal airflow. Yet the device represents a valuable experiment in this innovative endeavour. An art gallery had its own special requirements to be 'free' from internal partitioning to provide space for exhibitions. This particular project also aimed to address urban issues such as polluted air on the ground level and the fact that low-rise residences will have higher densities that inhibit typical window cross-ventilation. They are more prone to dust pollution caused by intensive surrounding urban construction and sources from traffic. One aim was to catch the less-polluted air 'higher up' and use fewer windows

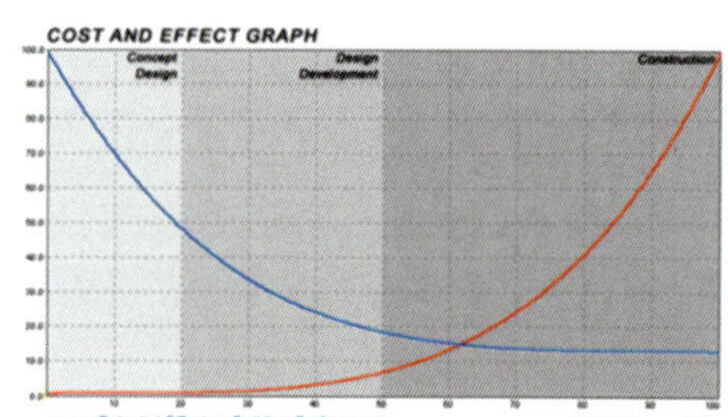

ABOVE
The Integrated Design Process (IDP) is significant in the Early Design Stage (EDS). It is estimated that 20% of decisions made during EDS influence 80% of later design impact (Source: Interoperability and Sustainable Design AEC bytes, 2008)

'lower down'. During post-occupancy monitoring it was found that occupants deviated from the expected opening and closing of doors and windows, and did not resemble the conditions of modelling inputs. Occupants left doors open towards the terraced patio to afford the view and ventilation to the courtyard garden. While full cross-ventilation across the length of the gallery could not be achieved, on days of higher ambient winds good internal wind speed occurred, and at times openings needed to be shut as some artwork would flap uncontrollably. During occupancy, data was collected to analyse the performance of the down-draft and measure the magnitude and direction of airflow across time.

Yeang's vegetative features such as linear parks, climbing vegetation, and ecocells demand a higher level of planting and landscaping maintenance (e.g., in the DiGi building and IBM Plaza). Yet such greenery inclusions are vital for the process of carbon capture, reduced carbon emissions and improved air quality in both the specific site and the surrounding urban context. There is a difference between a low-carbon target and a low-energy target, where the former is more long-term and relates to global levels of carbon emission. Ultimately, a low-carbon approach entails both carbon-reduction strategies– primarily through energy efficiency, and carbon-offset strategies – primarily through planting vegetation and greenery for carbon sequestration and absorption. The drive towards a low-carbon future cannot happen without a movement toward integrating more greenery into the urban environment and structures. There must be a balance between carbon emission and absorption. Features that integrate greenery must become a part of our long-term equation toward ecological balance.

In the TTDI Plaza and apartments, the challenge of high-rise development is to facilitate increased social and commercial activities within the urban structure by achieving acceptable comfort conditions for users without committing them to a life of air-conditioned spaces and high-energy consumption. The post-occupancy studies on airflow magnitude and distribution contribute to advancing knowledge on how to enhance thermal comfort without air conditioning. It also provides further understanding of the linkages between thermal comfort, human activities and semi-opened environmental conditions in a tropical climate.

Throughout the evolution of his projects, Yeang has developed an architectural language that emerges from his assemblies and subsystems. These technical 'eco-features' have been prototyped and fine-tuned from inherent processes. These ecologic and bioclimatic subsystems are products of a focused team working in an integrated mode of design. This typically involves interactions between architects, engineers, building scientists and ecologists whose work is supported by quantitative analyses that drive strategic design decisions. Eco-designs are modified and enhanced towards optimised subsystems. These represent a continuing progression and development from one project to another. The architecture of Ken Yeang emerges from these processes as one that continuously pursues discovery and innovation. It is an ethic that drives architectonic form and give rise to an eventual aesthetic. Fundamentally, it recognizes the straddling of design and performance. It is this iterative and knowledge-based process within an overall objective of environmental stewardship and mitigation of climate change that will aid in the eventual reduction of the effects of local and global environmental pollutants on humanity, and on the Earth.

APPLIED RESEARCH IN DESIGNING

Our work on ecoarchitecture is best described as 'RD&D' – a programme of research and development through designing, carried out as investigative and experimental work while concurrently delivering built projects in a professional design organisation.

This RD&D work is done at four general levels of investigation – on premises, on theories, on interpretations, and on aesthetic explorations of green design and ecoarchitecture. The premises are the axioms that are the starting basis for the reasoning underlying our work; these are the springboards enabling our deducing and inferring of other aspects that provide fundamental empirical bases for theoretical aspects of ecodesign. Theory is the general explanatory framework for green design that evolves from premises and ideas. Following this are technical interpretations by design, physical manifestations of theoretical work as applied research that demonstrate formal possibilities in built configurations, devices and sub-systems in the physical application and testing of theoretical propositions. Our preoccupation further involves aesthetic development as an endeavour to ascertain the visual imaging of what constitutes the aesthetics of ecoarchitecture and ecomasterplans, seeking to discover what these could look like, perhaps as a style.

In totality, our investigative work approximates a programme for research, discovery and invention. The developmental work on each is not sequential but generally done in conjunction with designing and delivering built projects.

In practice, such RD&D work is hampered by the vicissitudes of project-based activity, impacted by extraneous factors outside research work such as pressing external demands in a fast-tracked programme of delivery, not enabling complete testing of prototypes or the reiteration of simulations, the physical constraints of the project site by local constructional limitations, by budgetary limitations or by constraints arising from the need to comply with local governmental requirements as well as a multitude of other possibilities. As such, what might be a promising idea with potential could have its subsequent adoption, development and realization curtailed due to commercial circumstances or rejection by the project's sponsor. The emergent idea then has to be kept on hold, with the hope of being resurfaced and adopted on another occasion when a suitable opportunity appears that will offer amenable conditions for its inclusion and implementation.

The relevance and rationale underlying an ad hoc investigative programme of RD&D work are simply that an ongoing professional practice provides extensive and unique location-specific opportunities for experimentation and invention. This is not always found in the formality of a research laboratory. The demands in a project-based programme are by necessity the generation of rapid responses by the designer as insights and ideas. The pressure of this condition encourages serendipity in the creative design process and in unpredicted 'eureka' moments.

In our journey of experimentation and the continued maturing of work at these levels of investigation, we became aware of gaps in the field of ecodesign at each level.

KEN YEANG

These provide impetus and opportune areas for us to seek solutions. Discussed here is some of our work as applied research in design interpretations of axioms and theoretical frameworks as technical solutions and 'subsystems' in an endeavour to bridge the gaps between knowledge and practice in ecodesign.

The fundamental premise underlying our work on ecoarchitecture is the design objective to achieve a seamless and benign biointegration of our built environment and our activities within the natural environment. This includes everything that we make and produce, as well as everything that we do on land, on waterways and in the air.

The design approach is to bring together four factors holistically as a system – human society and its actions and activities, the ecology of the environment, the water cycle and its management and ecoengineering systems. These together become the broad theoretical framework for our ecodesigns, for which the challenge then is to find effective formal solutions that interpret the issues of each through design into built forms and working technical subsystems.

The first factor to be considered is us, humans. In seeking to achieve a sustainable future, there must be radical changes in ourselves, in our global society and its myriad of socio-economic, political and physical systems.

This involves radical changes to our current profligate ways of life and to our commerce, economic and social systems that have been prevalent over time, such as in our production of artefacts and food products for contemporary life, as well as changes to our industrial and mass-production systems, our mobility and transportation systems and to other activities such as recreation, all of which must become 'green' and environmentally responsive.

Just designing and delivering green buildings and artefacts is not sufficient – we need to extend the knowledge of ecodesign to the public at large, to educate and help them change their ways with respect to all of the above areas. This ambition requires an effort beyond the usual professional realm of the designer, but nevertheless we need to recognise that effecting these changes in society will require the involvement of others if we are to have a greater impact than just a few green building designs.

The second factor to be biointegrated is the ecology of the environment. Ecology is the branch of science dealing with the interrelation between the environment and organisms, but more fundamentally between humans and the natural environment. The natural environment is the biosphere, the thin film at the surface of the planet where organisms live and which provides the context for all our human activities, including all that we make, build, use and throw away.

ABOVE
C-Building

The issue here is that the planet is a closed system; there is no 'away'. Our discarded stuff and emissions have to go somewhere, and it is the impact of these unaccounted discharges, whether gaseous, liquid or solid, that cause much of the global environmental issues today, compounded by our other acts of impairment to the natural environment.

Then comes consideration of water, a factor that is fundamentally vital for all organic life and existence. We need to close the water cycle in as much as possible rather than have a throughput system of use and discharge. We need to manage it within its locality of use as a precious resource.

The final factor is engineering, crucial here because it provides the technological systems and subsystems that support human life and its expectations for comfort, mobility and commercial activity.

We can refer to all the above factors as armatures of sets of 'infrastructures', where green design is the biointegration of all four into a holistic functioning system.

The contents of our present built environment are mostly synthetic, artificial and denatured, besides also existing separately and alienated from nature.

Nature, prior to human intervention, existed in a general state of stasis even as its ecosystems went through stages of succession. Our built environment needs to mimic this stasis in a similar symbiotic state of stability within itself as a 'constructed ecosystem', and at the same time our built environment needs to become an integral part of nature rather than separate from it.

We can refer to this endeavour as 'biomimicry', designing to imitate the ecosystem's attributes, properties and processes. This includes, for instance, mimicking the way materials are recycled within ecosystems. There the waste of one organism becomes the food of another. Other aspects to mimic are the biological structure of the ecosystem, where there is a balance of biotic constituents and abiotic constituents acting together as a whole, and an ecosystem's renewable solar energy source.

This framework of the four sets of ecoinfrastructures and their biointegration as a system becomes, for us, a flexible 'platform' for green design. It provides the basis for designing beyond, for instance, the simplistic compliance to an accreditation system, which is essentially a checklist set of prescriptive items, or designing beyond carbon-neutral cleantech engineering systems.

The ecoinfrastructure platform for ecodesign is analogous to the DNA model of Francis Crick and James Watson, where the approach is to reduce the complexity of DNA to four simple sets of instructions. Here, our four sets of ecoinfrastructures provide a flexible structure and framework for a comprehensive approach to green design. Of course, successfully achieving this is easier said than done, but herein lies the challenge in finding design solutions and appropriate subsystems to interpret these into built form.

The key factor in ecological design starts with us humans. We need to question our own demands on the environment and our actions upon it. We need to start with this as the first crucial factor in design – simply stated, the less we need from the environment, the less we will impact it. We can refer to our human society and communities as human ecoinfrastructure, one of the four factors to biointegrate.

HYPER GREEN

- Ecological continuity from ground planes both vertically and horizontally
- Enhances biodiversity
- Ecocells
- Ecobridges
- Ecoundercrofts
- Green Roofs
- Green Walls
- Constructed Wetland
- Bioswales

HAPPY & PLEASURABLE ENVIRONMENT

- Parks and Open Spaces
- Safe Community
- Community Facilities & Amenities
- Barrier-Free Environment

INTEGRATED CONNECTIVITY

- 7-minute walkable neighbourhoods
- Links to roads and highways
- Safe parking spaces
- Parks and green spaces
- Public realm

THIS SPREAD
Green diagram

AESTHETICALLY BEAUTIFUL

- Biophilic
- Organic form engaging with the local ecology
- Blending with the site and surroundings
- Cultural identity

FUNCTIONAL

- Meets criteria
- Within cost
- High quality
- Strategic

SMART CITY

- Private and common information infrastructure
- Outdoor WiFi coverage and high-speed broadband on the go
- Technological sustainability
- Smart utility poles
- Public safety and security

Humans, although being only one of the multitude of species in nature, have immense power, literally moving hills and landforms and significantly changing landscapes, modifying and redirecting waterways and discharging gaseous, solid and liquid matter into the environment that affects global climate and ecology, all of which is generally made possible by the extensive use of non-renewable energy resources (such as fossil fuels). It is the culmination of all these callous acts on the natural environment that has resulted in today's global climate change, besides other attendant large-scale acts of impairment such as the destruction of natural habitats, causing extensive loss of biodiversity and topsoil and leading to surface run-off, siltation and the eutrophication of waterways.

We need to consider and quantify the extent of our needs and demands on the natural environment (on the land, waterways, atmospheric cycles and on the environment's natural resources, in particular the extraction and use of non-renewable energy resources). The less human society needs means less will be taken from the natural environment and there will be less we need to make and build, which in turn lessens the overall burden on the natural environment and its systems. This applies not just to society at large but must extend to the commercial world: our businesses, manufacturing, agro-food production systems, urban services, transportation systems, etc., essentially extending to all that we make and do that impinges on the natural environment.

All of our built structures (buildings, bridges, roads, etc.) and all of the artefacts that we make and fabricate (refrigerators, clothes, cars, etc.) all require materials and resources taken or extracted from the natural environment, which, at the end of their useful life, need to be green, and must be either reused or recycled (described earlier as ecomimicry) or be reintegrated benignly back into the environment, as opposed to being dumped into landfills or into the air or water.

Our human ecoinfrastructure must also include the intangible aspects of our human society, such as regulatory systems (laws, legislations, penalties, incentives, ethics, etc.) that society formulates to control and guide our activities (e.g., social interaction, business, construction, recreation, mobility, etc.). These must be changed to be environmentally responsive.

This infrastructure consists of all human communities, but consideration of their impacts is commonly missing in the endeavours of most designers, where built structures are the general focus. Consideration must be given to the impacts of all aspects of human life, including how we use these built facilities – not just what we do within the built structures but how we move about, how and what we are fed, what our habits are, how we service the structures, how we spend our related recreational and leisure time, etc.

We also need to change our mindset to depart from the present-day culture of consumerism that mass retailing encourages. This leads to the acquisition of material goods beyond that which is essential and adequate for living. We need to lower the Haves' excessive standards of living to reduce the impacts of manufacturing and disposal of commercial wastes and emissions into the environment. This is similarly applicable to our built environment through the conversion of polluting and high energy consuming industries into net zero energy built structures with net zero water and net zero waste systems. We as humans need to radically rethink and change all unsustainable activities.

In ensuring human health by design, we can adopt salutogenesis as a supporter of human well-being. The salutogenic model requires the creation, enhancement and improvement of society's physical, mental and social well-being through designing basic 'quality of life' features in our built environment.

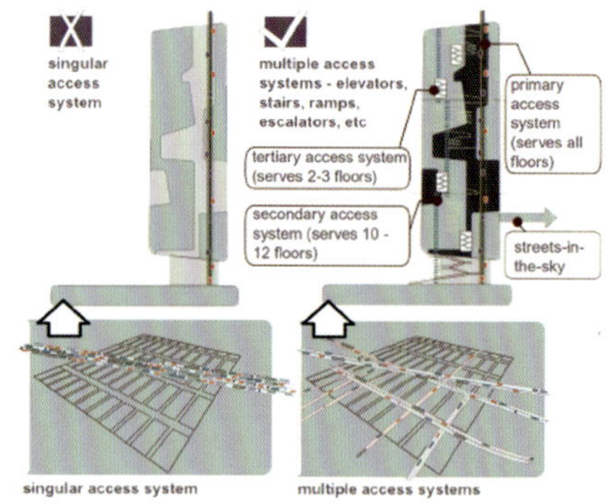

Providing multiple access systems

The first key salutogenic component is 'environmental comprehensivity', requiring environmental orderliness, predictability and legibility, such as creating visual order in the built environment with legible, intuitive wayfinding and the elimination of visual chaos, followed by the component of 'environmental manageability', requiring effective family and social support, and thirdly, 'environmental meaningfulness', requiring the provision of visual and aesthetic meaning, interest and satisfaction, as well as attendant spaces for contemplation in the urban environment.

Our human infrastructure needs to adhere to an ecological ethic. While this effort of changing society's worldview lies beyond the sphere of the designer's influence and capabilities, we need to recognise that this is a vital aspect for concerted societal changes at the global level.

In aggregate, our designing of human ecoinfrastructure means our departure from present-day 'one-way' demands on the natural environment to a reciprocal relationship where society gives back to the environment, where, besides reducing and eliminating our negative acts upon it, we design to have positive impacts on nature and to enhance ecology. Achieving this biointegration requires our built environment to be an integrated part of the natural environment, as opposed to existing in an environment alienated from nature.

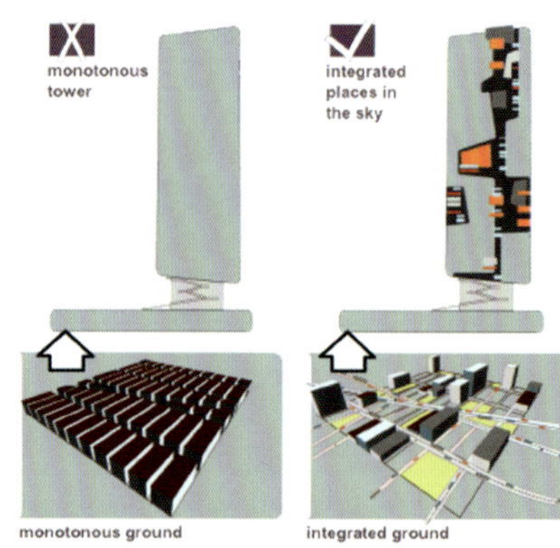

Creating places and gardens-in-the-sky

The next crucial factor to be considered in ecodesign is the natural environment itself, which we term here as 'green ecoinfrastructure'. Green ecoinfrastructures are 'nature's utilities'. These natural utilities provide 'common natural services' from ecosystems, which are crucial and beneficial for humans and wildlife alike.

Consideration of the environment's ecology is vital to all green design and planning work. This is, unfortunately, often neglected by many designers. This green ecoinfrastructure is of equivalent vitality and is crucially important for our sustainable future and more important than human-made urban infrastructure engineering utilities. Being organic, its whole is greater than the sum of its parts, whereas human engineering systems, being mechanistic, can be taken apart to fix any faulty components without affecting the whole.

This green infrastructure needs to be an interconnected network of ecological corridors and fingers across our landscape and urbanscape; it is the prime system in ecodesign as a device that links and reconnects the land into an ecological nexus where original greenfield areas had been fragmented by human action upon it and by other human-built interventions (such as roads, drains, dividing walls and barriers, impervious surfaces, constructed changes in levels, etc.).

Design ideas approach

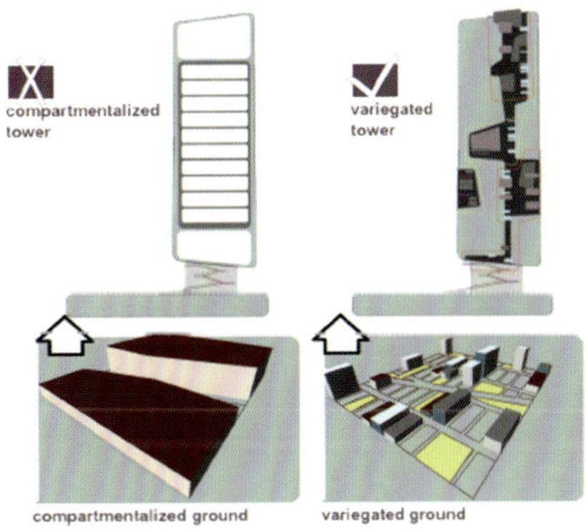

Avoidance of instant compartmentalisation of spaces

This approach to re-connect all the existent disparate green areas and habitats in cities and in urban areas into a network across the landscape and urbanscape should be the first step towards the greening of our cities, in concurrence with making all of their utilities sustainable. This re-connectivity enables green areas to flourish again as natural habitats, as being linked enables a greater pool of natural resources to be shared by all species within these ecosystems. This ecological nexus conserves the existent ecosystems' natural values and enhances their biodiversity while providing natural processes that deliver a wide array of beneficial ecological functions, including the provision of cleaner water, enhancement of existent water supplies, protection of source water, reduction of the heat-island effect in urban areas that is detrimental to all species, moderation of the impact of climate change, the enabling of cleaner air, the engendering of increased energy efficiency in the built environment and a multitude of other ecological benefits.

An unbroken linkage in ecoinfrastructure enables species to freely migrate across the landscape, whether to breed, to seek food and water or for refuge, enabling greater interaction between species and generally engendering a more diverse range of wildlife while promoting survivability and stability.

Reconnecting green areas in the landscape further enables larger habitats to exist in their own right, especially in newly linked woodland belts or wetlands, or newly linked natural features in the landscape, such as overgrown vegetation alongside railway lines and existent hedges. We must also take care to ensure that these new green infrastructures complement and enhance the natural functions of what already exists in the landscape.

Where there are other existent human-made infrastructures (such as roads, drains, impervious areas, barriers, etc.) that bisect or inhibit an ecological nexus, green connectivity can be achieved by using vegetated 'ecobridges' and 'ecoundercrofts', as well as other devices such as vegetated mounds and green ramps.

While the prime systems of nexus are ecological corridors and fingers as 'networks', ecobridges and ecoundercrofts are subsystems as 'connectors'. These subsystems then enable continuance of connectivity across the landscape, over and under conflicting routes of other built ecoinfrastructure.

We also need to make use of a locality's existent natural waterways and use edge greenery to link alongside them. Waterways as aquatic ecosystems also provide ecological services, such as providing natural drainage to attenuate flooding.

Green ecoinfrastructure as a network of ecocorridors and fingers becomes an ecologically vital networking and connecting device. Without it, no matter how advanced a design's ecoengineering systems may be, it remains biologically inert and isolated as an artificial built environment, separated and alienated from nature.

We must give precedence to green infrastructure as nature's utilities over and above the human-made 'grey' ecoengineering infrastructure. While being a new human intervention, green ecoinfrastructure reverses previous human fragmentation and interventions on the land, resulting in positive consequences and environmental benefits.

Its values are, as a green armature and framework for natural systems with natural functions, fundamental to the viability of the locality's floral and faunal life and habitats, as well as the quality of soil, water and air. This reconnectivity reverses impairment to the landscape by previous fragmentation and simplification of habitats and makes it whole again, providing a new green fabric for human society while safeguarding and enhancing the existent landscape's natural features.

The present built environment, with its current intensity of construction, needs to be further re-natured so that our new connectivity across the landscape via green ecoinfrastructure can extend into urban built forms. This greening balances the synthetic inorganic content of present built forms with biotic constituents – both as ecoinfrastructures horizontally across the urbanscape as well as vertically and internally within its built forms. This 'vertical landscaping' is a crucial aspect of green design. Green ecoinfrastructure becomes a vital constituent of our built environment, where our ecodesign extends the ecoinfrastructure vertically upwards and inwards in urban built forms, extending from the ground plane to create habitats in the sky. A combination of other subsystems, such as green walls, stepped and ramped vertical landscaping systems, green roofs and other areas within the built forms become new habitats, de-alienating the built form from the natural environment.

FACING PAGE
Incorporating vertical and continuous landscaping to the tower

A crucial aspect of ecomasterplanning is to ensure that, before making any physical act upon it (such as the clearing or remodeling of a greenfield site, land or construction, whether for roads, drains, buildings, etc,), we carry out an ecological analysis to ascertain the local ecosystem's characteristics and carrying capacity for human intervention. This analysis includes a deep understanding of the ecosystem's biological structure, inherent energy flow, species diversity, materials and nutrient flows, soils and edaphic factors and other internal ecological processes.

This ecological analysis of the site enables us to identify more precisely which parts of the terrain can permit un-detrimental, irreversible acts upon it, which types of built structures and human activities may be imposed, which parts of the land are ecologically sensitive and susceptible to human intervention and construction, what the natural drainage patterns to avoid future flooding of our built systems and to guide the designing of sustainable drainage systems are (such as identifying appropriate locations for bioswales, rain gardens, retention ponds, etc.) and the location of constructed wetlands for the natural treatment of black water. This approach is an anticipatory one, in advance of the likely ecological impacts of intended construction of built forms and interventions. However, we need also to be aware of the consequences after construction, of subsequent use and operation over time and at the end of useful life.

This type of ecological analysis needs to be ideally done diurnally and, in some instances, over several years. In seeking ways to reduce this lengthy effort, an abbreviated approach could be implemented through the 'sieve-mapping' technique currently used as the basis for ecological land-use planning.

We must caution that this method is a simplified approach to understanding the ecology of a terrain, and tends to regard the site's ecology statically. We need to ensure that we do not ignore the dynamic forces taking place within the ecosystem, between each of our mapped layers, where there are complex interactions. Mapping needs

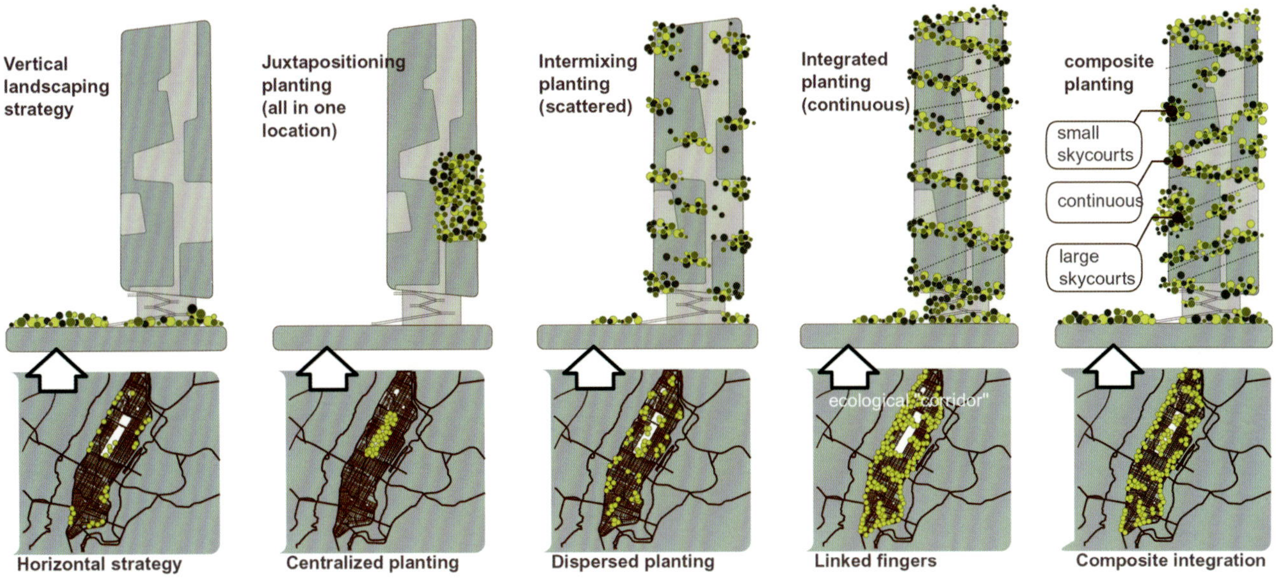

verified by periodic assessment of its dependability and to be monitored and studied using conventional methods. Nevertheless, the ecological sieve-mapping technique provides a good basis for ecomasterplanning.

The third factor in ecodesign and planning to be integrated with the other factors in our framework is engineering. Ecoengineering systems (whether within buildings or external urban infrastructural utilities such as roads and other transportation networks) are essential for contemporary human life, comfort, health and safety. The internal environmental engineering systems for our built forms must include passive-mode, mixed-mode, full-mode and productive-mode systems for creating conditions conducive to comfort for human inhabitants.

The usual external engineering ecoinfrastructure of utilities in urban developments includes items such as roads, drains, sewage systems, water reticulation systems, telecommunications, IT, energy and electric power distribution systems. To avoid obsolescence we need not prescribe specific engineering systems here, but should design these to be clean technologies as net-zero-energy systems, as carbon-neutral with zero emissions, as having lowembodied energy, as net-waste materials systems. It must at the same time be integral with other ecoinfrastructures, giving precedence to green ecoinfrastructure over others rather than vice-versa. These provide design opportunities for creating new subsystems.

The fourth factor in ecodesign and planning that needs to be integrated into our design framework is water infrastructure. This parallels in significance to our green ecological infrastructure and needs to be managed to enable the water cycle of the locality to 'close its loop' as much as possible, although this is not always possible in all localities (e.g., due to dry climatic conditions, evaporation, low rainfall or leakages in existing systems).

The locality's rainfall needs to be harvested and the built environment's greywater must be treated for reuse and recycling. The locality's rainfall and excess surface water must be retained within the site and the surplus returned to the ground to recharge aquifers via subsystems such as bioswales, filtration beds (as 'rain gardens'), pervious roadways and pervious built surfaces and retention ponds. Consideration must be given to the locality's groundwater table, its location and natural drainage patterns, as well as how to provide appropriate surface-water management so that rainfall remains within the locality and does not drain away into rivers and other water bodies.

Stormwater management must enable surface water to be harvested or infiltrated using natural processes, or by evapotranspiration on or near the site where it falls, while potentially generating other environmental benefits.

Black water must be treated using natural processes, as opposed to mechanical means that require energy input.

Waterways should not be culverted as engineered waterways, and existent culverted waterways should be replaced with 'constructed wetlands', rain gardens and buffer strips to become ecologically functional meadows and woodland habitats.

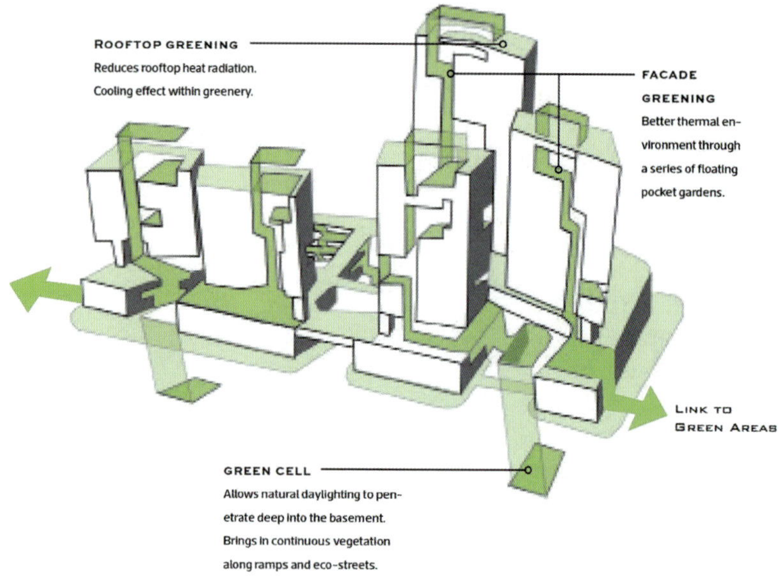

ABOVE
Continuous greening concept

FACING PAGE
Biodiversity matrix as basis for designing buildings as constructed ecosystems

Design needs to avoid the impervious sealing of ground surfaces, as this tends to reduce soil moisture and leave low-lying areas susceptible to flooding from their run-off.

Design can provide green buffers that can be used together with green ecoinfrastructure to maximise habitat potential.

The site's wetland greenways need to be designed as part of sustainable drainage systems to provide vital natural ecological services. These sustainable urban drainage systems can function as constructed wetland habitats. Designing for surface-water management should maximise their habitat potential. These not only alleviate flooding, but also construct buffer strips for habitat creation. While the width of green buffers may be constrained by existing land use, their integration through new green corridors as linear green ecoinfrastructures can allow for wider widths. Intermittent waterway tributaries can be linked using bioswales.

In aggregate, the above four ecoinfrastructures – human society, the water cycle and its management, the land as a network of ecological corridors and fingers and eco-engineering clean-tech systems – need to be biointegrated into a complete, seamless system, whether we are designing a single built form multiple built forms, or an entire area or region. Green design requires us to bring all of the above together to achieve a seamless and benign biointegration of our built environment and the natural environment.

This framework provides a flexible platform for a comprehensive approach to green design, planning and designing our built environment as a compilation of 'constructed ecosystems' in ecomimicry of the stasis of ecosystems in nature.

PLAN

Discription of overall habitat design and aims, wider contextual associations, visual and economic aesthetics

More explanation.... possibly little graphic to show habitat linkages or this could be on the wider landscape description- to include sections of how the architectural landscapes will relate to ground level landscapes...

KEY

Description of the approach to the layout and key

- DPS — Dominant plant species
- WQ — Water Quality
- WB — Water Balance
- J F M A M J J A S O N D — Season which they occur- If full means resident
- (Breeding icon) — Breeding
- F — Feeding
- P — Prey

		Shrub Roofs	Grassland Roofs	Planted facades	Densely wooded area	Wet Woodland	Reeds	Marsh	Polishing Pond with Rafts	Flowing Water and Still Ponds-Urban	Streetscape Planting
	Biodiversity Target	DPS WQ WB	DPS WQ WB	DPS WQ WB	DPS WQ WB	DPS WQ WB	DPS WQ WB	DPS WQ WB	DPS WQ WB	DPS WQ WB	DPS WQ WB
	Indicator of Biodiversity and Primary Associated Species										
MAMMALS	Siberian Weasel *Mustela sibrica* (J F M A M J J A S O N D)				Breeding F	Breeding F	F	F			
MAMMALS	Shrews *Crocidura lasiura, Crocidura suaveolens* (J F M A M J J A S O N D)				Breeding F P	Breeding F P		Breeding F P			
MAMMALS	Rodents *Severall species* (J F M A M J J A S O N D)				Breeding F P	Breeding F P	Breeding F P	Breeding F P			
BATS	Northern Bat *Eptesicus nilssonii* (J F M A M J J A S O N D)	F	F	F	Breeding F	F					F
BATS	Daubenton's Bat *Myotis daubentonii* (J F M A M J J A S O N D)				Breeding	Breeding			F	F	
BATS	Big-footed Myotis *Myotis macrodactylus* (J F M A M J J A S O N D)			Breeding					F	F	F
BIRDS	Moorhen *Gallinula chloropus* (A M J J A S)						Breeding F	F	Breeding F	Breeding F	
BIRDS	Eastern Spot-billed Duck *Anas zonorhyncha* (J F M A M J J A S O N D)								Breeding F	Breeding F	
BIRDS	Little Egret *Egretta garzetta* (A M J J A S)					F	F	F	F		
BIRDS	Eurasian Sparrowhawk *Accipter Nicus* (J F M A M J J A S O N D)	F		F	Breeding F	F					
BIRDS	Eurasian Kestrel *Falco tinnunculus* (J F M O N D)				F	F	F	F			
BIRDS	Turtle Dove *Streptopelia orientalis* (J F M A M J J A S O N D)	Breeding F	F	Breeding							Breeding F
BIRDS	Oriental Scops Owl *Otus lettia* (J F M A M J J A S O N D)	Breeding		Breeding	Breeding F	F		F			F
BIRDS	Collarded Scops Owl *Otus lettia* (J F M A M J J A S O N D)	Breeding		Breeding	Breeding F	F		F			F
BIRDS	Hoopoo *Upupa epops* (A M J J A S)		Breeding F		Breeding	F		F			
BIRDS	Pygmy Woodpecker *Yungipicus kizuki* (J F M A M J J A S O N D)	F			Breeding F	Breeding F					F
BIRDS	Brown Shrike *Lanius cristatus* (A M J J A S)	Breeding F			Breeding F	Breeding F	F	F			F
BIRDS	Eurasian siskin *Carduelis spinus* (J F M N D)										
BIRDS	Azure-winged Magpie *Cyanopica cyanus* (J F M A M J J A S O N D)	F	F		Breeding F	Breeding F	F				F
BIRDS	Brown-eared Bulbul *Microscelis amaurotis* (J F M A M J J A S O N D)	Breeding F		F	Breeding F	Breeding F					
BIRDS	Oriental Reed Warbler *Acrocephalus orientalis* (A M J J A S)						Breeding F	F			
BIRDS	Penduline Tit *Remiz consobrinus* (M A S O)						F	F	F	F	
BIRDS	Red-rumped Swallow *Cecropis daurica* (A M J J A S)	F		Breeding	F	F	F	F	F		
	Dybowski's frog *Rana dybowskii* (J F M A M J J A S O N D)				F	F P	F P	P		P	
	Dark-spotted Frog *Pelophylax nirgomaculatus*					F	F	F	Breeding F		
	Dragonflies *20+species*			F	F	F	Breeding F	Breeding F	Breeding F	Breeding F	
	Yellow-tip *Anthocharis scolymus* (A M J J A S O)	F P	F P	F	Breeding F	F		Breeding F	F		Breeding F
	Scarce Heath *Coenonympha hero* (A M J J A S O)	Breeding F P	Breeding F	F	F			Breeding F	F		Breeding F
	Golden Emporer *Dilipa fenestra* (A M J J A S O)	F P	F	F	Breeding F	Breeding		F			F
	Invertebrates *Many ubiquitous* (J F M A M J J A S O N D)	Breeding F P	Breeding F P		Breeding F P	Breeding F P	Breeding F P				Breeding F P

IDEAS AND SUBSYSTEMS

Ecocell

DESIGN IDEA

Serving as a 'vertical eco-integrator' of the multiple layers of building design, the ecocell is principally a 'landscape sandwich'. The device inverts the vertical stratification of a built form as a cell-like void that cuts through a built form (i.e., slicing down through all floors, from the uppermost level to the lowest level of the basement) or a void that is located at regular intervals within the built form. An ecocell has multiple functions: it affords daylight (like an air well), it affords natural ventilation opportunities to the inner parts of a building, and its continuous vegetated ramp enables greenery to flow in an ecological nexus from the roof's gardens down to the lowest basement. By being open to the sky, it can potentially harvest rainwater and surface water as part of the built form's water recycling system. If located at the base of a built form, an ecocell functions as a component of the building's water management system, such as in algae sewerage treatment tanks that convert sewerage waste (black water) into pure water (e.g., Todd's 'Living Machine') as a compact 'constructed wetland', and can be used for storing harvested rainwater tanks, for the collection and recycling of greywater, for bioswales to recharge aquifers and many other uses.

BELOW
Ecocell concept

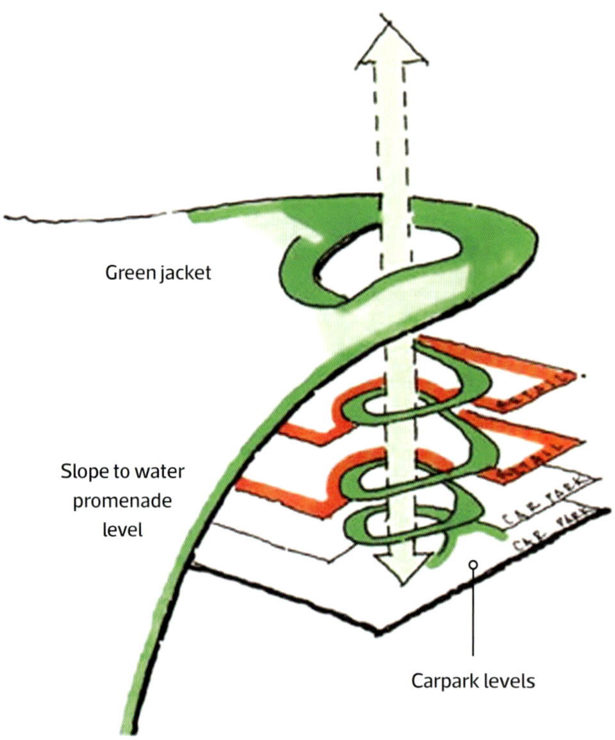

FAR RIGHT
Section through eco-cell for West Kowloon

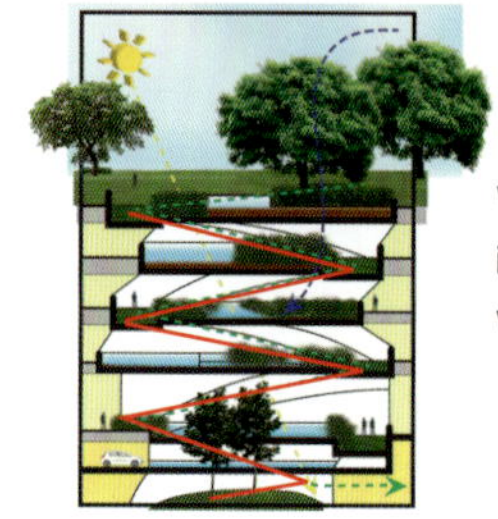
Vertical integration of vegetation

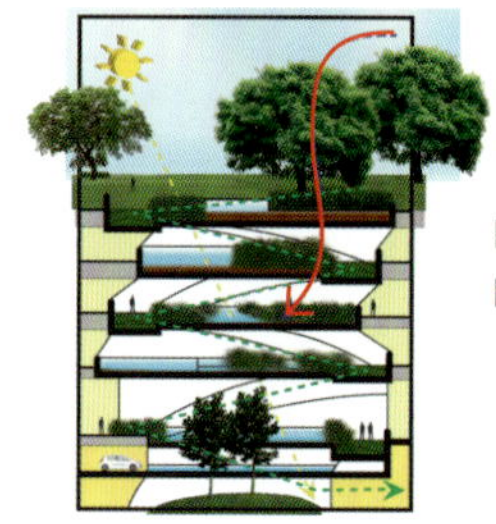
Rainwater harvesting

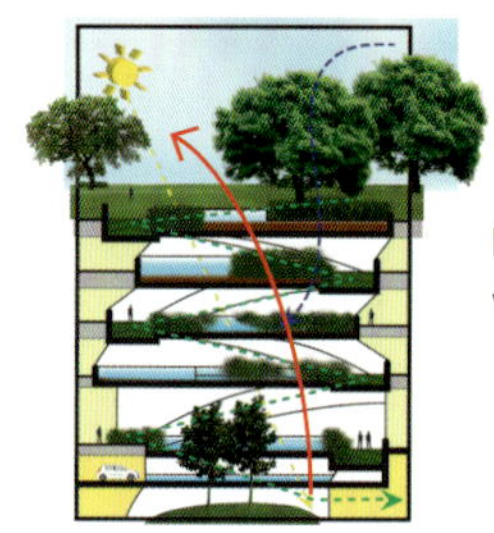
Natural ventilation

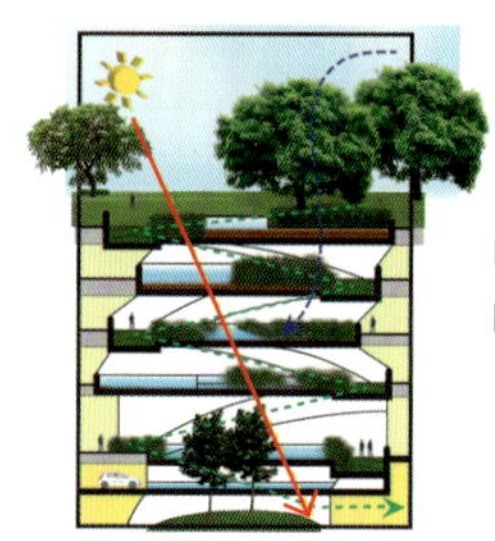
Daylight penetration

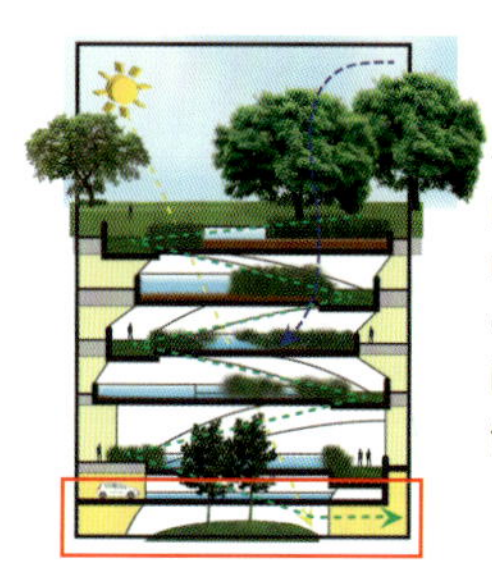
An opportunity to provide a 'living machine' or constructed wetland for sewage treatment

RIGHT
Ecocell from ground level to basement in Solaris

BELOW
Section through Ecocell at the basement of Solaris

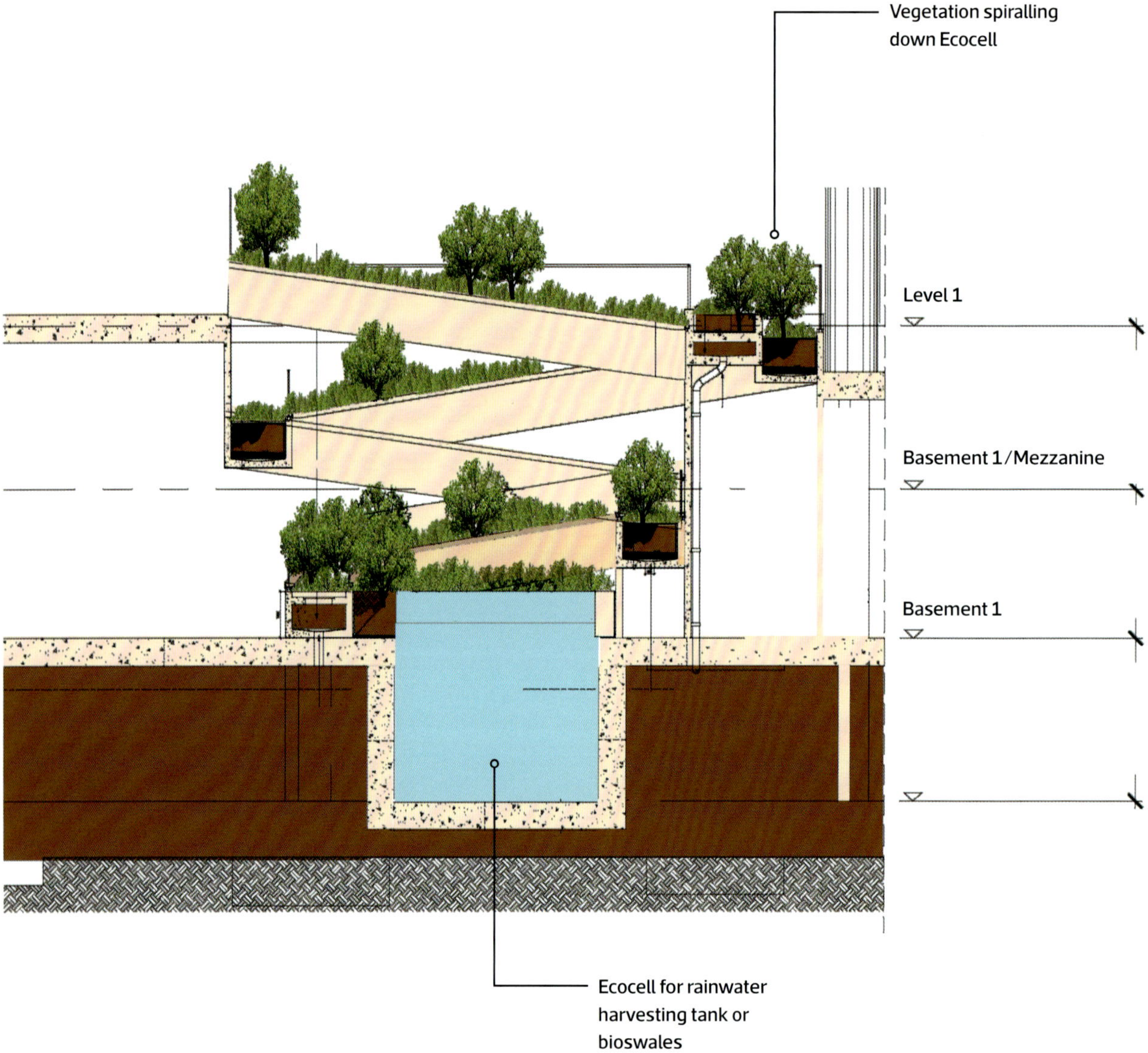

TTDI Plaza
Escalating planters
Extractor fans as mixed-mode cooling systems
Naturally ventilated retail public plaza

TTDI PLAZA

TTDI Plaza is a mixed-development project located in a middle-class suburb in Kuala Lumpur, Malaysia, with a site area of 3.4 acres. The complex was completed in 2006 and consists of a 21- (6D1 tower) and 26- (6D3 tower) storey high-rise apartment and two rows of three-story shop houses with a 2,200m^2 covered canopy.

In the TTDI plaza, the ecocell is a sunken courtyard in a publicly accessible area. It connects upper pedestrian thoroughfares with lower utility areas and carpark levels. The plaza represents a functional focus for the development with the ecocell acting as a thermal modifier, helping to create a kind of micro-climatic oasis within a plaza as a public area in a large mixed-development complex.

SIMULATIONS

The climatic performance of an ecocell was tested with boundary conditions modelled on external conditions and the impact of the thermal mass of surrounding shop lots and concrete walls. Internal temperatures were predicted using computational fluid dynamics (CFD) simulation. The boundary conditions took into account external weather data provided by the nearest meteorological department.

Temperature contours and resulting simulations assisted in providing an instantaneous snapshot of the thermal performance of the plaza and sunken ecocell during the design development process. Representing a specific instance in time, thermal comfort and temperature distribution over an average day are reflected from the results related to the hottest scenario under the Malaysian climate (i.e., at 2 pm on an average day).

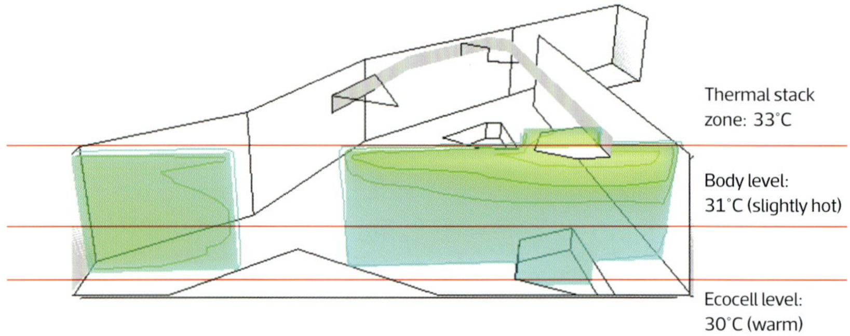

FIGURE 1 Simulated stratified temperatures in the plaza and ecocell at body level with air extractor *off* (vertical view)

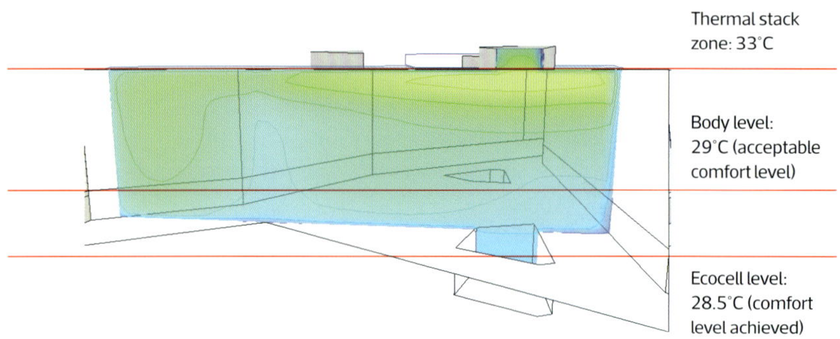

FIGURE 2 Simulated snapshots of predicted temperatures at body level with air extractor *on* (vertical view)

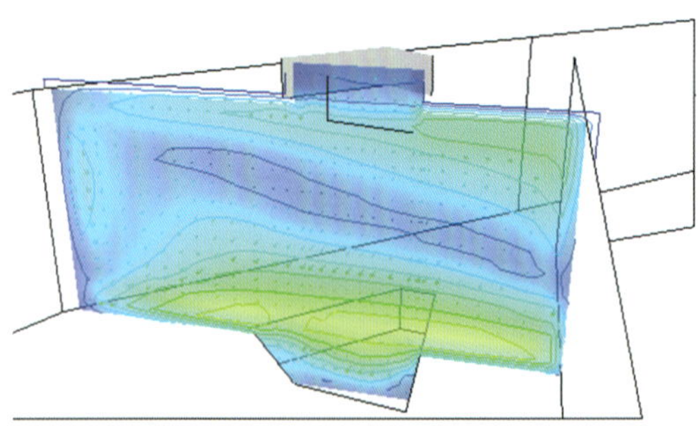

FIGURE 3 Simulated air velocity distribution in the plaza and Ecocell (Vertical Distribution)

RIGHT
Looking up to the canopy skylight

FAR RIGHT
Atrium below extractor fans

BELOW
Wireframe model showing conceptual integration of an ecocell in TTDI Plaza. For analytical pusposes, the space is split into six stacked thermal zones:
1 ecocell zone
4 stacked concourse zones
1 thermal stack zone

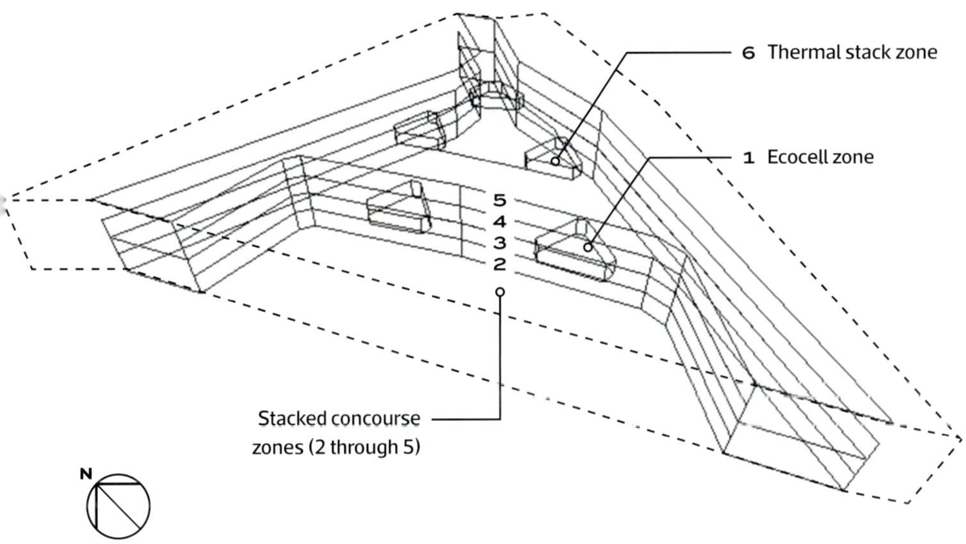

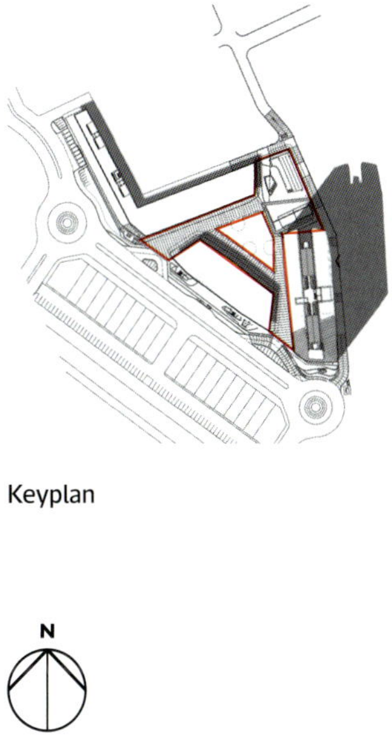

Keyplan

Figures 1, 2 and 3 demonstrate how the ecocell itself performed under con ditions of the plaza and how its internal temperatures were affected by its surrounding walls, essentially protected from heat gain throughout the day and acting to some extent like a heat sink. The results and the post-occupancy data demonstrate the effectiveness of the ecocell as a heat sink due to the protected nature of the surrounding concrete walls as a thermal mass in the centre of the plaza. Comfort depends of four main parameters other than metabolic rate or type of clothing, i.e., dry-bulb temperature, humidity, air movement and mean radiant temperature (MRT). In the TTDI, the shape of the plaza, to some extent, had modified the flow and magnitude of the incoming air movement, while the roof glass specifications ameliorated the incident solar radiation, the overall temperature gains were affected by the glazed areas and the surrounding shaded walls, which act as a heat sink, resulted in a reduced temperature zone within the ecocell. The ecocell thermal conditions demonstrate the ability of a thermal mass feature and component to utilise shaded conditions, including the heat sink capabilities of the concrete walls, which are protected from solar radiation. Results of the thermal stratification effect of the entire plaza are also illustrated in Figures 2 and 3. The results verified the expected performance, where the combination of surrounding mass and generally protected positions caused temperatures to be reduced within the sunken ecocell areas.

SOLARIS, SINGAPORE

Located at the building's northeast corner, the ecocells here are generally at regular intervals throughout the built form and are placed in such a manner that they link to the indigenous peripheral vegetation. Located at the heart of the built form and going down to its lowest floors, each ecocell could also be a component of the building's water-management system, possibly a bioswale to recharge the site's aquifers or integration with algae sewerage treatment tanks that convert sewerage waste (black water) into useable water as a compact 'constructed wetland'. The base could also be a location for placement of rainwater tanks for the collection and recycling of greywater and surface water, which could be stored and recycled for irrigation or cleaning purposes.

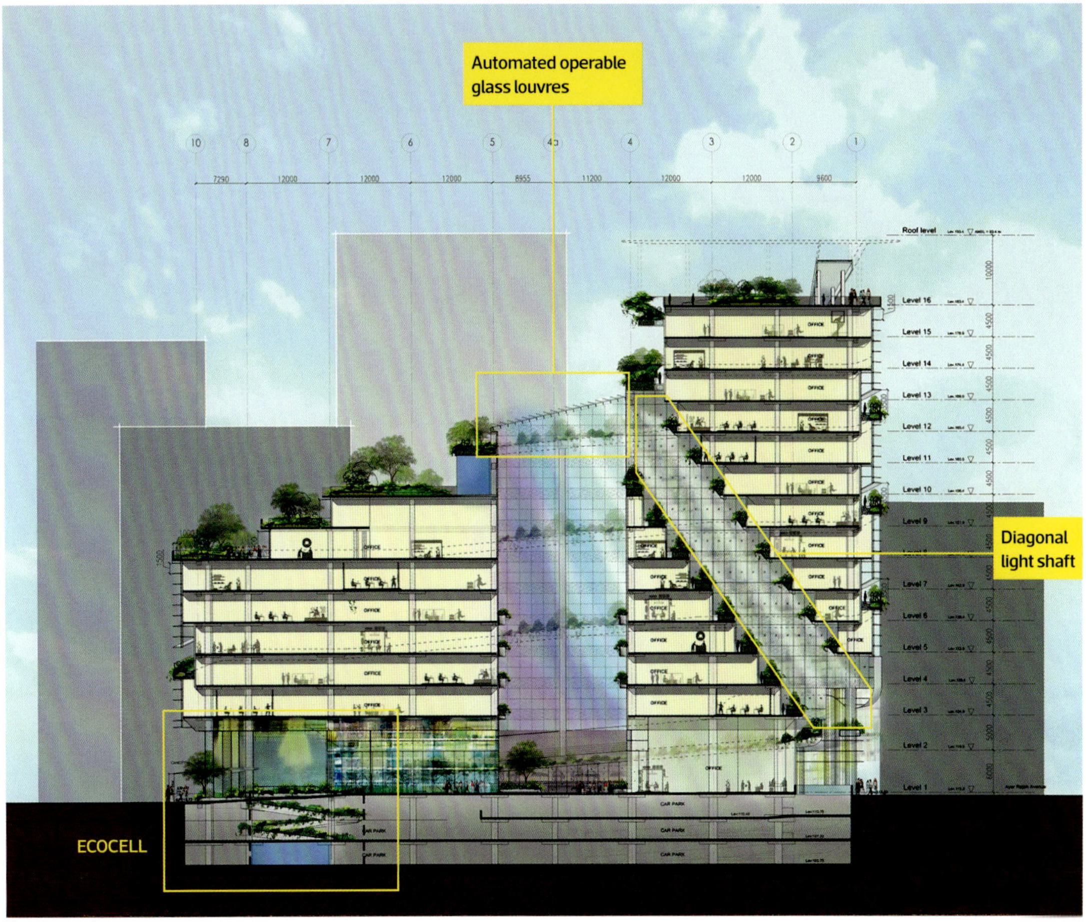

Northeast Section

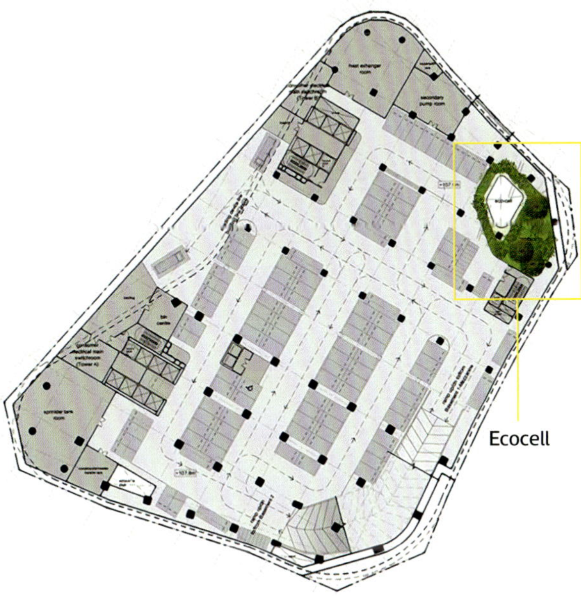

Basement Level 1

Basement Mezzanine

BELOW
Section through West Kowloon

BOTTOM
West Kowloon Waterfront Masterplan

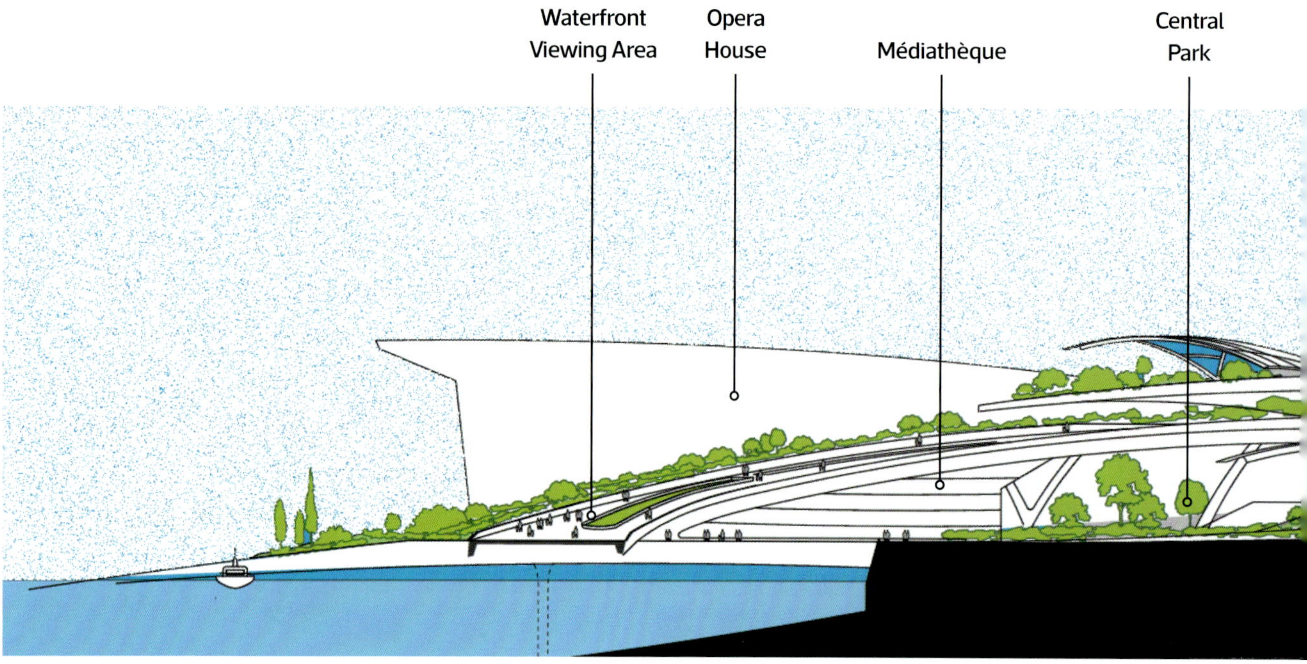

KOWLOON WATERFRONT, HONG KONG

Besides serving as an eco-integrator, an ecocell can have several other functions: it can bring daylight into the inner parts of a building (like an 'air well') or could be used to provide natural ventilation opportunities to inner areas. Its continuous vegetated ramp enables greenery to flow in an ecological nexus from the built form's rooftop vegetated gardens through to the lowest basements. The extensive vegetation enables it to function as a sustainable passive airfiltration system that, by removing air pollutants and VOC within its vicinity, improves IAQ (Indoor Air Quality) at zero cost. The vegetation helps to cleanse the air in its surrounding subterranean spaces and contributes to the lowering of ambient temperature.

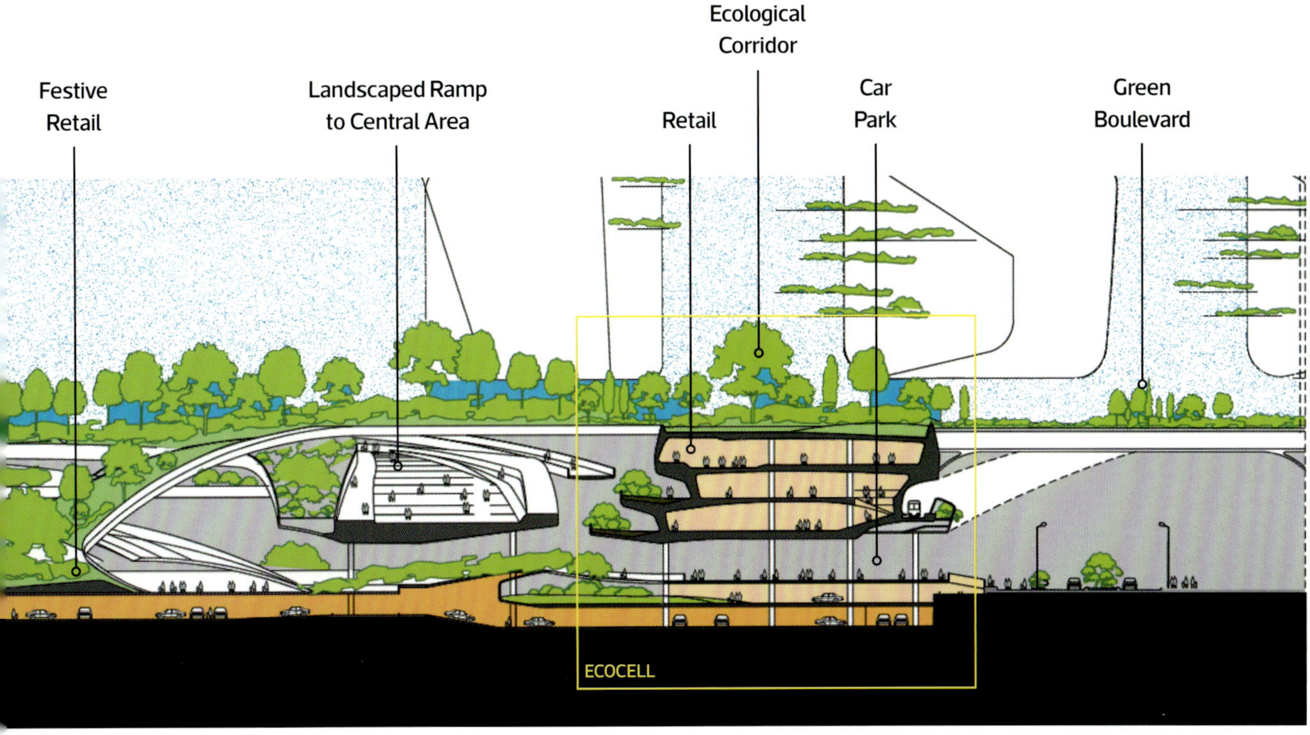
Ecological Corridor
Festive Retail
Landscaped Ramp to Central Area
Retail
Car Park
Green Boulevard
ECOCELL

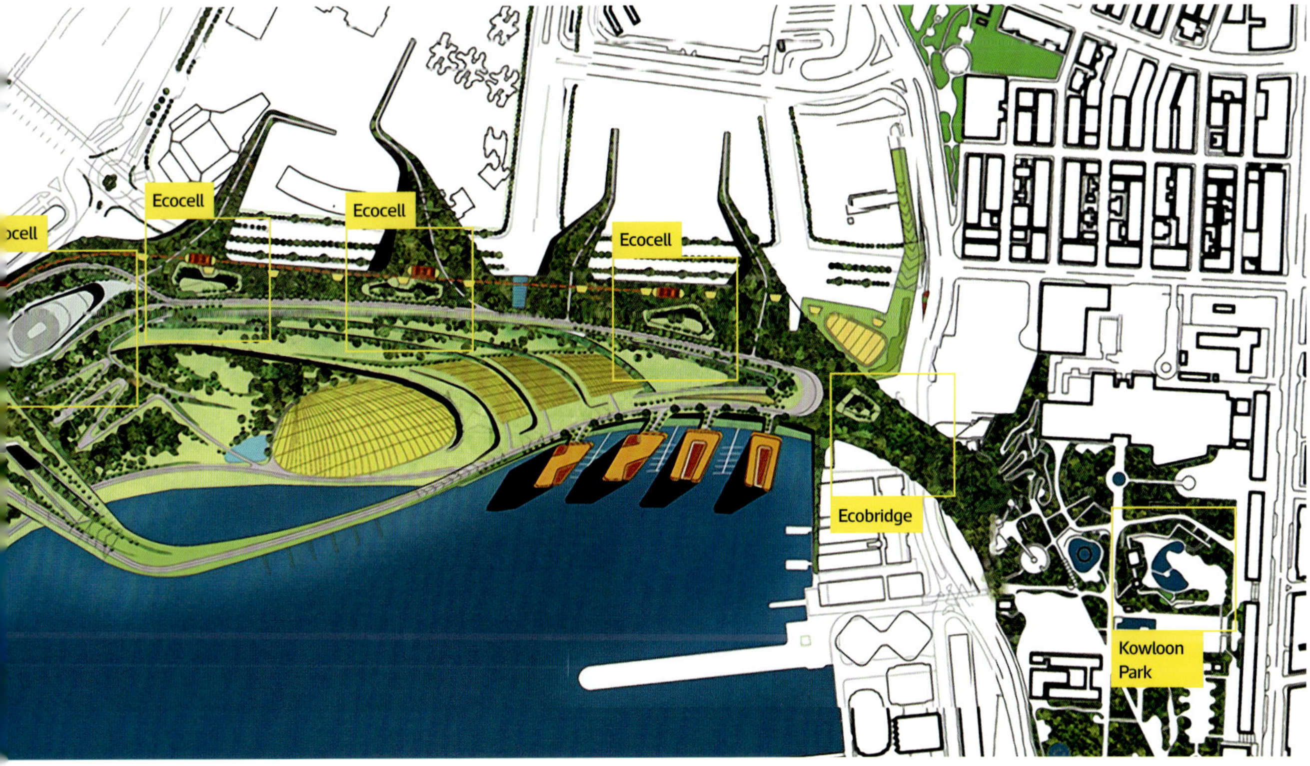
Ecocell
Ecocell
Ecocell
Ecobridge
Kowloon Park

NATIONAL LIBRARY, SINGAPORE

This design intent is to provide the NLB with a state-of-the-art and innovative library for the tropics that serves as an icon for the region and its locality. It is to be a facility that meets the client's requirements and objectives, simultaneously a cultural space and a unique, enjoyable civic space for Singapore. The NLB building's built form consists essentially of two blocks that are separated by a day-lit, semi-enclosed internal 'street' and are connected by bridges at the upper levels

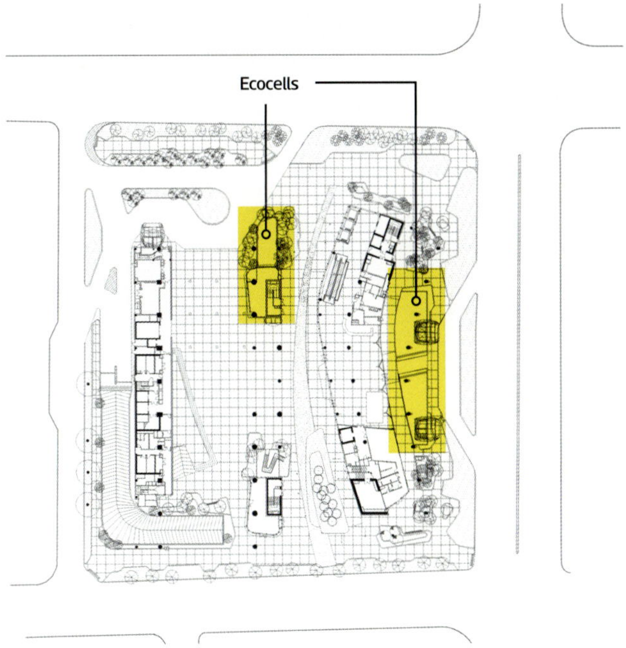

over the 'street' below. The larger block contains the library's collections and sits over an open-to-the-sky, naturally ventilated civic plaza, providing opportunities for 'outdoor' events and cafés (as well as another plaza for multimedia, programming, etc.). The trees and shrubs incorporated on the ramp can be selected to replace and replenish native species existing on and around the site, some of which may have been lost during construction. The ecocell concept can be further developed by seeking to achieve greater integration of its organic mass with the inorganic mass of the built form, the combination becoming a constructed ecosystem.

TOP LEFT
Ecocell brings daylight into the basement level of the National Library

TOP RIGHT
Location of Ecocells

BOTTOM
Upper level of Ecocell

Down-draft Cooling Shaft

DESIGN IDEA

The Down-draft Cooling Shaft is an experimental device meant to function as a down-draft shaft that channels wind from the upper parts of a building down the shaft to spaces below in order to provide comfortable cooling and enhance natural ventilation within a building. Within dense city areas, at times, wind-induced ventilation at ground level has been known to bring pollution and dust into buildings from the surrounding areas and activities. At times of higher-than-average winds it acts to promote stack effect. However, this technology has never before been used in the tropics of Malaysia. Though Malaysia is known as a humid climate with low winds, as cities continue high-density development there will be an increasing difficulty for typical windows to achieve effective cross-ventilation, and dust pollution in cities caused by frenzied development and traffic activities will raise interests in catching less-polluted air 'higher up' and using less windows 'lower down'.

BELOW
Conceptual sketch of down-draft chimney

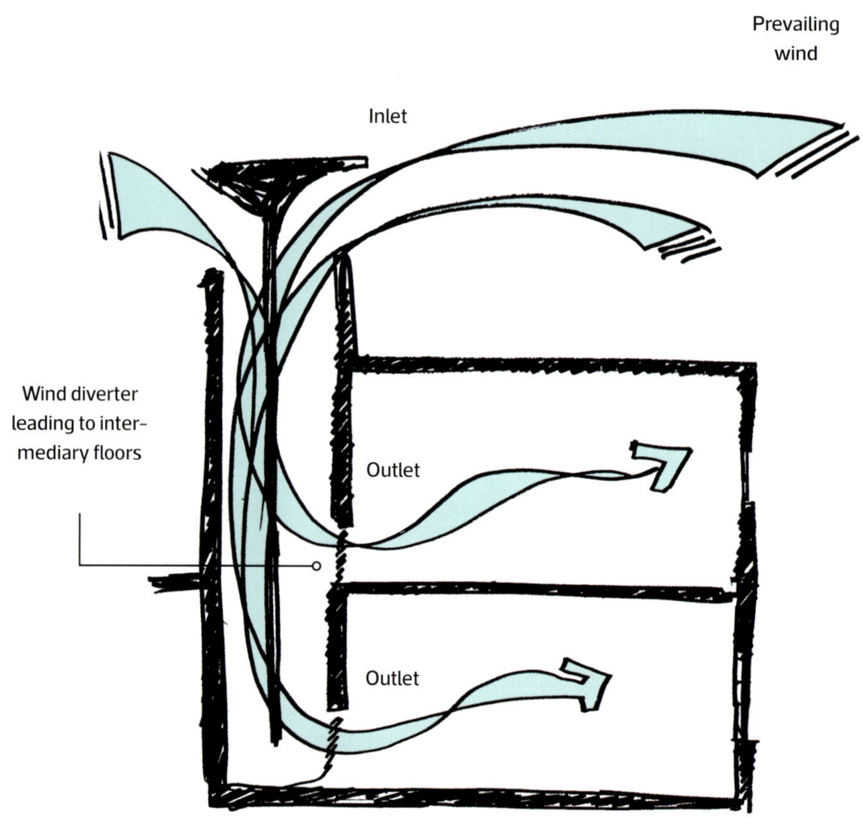

Top of down-draft wind scoop
Main entrance

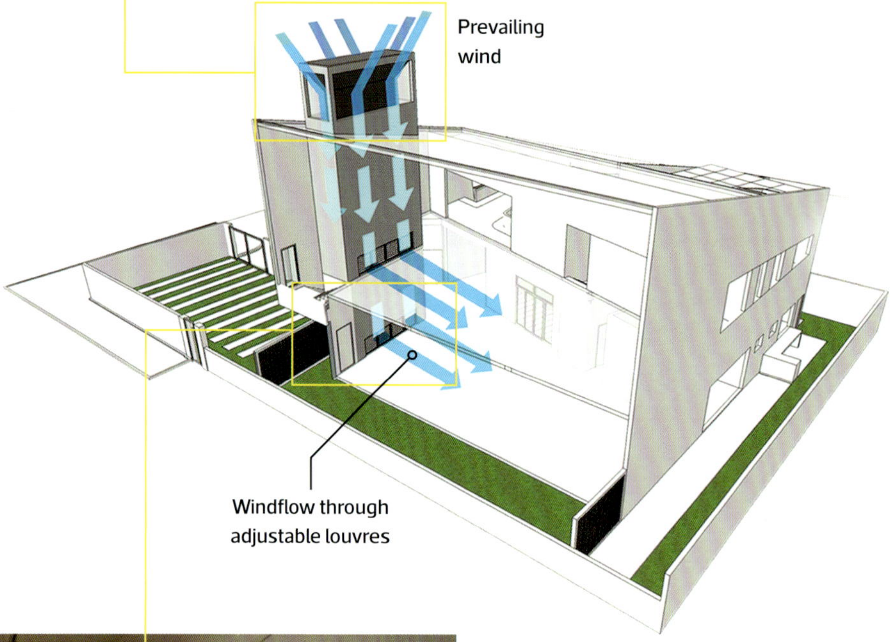

ABOVE
Top of down-draft wind scoop

RIGHT
Cross-section of down-draft chimney

BELOW
Interior view of gallery

Level 1 gallery,
The Ganendra Art House

THE GANENDRA ART HOUSE

The Ganendra Art House (GAH) is a combination of residence and art gallery. The two-storey bungalow is located in the suburban area of Petaling Jaya in Selangor, Malaysia, with a site area of 0.19 acres. Just over 63% of the building is devoted to gallery space and 36.7% is for other uses, with a total floor area of 633.4m^2.

Even from the initial conceptual stage, the client insisted on achieving comfort through passive means without air-conditioning. The challenge was to introduce airflow into the building without compromising or reducing the vertical wall sapce needed for exhibition purposes.

The basic layout of the house is comprisesed of two levels, the ground floor and level 1. There are two main spaces at both levels where all the artwork is to be displayed. Apart from that, it has two bedrooms and a toilet at level 1. The ground floor also features an office, a multipurpose room, a kitchen and a toilet. The chimney is essentially a rectangular box inserted into the roof massing. The outside has vertical walls while the inside has a 'Y' profile. The longer sides of the chimney 'box' face north and south, aligned with prevailing winds.

JUSTIFICATIONS

As cities continue higher-density development, it will be increasingly difficult for typical windows to effectively cross-ventilate. The Ganendra down-draft wind shaft is a reflection of similar down-draft features in other regions of the world. These essentially aim to 'catch' windy, cleaner air high up in the urban environment.

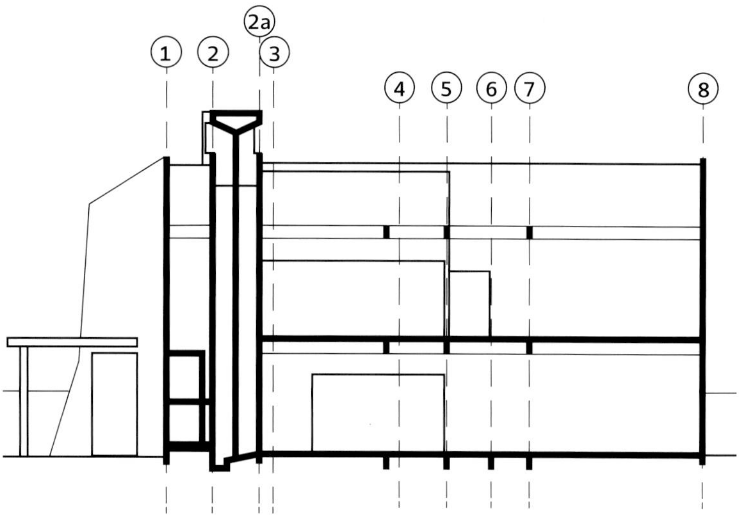

FIGURE 1
Original cross-section of the chimney and 'Y' deflector

An art gallery has its own special requirements, notably the need to be 'free' from internal partitioning in order to provide space for exhibitions. The gallery affords the opportunity to test such a strategy with the initiative and vision of both the client and architect. The initial direction of increasing building height was not possible due to height restrictions mandated by local authorities.

The Ganendra experimental wind scoop is inserted into the roof profile to assist and admit natural ventilation to gallery spaces without depending on vertical windows. This affords the ability to 'free up' walls and vertical surfaces for exhibiting works of art. CFD simulations were undertaken to test the concept, then sectional design and detailing was fine-tuned.

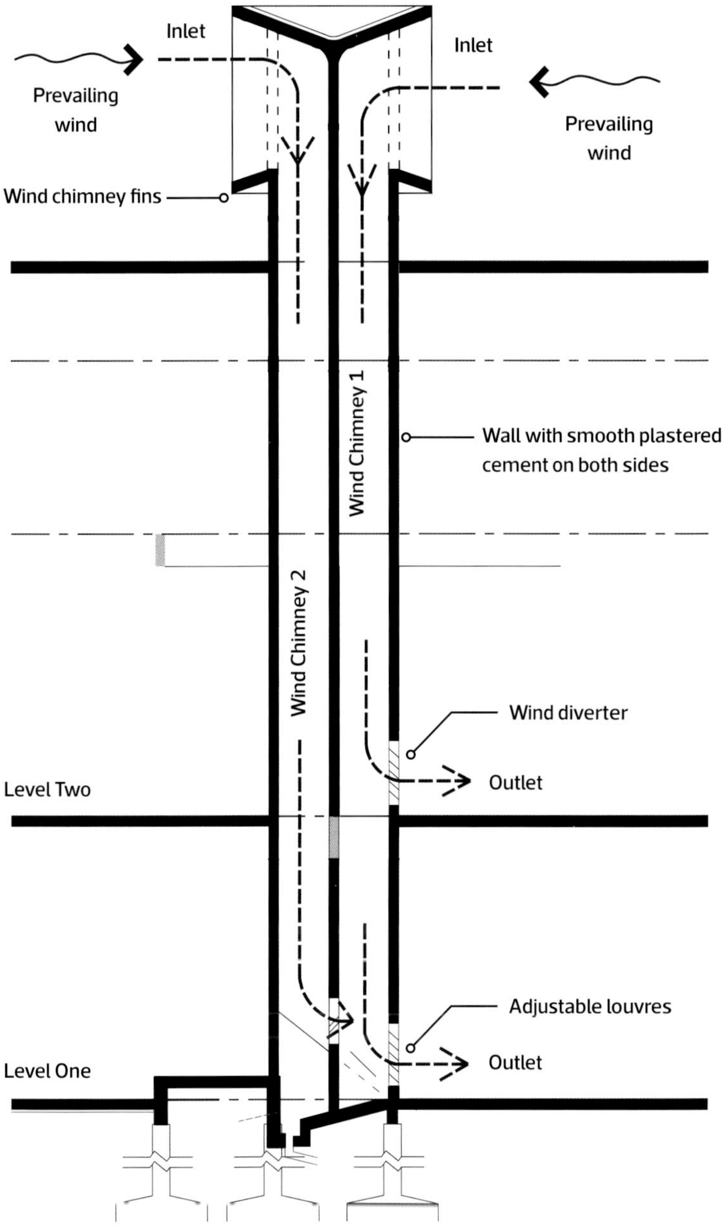

FIGURE 2
Improved design, double chimney assembly to capture wind from all directions

APPLIED RESEARCH & SIMULATIONS

The innovative 'Y'-deflector chimney was designed to divert windflow from above the rooftop to the lower floors of the bungalow. An on-site post-occupancy monitoring study was conducted to compare predicted airflow to actual airflow performance. Typically, only 60% of the time the passive approach can be depended on. At times when external wind speeds were not sufficient (40% of the year), mechanical fans were needed to achieve comfort under such hot, humid conditions.

Under simulated conditions, a wind speed of 1.32 m/s was introduced in order to test the performance of the deflector; a wind speed average of 0.5 m/s was found within the gallery spaces. The sectional profile was improved to 'catch' winds from opposing directions.

THE ORIGINAL 'Y'-DEFLECTOR PROFILE

The original roof has a 'Y' deflector connected to a simple chimney-like volume, such as in Figure 1.

The original 'Y' deflector is mainly a chimney that brings airflow into the living room areas. However, it was found that air short-circuited through the chimney itself and did not properly divert into the living areas.

Figures 2 and 3 exemplify the concept of the improved design. The aim was to catch winds in both prevailing directions and divert them to both of the living rooms as well as the first floor of the house. Hence, openings 1A and 1B are connected to Chimney 1, which is intended to catch northwest winds, while opening 2 is connected to Chimney 2, intended to divert southeast winds.

SIMULATIONS

The original design consists of a simple chimney that connects to both the ground floor and upper floor. The improved design consists of an improved cross-section of the chimney. CFD simulations were used to predict the magnitude and distribution of airflow based on a 1 m/s external average wind speed. Results, as in Figure 4 and 5 below, were based on the scenario of the wind chimney being 'entirely opened' and connected directly to both ground and living areas. The openings in these areas were modelled as 'partially' closed – only the windows on the opposite walls of the living rooms were open.

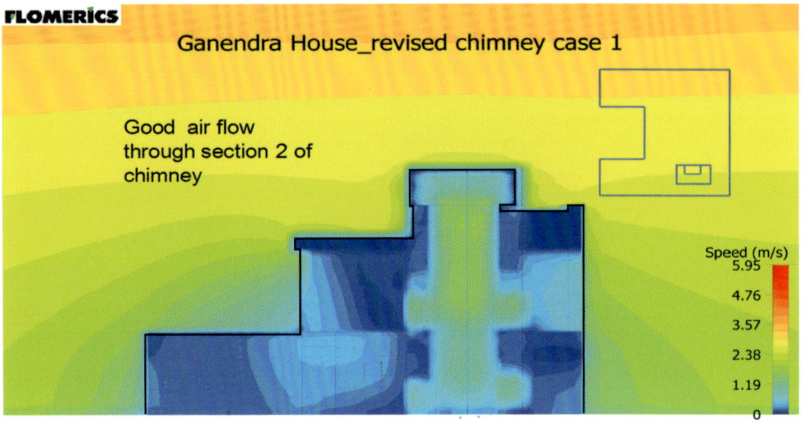

FIGURE 3 Revised Chimney Case 1 (Jahnkassim & Abkr, 2015)

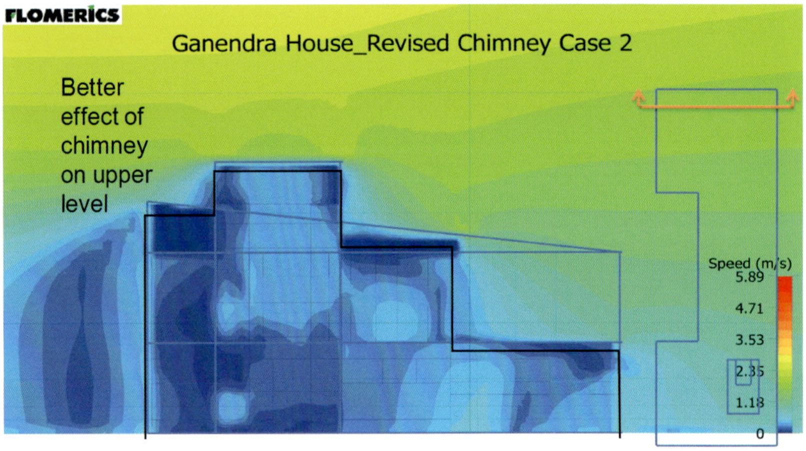

FIGURE 4 Revised Chimney Case 2 (Jahnkassim & Abkr, 2015)

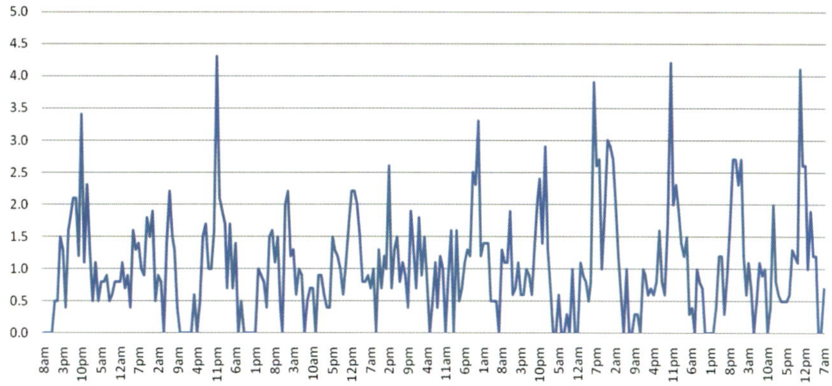

CHART 1
External wind speeds from 24 Feb – 7 Mar 2011 (recorded hourly at Petaling Jaya Meteorological Station) (Jahnkassim & Abkr, 2015)

POST-OCCUPANCY PERFORMANCE

During the post-occupancy phase, it was found that the actual conditions differ slightly from what was in the modelling assumptions. The sliding doors towards the terraced patio were left open to afford views and ventilation to the court-yard garden, but full cross-ventilation across the length of gallery could not be consistently achieved. This caused a short-circuiting of the airflow, flowing out of the chimney opening and through the open sliding doors rather than falling and distributing into the living room. There was also an overwhelming wind influx during periods of wind preceding monsoon storms, whereas during periods of low wind external conditions and wind speeds did not cause enough internal airflow.

On days with higher ambient wind it was found that good wind speed occurred within the gallery, and occupants at times needed to shut the wind louvres due to fabric and canvas flapping uncontrollably. Occupants also tended to shut the middle louvres while leaving the side louvres open, remarking that this increased louvre performance. In a simulation based on the external input of windflow, airflow inside the chimney ranged from 0 to 0.8m/s, with the upper levels being more intense air. The airflow measured ranged from 0.12 m/s to 0.7 m/s.

In terms of temperature variation, the average dry-bulb temperature within the gallery space was 28.6°C with an average relative humidity of 72.7%. The air movement in Chimney 1 averaged, on 4 March 2011, at 0.43 m/s (MS 1525 is 0.15 m/s to 0.50 m/s). The air movement in Chimney 2 on the 4 March 2011 averaged at 0.58 m/s.

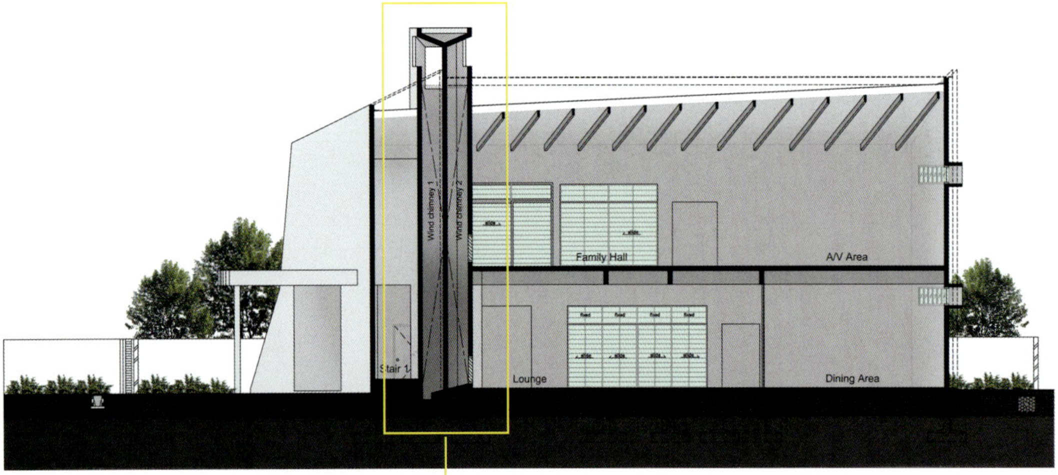

Section A-A

No.	Temperature (°C)	Humidity (%RH)
1	28.3	74.3
2	27.5	81.3
3	28.3	73.4
5	28.8	69.9
6	28.2	73.8
7	28.5	71.1
14	28.4	74.7

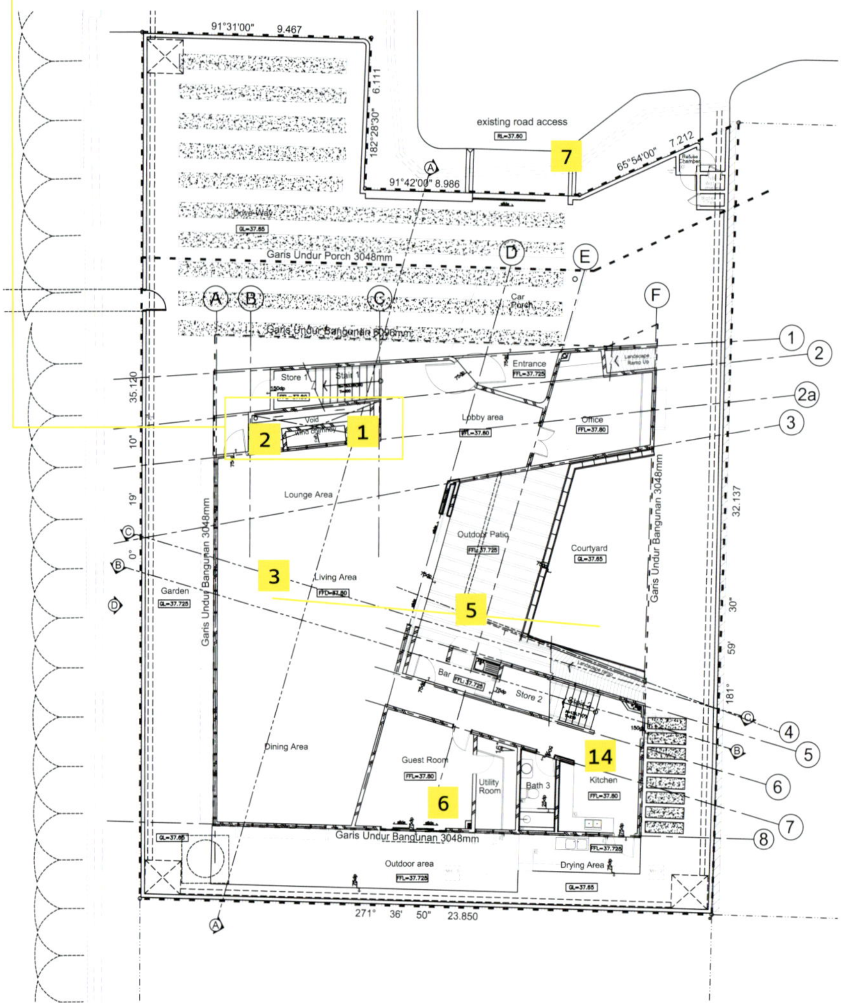

FIGURE 6
Level 1 plan with temperature and humidity readings (measured at 2pm, March 2011)

Note: location markers 1 and 2 correspond to chimneys 1 and 2 respectively.

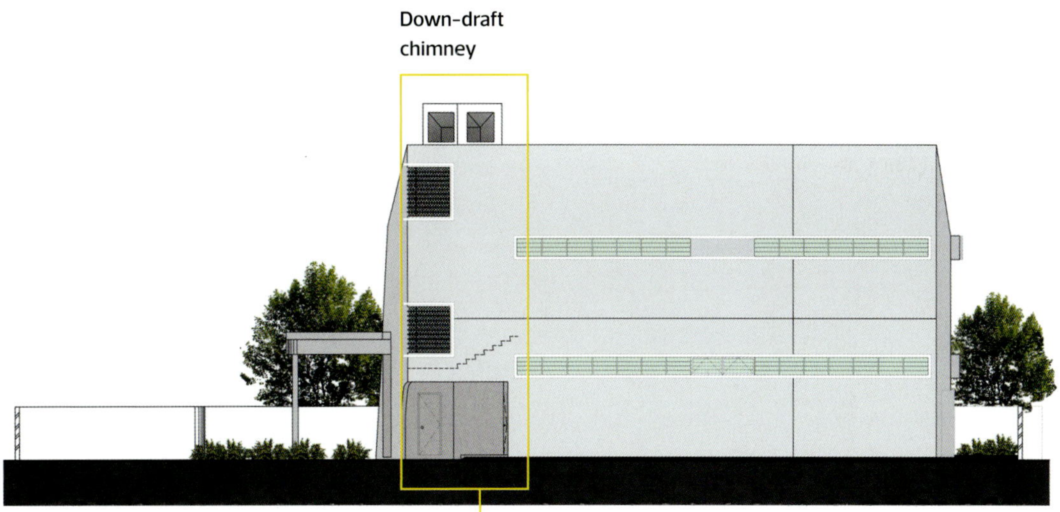

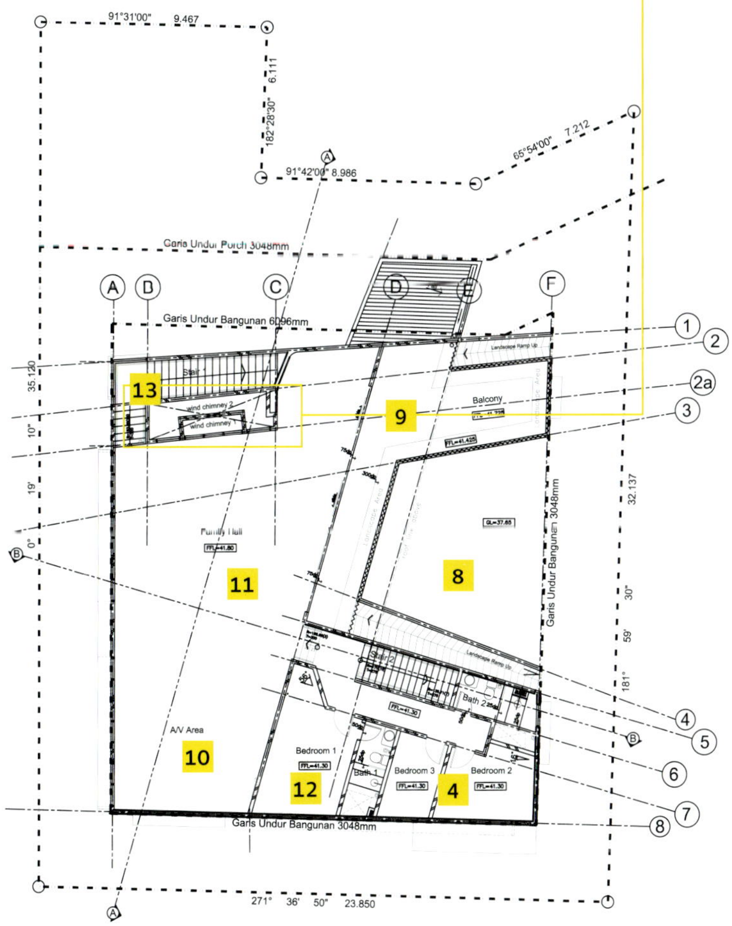

No.	Temperature (°C)	Humidity (%RH)
4	29.5	70.1
8	28.8	72.1
9	29.0	68.7
10	28.8	71.5
11	28.8	69.8
12	28.3	75.9
13	28.3	70.5

FIGURE 7
Level 2 plan with temperature and humidity readings (measured at 2pm, March 2011)

ABOVE
North elevation

LEFT
A close-up of the south and east windows with sunshading

FACING PAGE
Deep overhangs to keep out sunlight while permitting cross-ventilation

Sunshading hood
Landscaped ramp

Double Roof

DESIGN IDEA

Inspired by the umbrella, the double roof is an open system but an enclosing layer meant to protect a building from overhead solar radiation while allowing airflow within the double layering of roofs. The principle of the double roof is a variation of the principle of double-skin façades. The outermost roof layer performs a protective function as an environmental sieve to the inner layer.

Working like a pair of louvred sunglasses, the double roof is a 'baffle' roof that sweeps over not only the actual flat roof of the upper floor of the built form, but also over the pool terrace area. This secondary roof shades the roof terrace immediately underneath the pool, enhancing the cooling breeze to the lower floors. A building's enclosure system can be regarded as an operable 'valve' that filters out undesirable climatic elements (in this instance, solar radiation) but allows in that which is desirable or conducive to comfort (e.g., cross-ventilation). By comparison to other vernacular architectural approaches that respond to the local climate, the concept of the double roof differs in that it is intentionally designed not as a passive structure but as a system of working parts at the façade (hence its valve analogy).

In addition to the outer louvred roof as an overhead environmental filter, there is a secondary system of sliding grilles, glass panels, solid panels and adjustable blinds at the built form's vertical façades. Users can control and adjust the levels of environmental articulation to provide privacy, cross-ventilation, natural lighting, space usage, security and comfort.

BELOW
Drawing by Beverly Yeang at four years old

BOTTOM
Concept image: louvred glasses

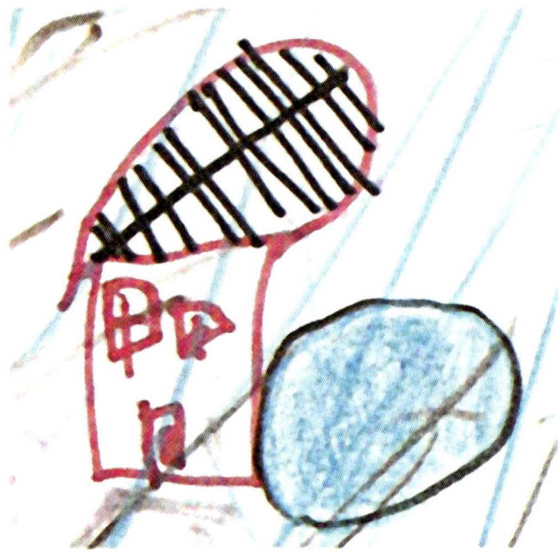

Roof-Roof House,
Southwest elevation

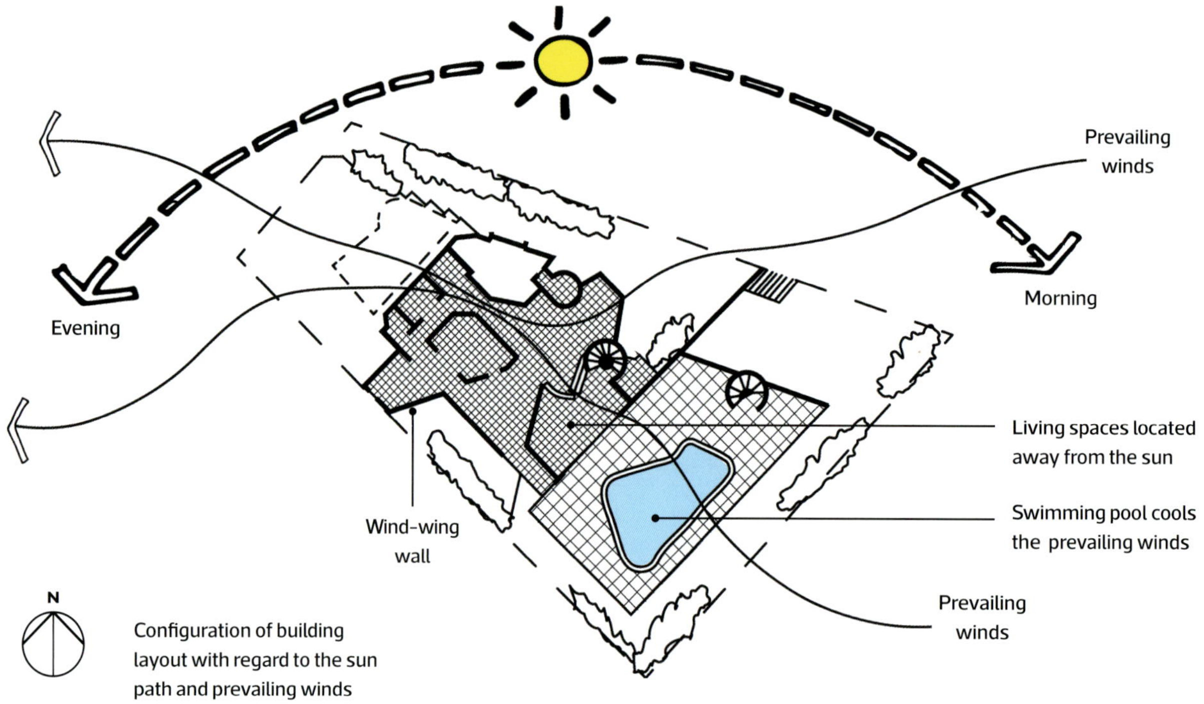

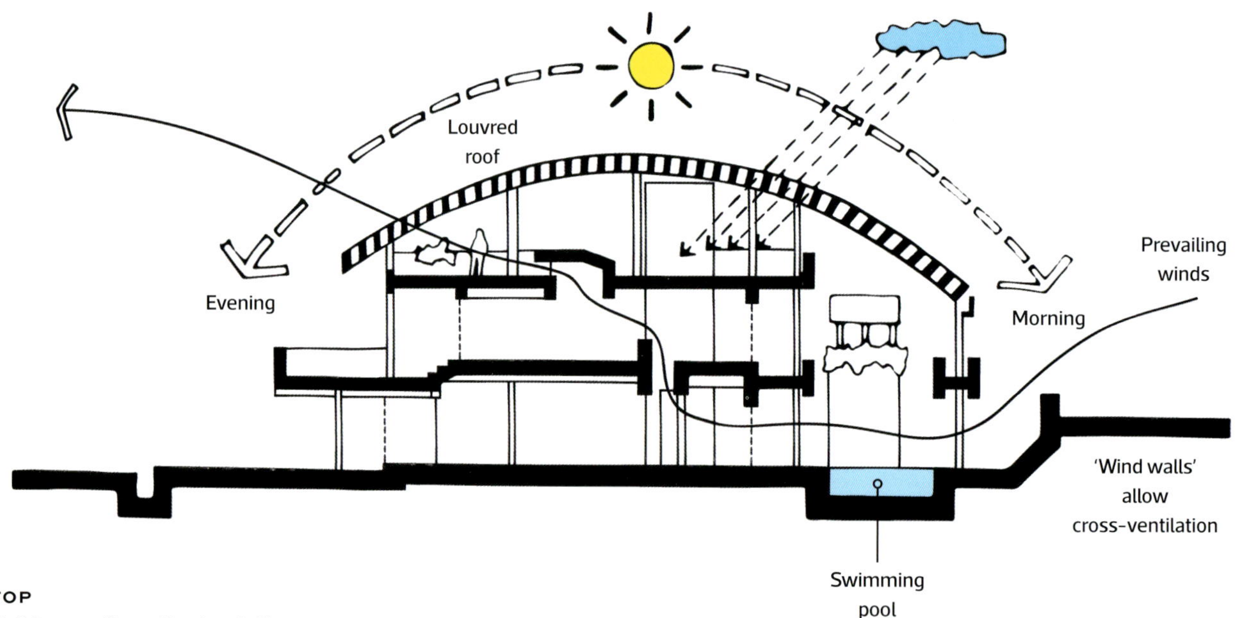

TOP
Building configuration in relation to sun path and prevailing winds

ABOVE
Cross-ventilation

ABOVE
The overarching 'second roof'

RIGHT
The Roof-Roof House's swimming pool is oriented south.

ROOF-ROOF HOUSE

The Roof-Roof House is located in Ampang, Selangor, with a total built-up area of 3,500 square feet. Ken Yeang was his own client for this house, which was completed in 1984, a decade after Yeang left Cambridge University and started practice in Malaysia. This 2-storey house with a roof terrace is designed as a life-size working prototype of the architect's bioclimatic design ideas. The Roof-Roof House is perhaps the most well-known and publicised of Yeang's residential designs. It consists of a series of spaces arranged loosely as 'archetypical volumes' and punctuated with openings.

The double roof in this project is curved and constructed of reinforced concrete, hovering above the main roof. In this case, this outer, curved roof represents the house's most expressive element. Its curvature simulates and alludes to the overhead path of the tropical sun. The roof has both an underlying climatic and poetic intention. The curved element is comprised of louvres angled to reduce direct solar radiation from the midday sun while still admitting the morning sun. Because its louvres are angled to intercept the sun – rather than blocking it completely – they cause a play of light and shadow across the communal space.

BIOCLIMATIC FUNCTION AND INTENTIONS

The double roof is based on the tropical umbrella. This component, in principle, involves a second-layer roof over a primary roof. Climatically, the double roof is both an open system and enclosing layer, protecting a building from overhead solar radiation yet allowing airflow. The roof is also a variation of the principle of the double-skin façade.

DESIGN AND PRINCIPLES

Powell (1999) observes how, in aesthetic terms, this approach enriches the underlying Modernist theme of 'white-washed' reinforced concrete. He says:

> *The play of light as the sun moves across the louvered roof and the secondary forms is delightful....the juxtaposition of one element over another is breath-taking, as is the clarity of edges, shadow lines and dark recesses.*

To maximise cross-ventilation effects, the planning of internal spaces is based on a radial arrangement along the

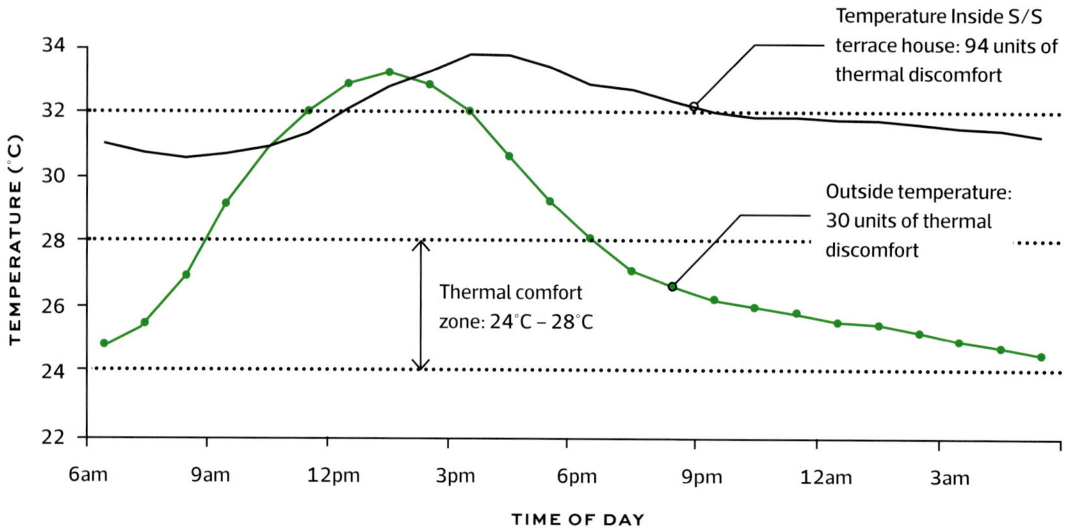

FIGURE 1 Temperature inside a concrete house, February 1998 (Chan, 2005)

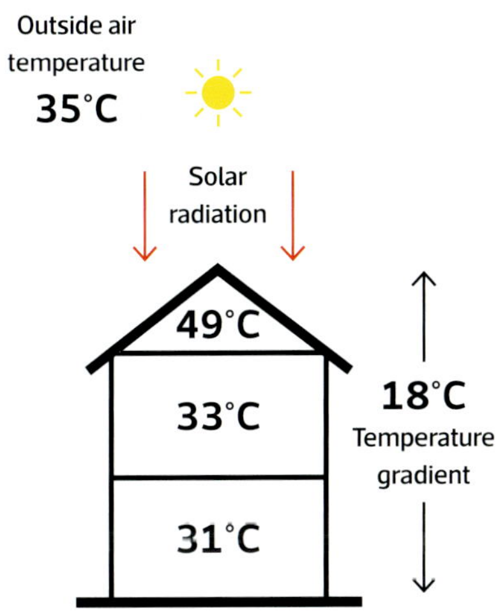

FIGURE 2
Indoor temperature versus outdoor ambient temperature (Chan. 2005)

east-west axis. The ground floor spaces that face east are open to the swimming pool. Throughout the day, the pool is intended to cool the air as it enters from the prevailing south-easterly and north-westerly directions. The movable internal glass partitions and panels act to control the flow of air and improve the internal micro-climate of the house.

THE SIGNIFICANCE OF THE ROOF IN PASSIVE DESIGN

Under the Malaysian climate, due to the intensity of solar radiation from the overhead sun path throughout the year, an enclosed roof or a typical attic space below a sealed roof surface will overheat throughout the day. Temperatures in these spaces are typically 10-14 degrees hotter than the ambient temperature. The roof space, or plenum, can heat up to 49 °C when external temperatures are peaking (i.e., 33 °C). The heat builds up during the day due to absorption by tiles and decking. Typically, insulation is used to reduce heat conduction or ventilation features are introduced to exhaust the heated air. The roof space also accumulates moisture, leading to mould occurrence issues and health issues as well as potentially harboring pests and vermin. Typical strategies to reduce heat and moisture build-up include the installation of ridge vents and turbines into the attic roof for exhaustion.

TYPICAL PERFORMANCE OF A CONCRETE HOUSE IN MALAYSIA

Typical thermal performance of a concrete house suggests that internal temperatures are generally higher than outside, due to the capacity of concrete to absorb heat. It is typical for attic temperatures to reach 40 °C or higher, the first floor to reach about 33 °C, and the ground floor to reach about 31 °C. Studies (such as those by Chan Chee Hong, 2005) have highlighted the importance of the roof in the control of heat gain and its consequent impact on passive cooling in low-rise housing in the tropics.

Additional studies, such as those conducted by Francois Garde, Leatitia Adelard, H. Boyer and C. Rat. (2004), further highlight the significance of the roof as a prime passive measure in the tropics. Also, studies such as those conducted by S. Ahmed, S. Abduli and A. Zain-Ahmad (2005) demonstrate not only that the enhanced performance of the roof is critical to cooling a house but that the exhaustion of hot air within the roof space (i.e., between the roof's constructed layers) is equally important. Ideally, there should be continuous airflow between a double layer of roof construction. In a study by D. Harimi, M. Harimi, V.J. Kurian, N. Bulong, I. Zakaria and I. Gungat (2005), the heat gain absorption impact of concrete tiles on the roof was highlighted. A further study by Hui Seng Kin (1998) highlighted the importance of implementing wind-induced cooling to achieve passive cooling systems and reduce daytime temperatures in residential concrete houses.

PERFORMANCE IN USE OF THE ROOF-ROOF HOUSE

A final-year thesis by UTM final-year architecture student Zulkifli Ismail in 2002 monitored the performance of the house by assessing internal spaces. Thermal comfort measurements were conducted for two full days, throughout the day and night on the 13th and 14th of September. Ismail found on Day 1 that when the external temperature was at a peak of 35 °C the internal temperatures of the house were lower, at peaks of 30.5 at the ground floor, 30.6 at the first floor, and 33.8 at the roof level. On Day 1 of the assessment, when the external weather was cloudier and the average temperature during the day was 31 degrees, the ground floor was 29.1 degrees, the first floor was 29.4 degrees, and the uppermost floor was 30.7 degrees. Zulkifli found that from 11 am onwards there was a decrease in solar radiation by 250 w/m² within the terrace areas of the roof compared to the external solar radiation values, which ranged between 500 and 800 w/m². At points just above the swimming pool the decrease is higher, and at about 11 am the highest recorded solar external reading was 775 w/m² while at different exposed areas around the house the solar intensity decreased to 675 and 664 w/m² respectively. On Day 2 of measurement, the external solar radiation levels were measured at 774 w/m² and the peak reading was also around 11 am.

Air temperature recorded was lowest around the swimming pool and found to be about 27 °C. However, due to heat absorption of the concrete mass, between 8:30 am to 3: pm the external temperatures were higher than the internal temperatures. At peak temperatures there is about a 5-degree difference between internal and external areas, with the maximum temperature outside peaking around 31.1 °C.

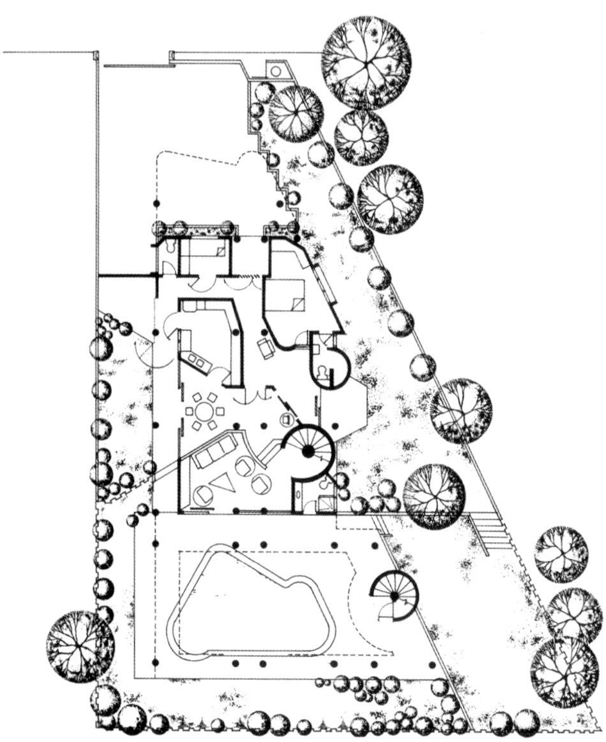

Ground Floor Plan

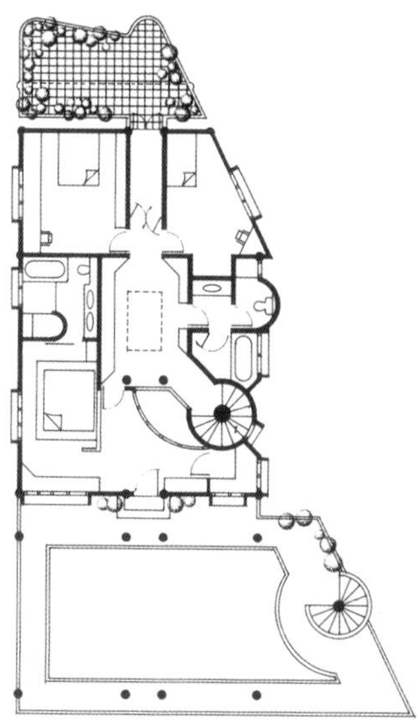

First Floor Plan

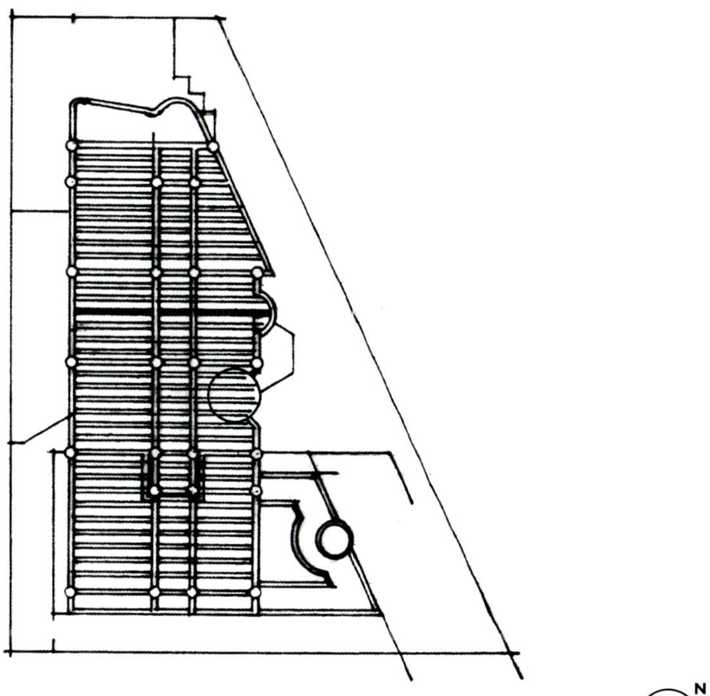

Roof Plan

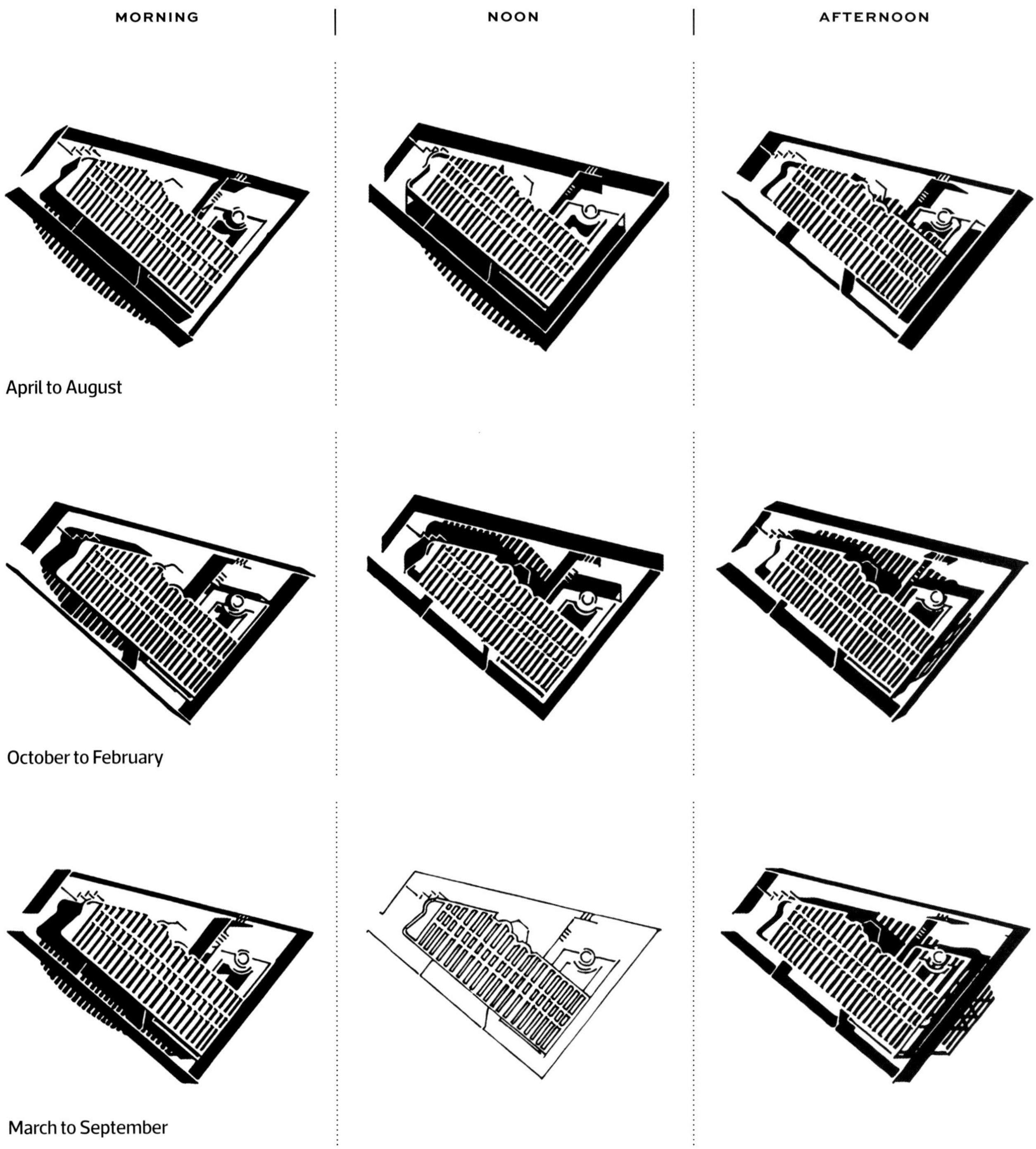

ABOVE

Plan view of shading diagram

The swimming pool in Roof Roof House also doubles as an evaporative cooling device.

Vertical Landscaping

DESIGN IDEA

'Vertical landscaping' is a constructed subsystem that brings landscaping and planting up the walls and façades of a building, linking the vegetation at the ground plane to the upper horizontal surfaces, terraces and roofs in the built form.

To enable a vertical ecological nexus and connection, we need a system of planter boxes or trellises that starts from the ground plane (linked to the landscape at the ground level and, if possible, to the hinterland) and extends up the face of a building. At mid-level, planters can traverse horizontally across a built form's floor and then climb upwards again, at the same or another façade, to link to vegetated, landscaped terraces. A large mass of vertical planting is designed to work in tandem with a building's mechanical systems, to perform as insulation to reduce the energy load and to scrub external incoming air before it enters the building's M&E systems. Robotic devices akin to cherry pickers can be incorporated into the architecture of the built form as landscape maintenance; these systems could also be used to clean and maintain the façade's glazing, cladding and outriggers. The greenery enhances the microclimate around the built form near its facade by absorbing air-polluting VOCs and carbon dioxide while producing oxygen through photosynthesis. The aim is to contribute to enhancing biodiversity, and in some cases even bring back native species that are believed to have disappeared from a locality. Vertical greening balances the inorganic mass of the built form, and its integration advances the idea of creating buildings that are constructed ecosystems.

BELOW
Concept section for IBM Plaza

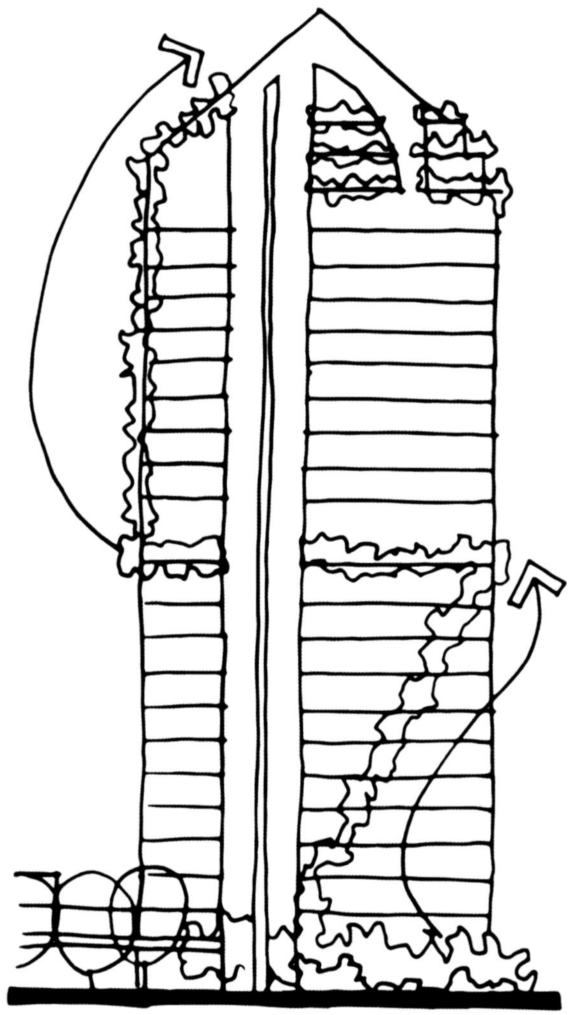

IBM Plaza
Stepped planters
Elevated core on west side as solar buffer
Interlinking bridge

Centralised planting

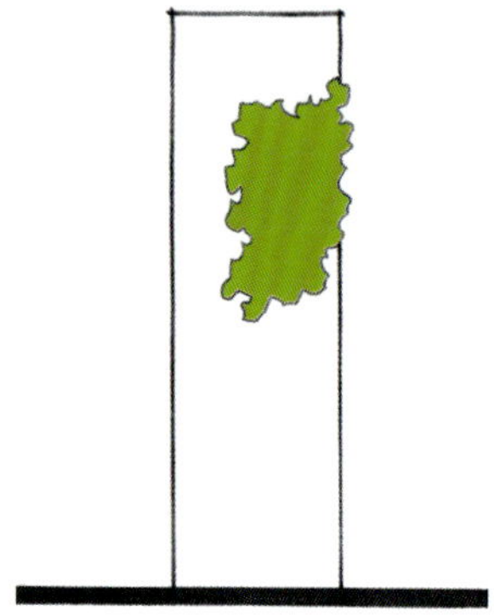

Juxtapositioning

Dispersed planting / 'spotty' pattern

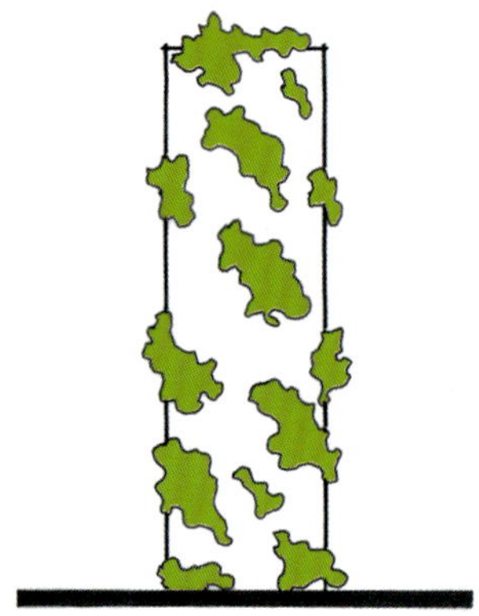

Intermixing

Dispersed planting / 'stepping stones'

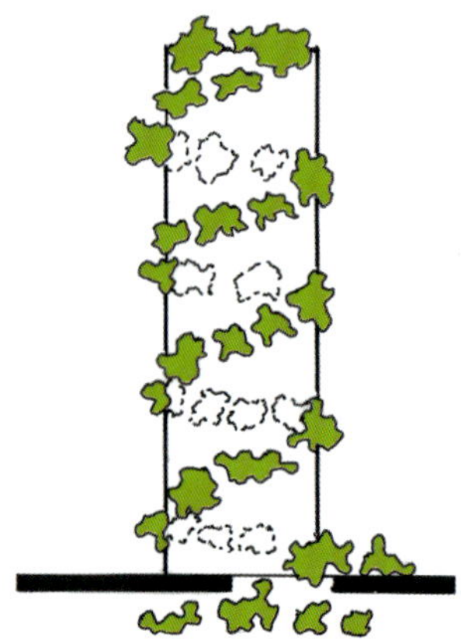

Linear intermixing

Continuous planting

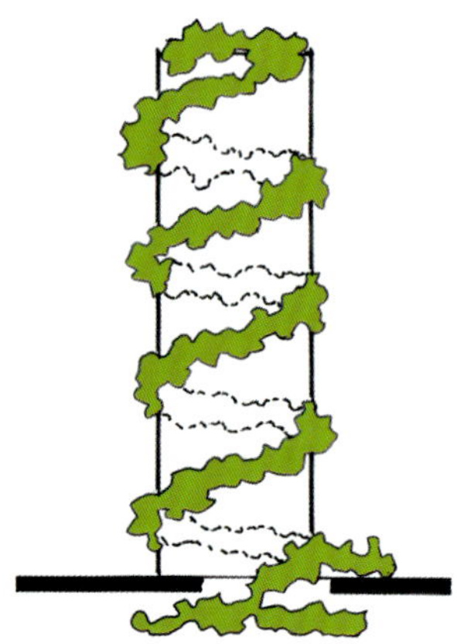

Integrating

Linear spine

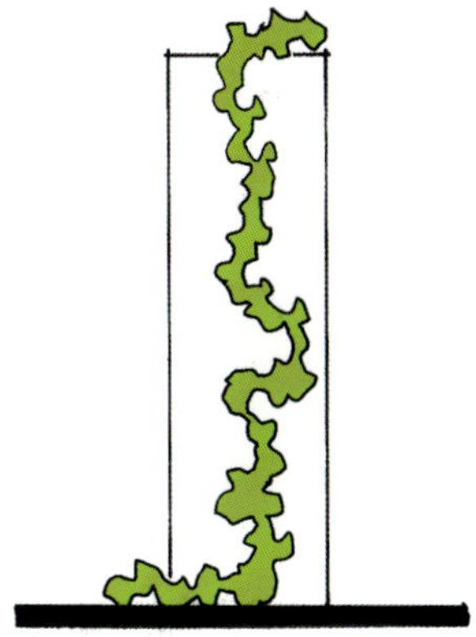

Linear spine

Linear spine
with fingers

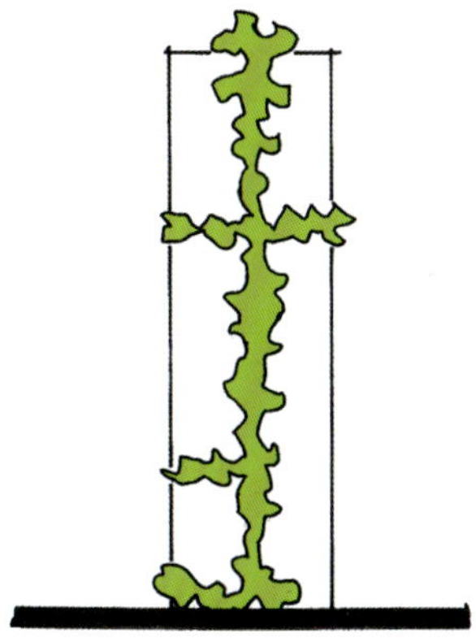

Linear spine
with fingers

Double
linear spine
with fingers

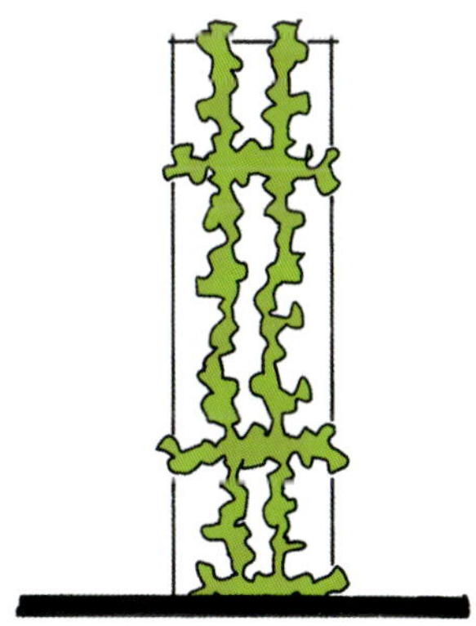

Double
linear spine
with fingers

Integrated
linear spine

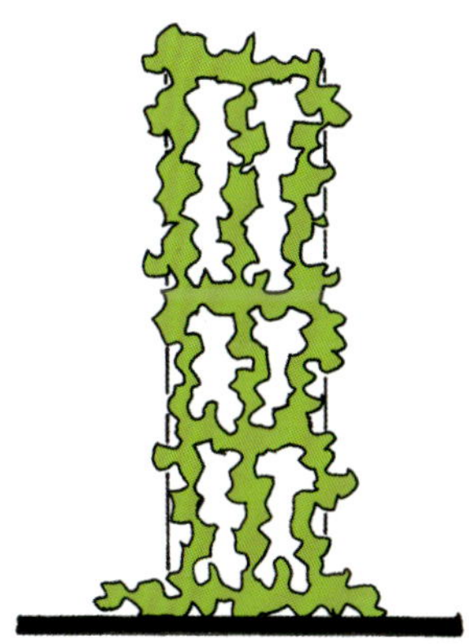

Integrated
linear spine

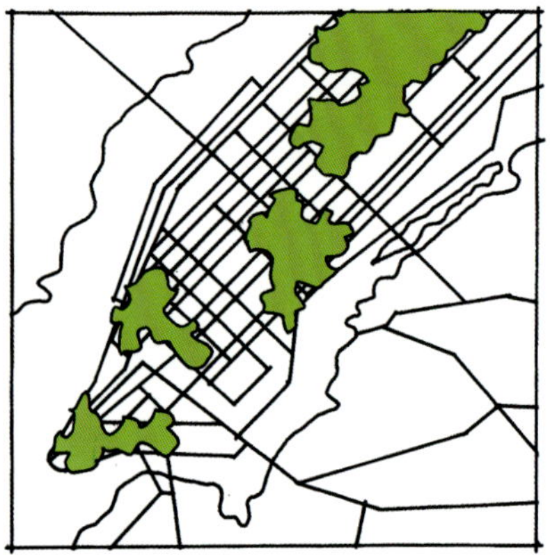

Clumps

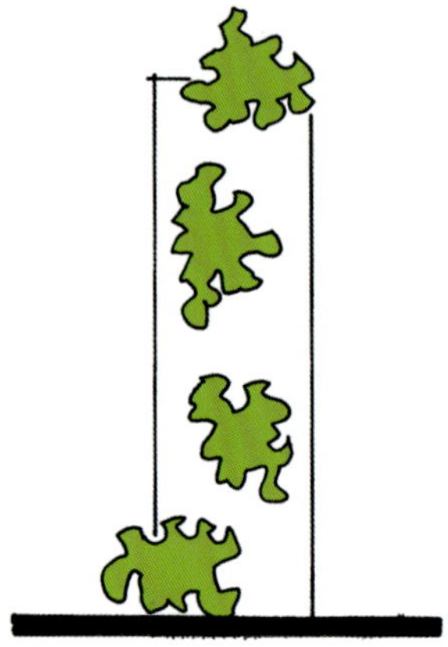

Clumps

Linear spine
with clumps

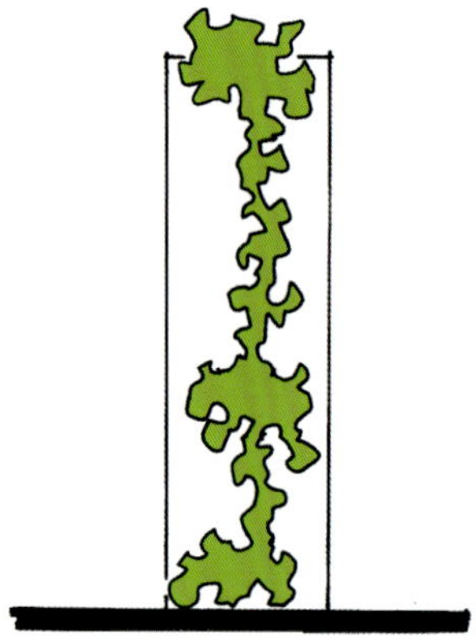

Linear spine
with clumps

Continuous
clumps

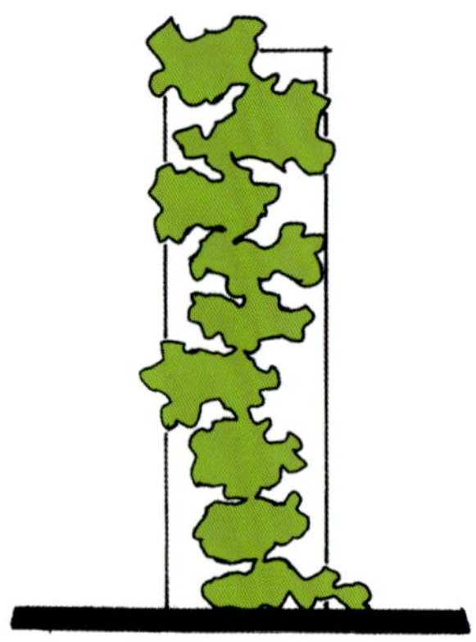

Continuous
clumps

Mixed linear
clumps

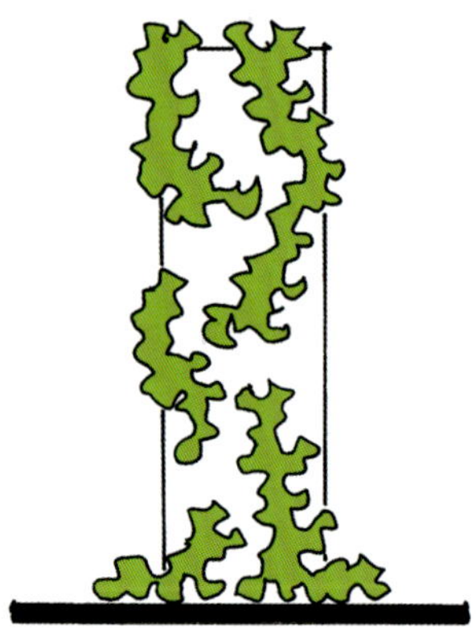

Mixed linear
clumps

FACING PAGE, LEFT
Greening patterns for masterplan

FACING PAGE, RIGHT
Greening patterns for built forms

ABOVE
View of IBM Plaza showing vertical landscaping: linear intermixing

IBM PLAZA

The IBM Plaza consists of a 24-storey office tower and a three-storey annexe block, which houses a single-storey restaurant / food court that is linked by a curvilinear bridge. The tower is located in the centre of one of the affluent suburbs of Kuala Lumpur. Adjacent buildings that surround the IBM Plaza include three-storey shop/houses and shop/offices, linked townhouses and low- and medium-rise condominiums.

Yeang explains the principles involved in this design:

> *The building does four things. It sets out to respond by both plan and form to the climate. It responds to the requirement for landscaping by introducing planting diagonally upwards across the face of a high-rise built form. It seeks to break away from the conventions of a straight plan, a curtain-walled, modernist tower block. In terms of urban design, it provides linkages to the surrounding base.*

Yeang's initial concept for the building was integrating 'open-air' sky gardens at the ground level, the middle level, and at the rooftop of the tropical high-rise. The vegetation was designed to appear to be 'climbing the face of the tower' (as shown in Figure 3) - it ascends from the ground-floor garden or the landscaped base that surrounds the main tower block. This vertical landscaping climbs in a zig-zag manner through an escalating system of planter boxes, which rise diagonally up the building. Mid-way, these planters continue on the opposite face of the building, culminating in a roof garden.

In the initial stages of design, Yeang

FIGURE 1 Stepped planters on IBM Plaza

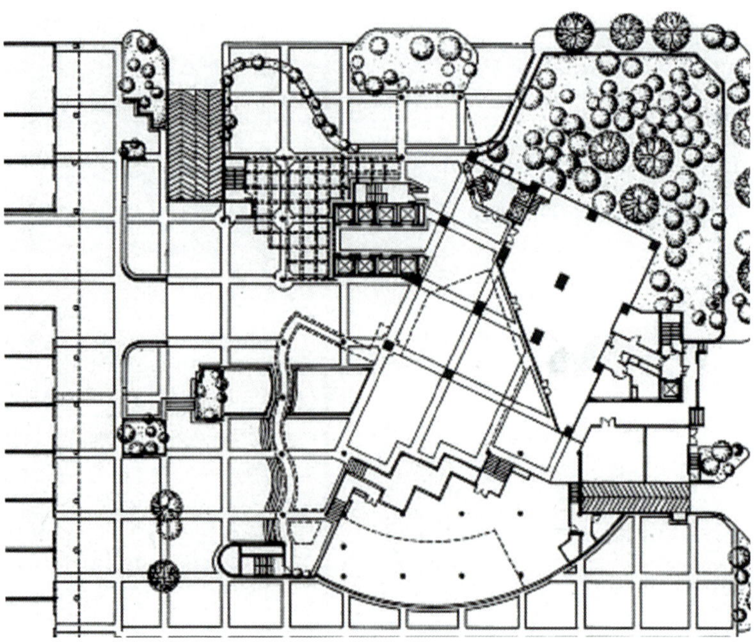

FIGURE 2 Plan of typical floor showing orientation of building

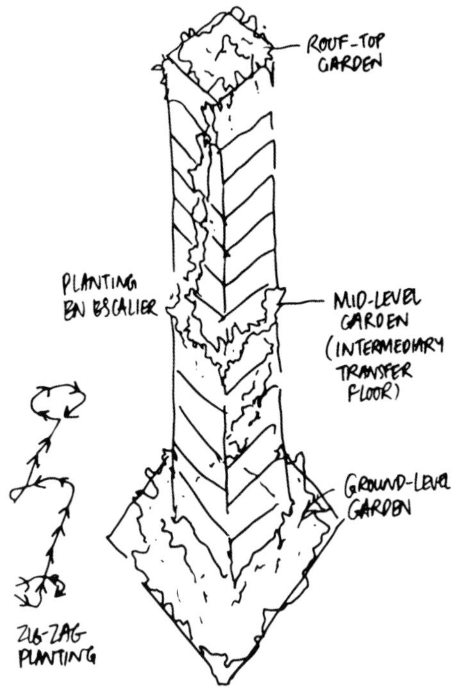

FIGURE 3 Yeang's concept for vegetation strategies in IBM Plaza

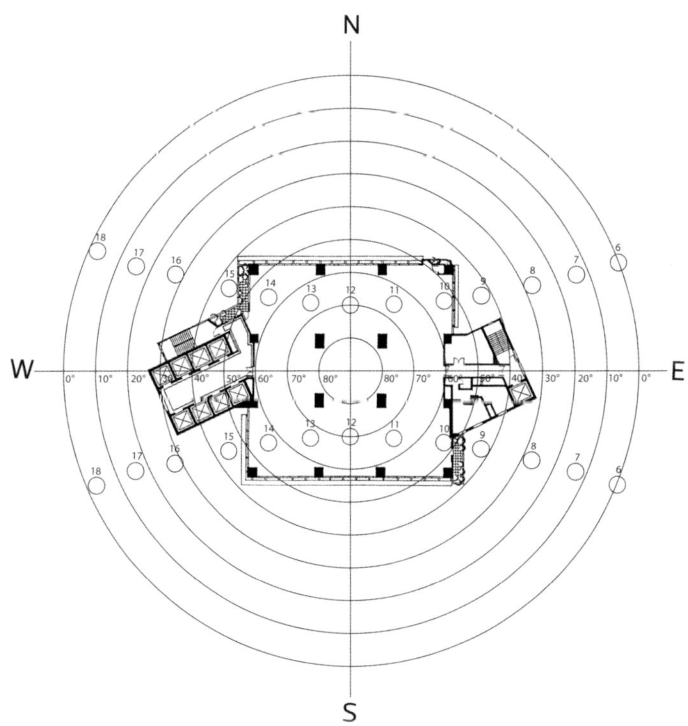

FIGURE 4 IBM Plaza- Typical floor plan showing orientation of tower according to sunpath

recognised that the sun's geometry and the contextual geometry of the building and site did not coincide. The orientation of the main tower was then adjusted to adhere to the sun's geometry, while subsidiary elements (service cores that house the toilets and lifts) remained oriented towards the geometry of the site. The service cores, fire escape areas and toilets are located on the hot east and west sides of the tower.

SIMULATION STUDIES: IBM PLAZA

Using dynamic thermal simulation tools, cooling and total energy consumption were observed to assess the cooling load impact of the above strategies in comparison with generic models. The key issue of the investigation was the extent of impact in adding balconies and vegetation to a generic form of the tower, a 'baseline' tower with a conventional, homogenous facade and a 'central core' layout. Cooling load impact was analyzed and compared to a baseline option with no vegetation.

SIMULATION STUDIES: MENARA MESINIAGA (GENERIC STUDIES)

Similarly to IBM Plaza, here the impact of vegetation was assessed based on an addition of 0.5m to the height of the balconies (which were 1.0m) that surrounded the perimeter and shaded the windows below.

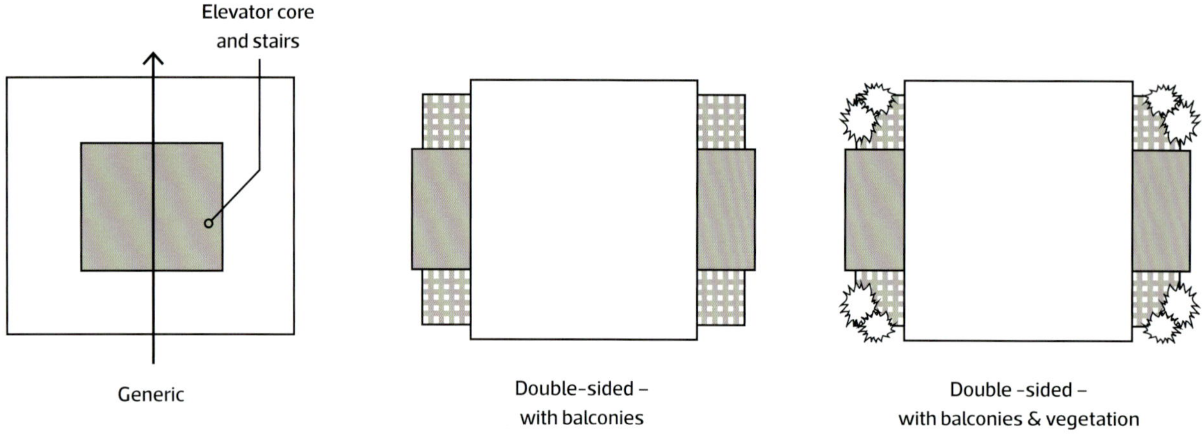

FIGURE 5 Typical layout plan of generic, 'with balconies' and 'with balconies and vegetation' models for IBM Plaza (Jahnkassim, 2004)

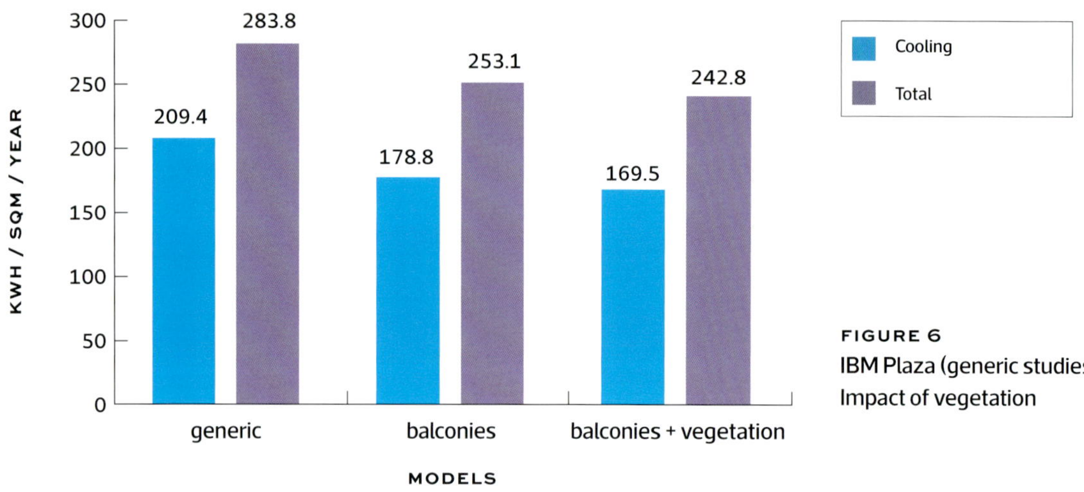

FIGURE 6
IBM Plaza (generic studies) – Impact of vegetation

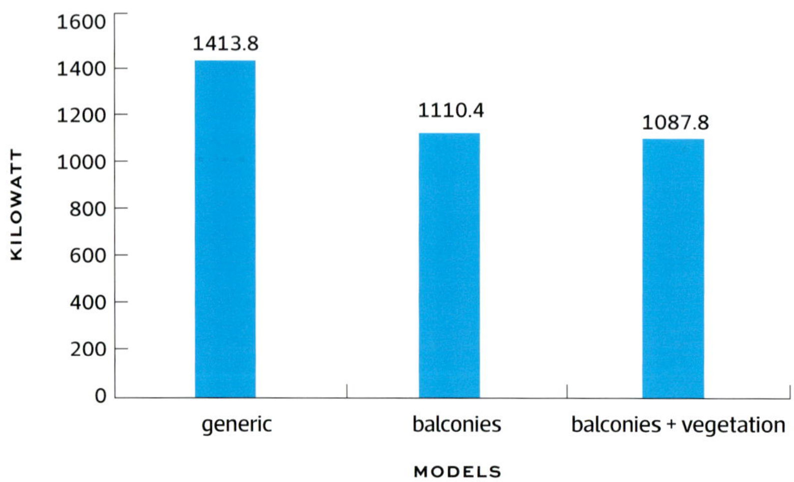

FIGURE 7
Plaza IBM (generic studies) – Peak cooling impact of vegetation

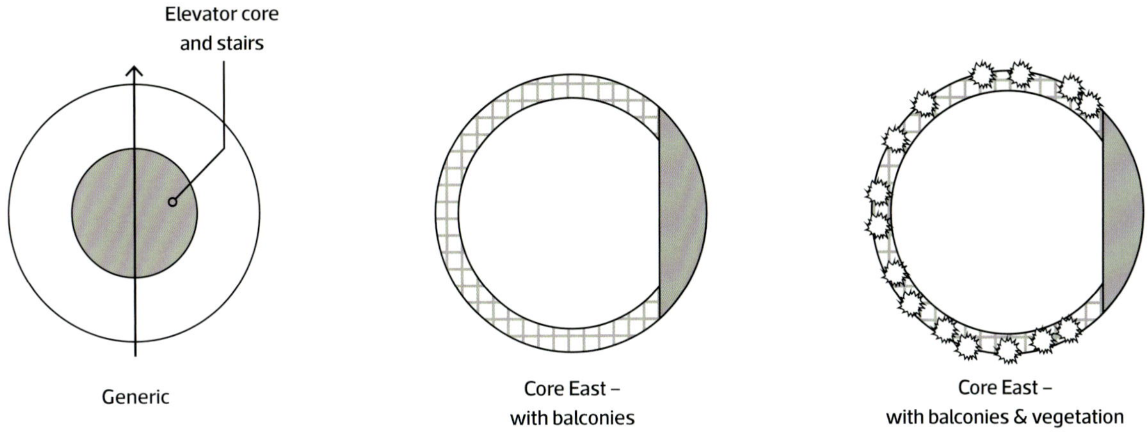

FIGURE 8 Typical layout plan of generic, with 'balconies' and 'with balconies and vegetation' models for Menara Mesiniaga

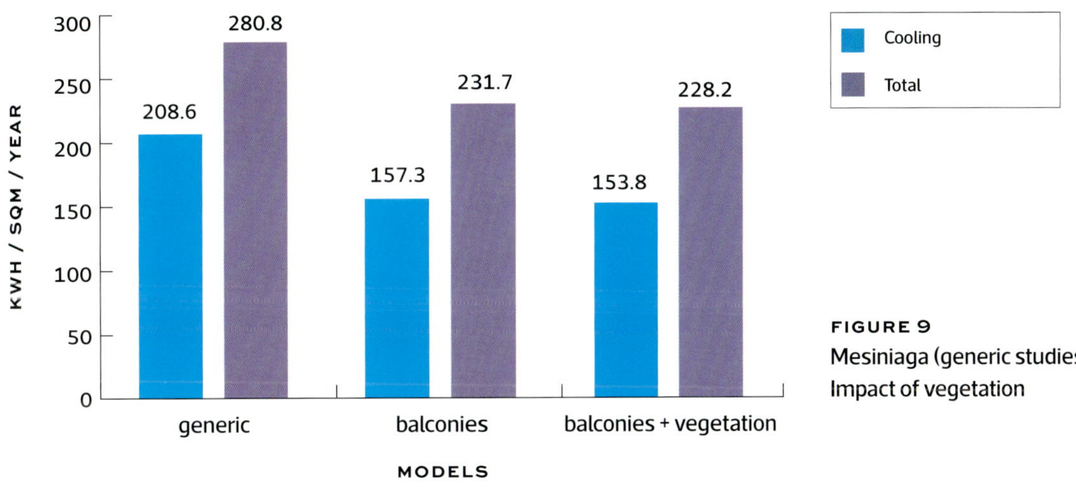

FIGURE 9
Mesiniaga (generic studies) – Impact of vegetation

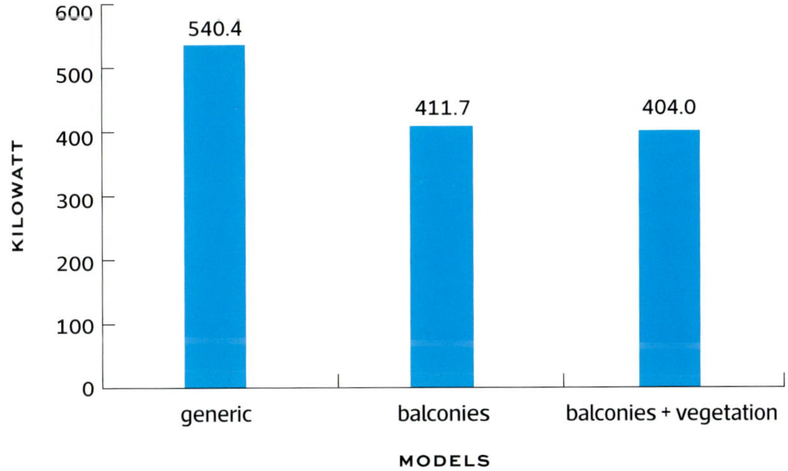

FIGURE 10
Mesiniaga (generic studies) – Peak cooling impact of vegetation

SIMULATION STUDIES: MENARA MESINIAGA (FINAL DESIGN)

In the final phase of study, vegetation was modelled as an obstruction placed at the edges of the large skycourts. This feature was modelled after an addition of 0.5m to the height of the balcony (balcony width 4.5m).

The average height of vegetation in the simulation studies was 1.5m, including the balconies. It was generally found that the effectiveness of vegetation in reducing heat gain is dependent on its impact as an opaque obstruction to the window wall. This determines the amount of shading on the façade, which can obstruct incoming solar gains. This, in turn, depends not only on the height of vegetation but also the distance of vegetation from the window wall. In IBM Plaza, the vegetation is designed with narrower balconies – located about 1.5m away from the window wall. However, in Mesiniaga, where vegetation is placed in the larger skycourts, they are located about 4.5m away from the window wall. Hence, when used in conjunction with sky-garden strategies, vegetation's cooling effectiveness on the high-rise envelope decreases.

BENEFITS OF 'LANDSCAPING IN SKYCOURTS': SURVEY

A detailed assessment of user responses was undertaken in Mesiniaga – users were simply asked to indicate their responses, on a general scale, to the landscaping feature – to what extent did they agree that the landscaping 'outside' contributed positively to the office atmosphere 'inside' the building. IBM Plaza was not included in the assessment because there are no skycourts with landscaping – it only has smaller balconies. The responses are summarized in Figure. 13 and the trend is positive.

SUMMARY & DISCUSSIONS

Vegetation components are intended by Yeang to primarily improve air quality and balance the organic and inorganic mass of the tower. However, when integrated as green elements in balconies, skycourts or façade systems of air-conditioned high-rises, their advantage of affecting indoor air quality is almost secondary, the primary advantage being limiting heat gain under the tropical climate.

Yeang has mentioned:

> *Besides providing shading to the internal spaces and to the external wall, it also minimizes heat reflection and glare into the building.* (1992)

Vegetation has a variety of benefits, not only energy efficiency. Greenery helps to reduce pollution and increases evapotranspiration while having a cooling impact on buildings, people and surroundings. In a high-rise, planting vegetation on the façade has more potential for cooling and shading than the roof. In order to analyse the impact of vegetation, this feature was tested based on a generic square.

The extent of the effectiveness of vegetation as a cooling strategy to control solar heat gain in the tropics is dependent upon vegetative height, opacity and average distance from window walls. Although it gives a form of thermal protection, the advantages of vegetation are not only environmental but psychological. Occupants have commented how they enjoy the opportunity to see greenery in high-rise office environments. Perceptions of the interior by building occupants and their responses were clearly more positive in the presence of plants and vegetation.

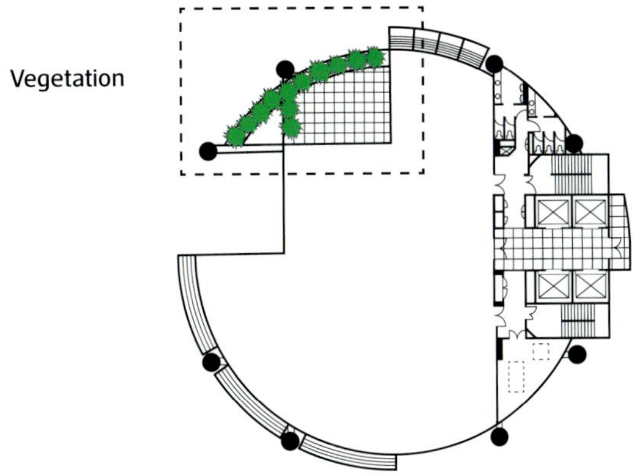

FIGURE 11
Floor plan of Menara Mesiniaga

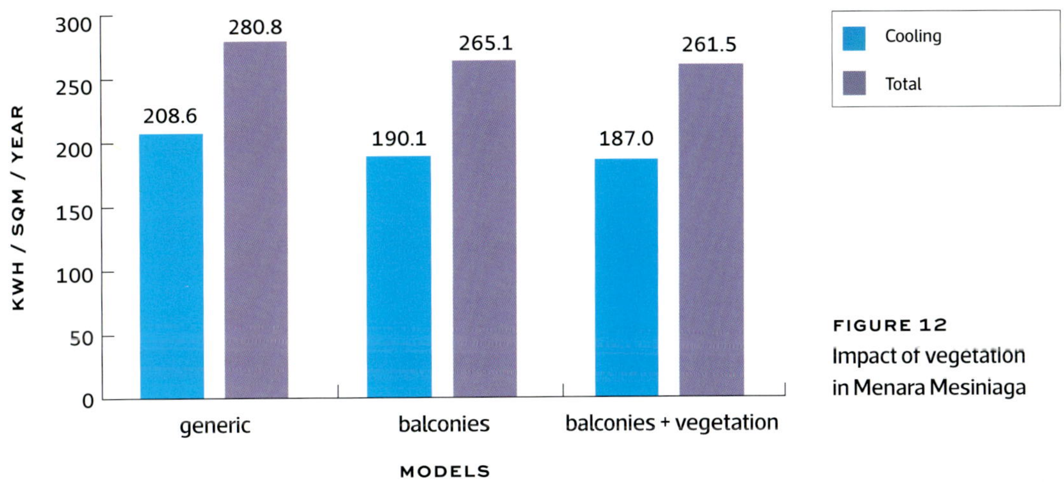

FIGURE 12
Impact of vegetation in Menara Mesiniaga

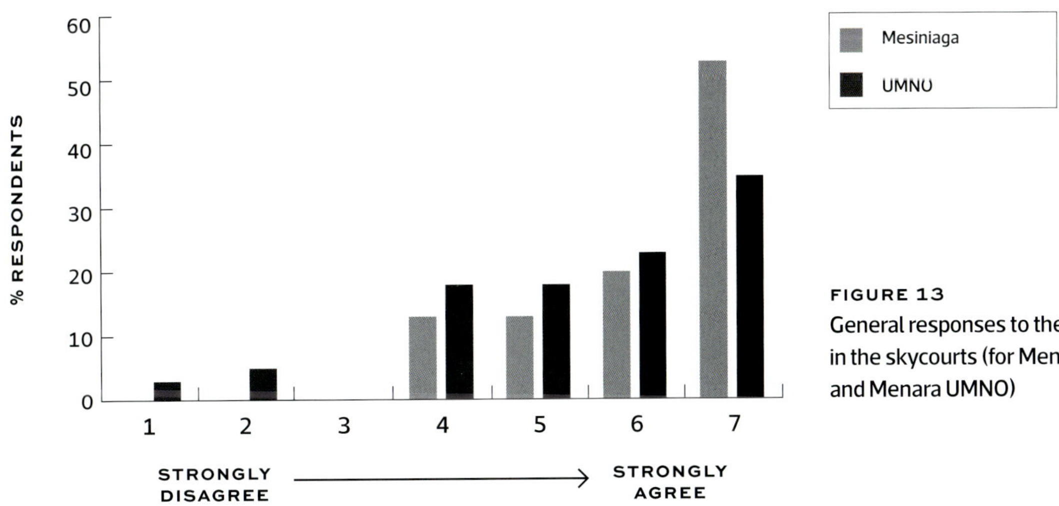

FIGURE 13
General responses to the landscaping in the skycourts (for Menara Mesiniaga and Menara UMNO)

LEFT
The orange 'ribbon' marks the presence of the internal planted ramp

BELOW
Section through landscaped ramp

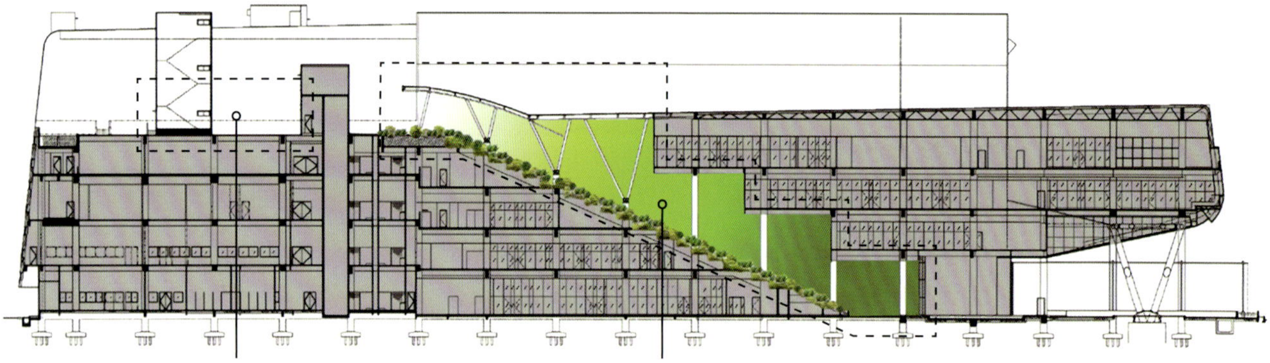

MEWAH OILS HEADQUARTERS, SELANGOR, MALAYSIA

The significance of this project is that here the vegetation becomes internalised, in contrast to other tropical projects where the planting is largely located on the outside of buildings within recesses or skycourts, or within inside/outside transitional spaces.

The main feature of Mewah Oils Headquarters is a continuous landscaped ramp, which rises from the ground level to the roof and acts as vertical landscaping for the building. The ramp is thickly

CLOCKWISE, FROM TOP LEFT

1 Landscaped ramp adjacent to roof

2 Landscaped ramp and water feature

3 Landscaped ramp at mid-level

4 View of cafeteria from entrance

vegetated with tropical plants, which are maintained using recycled rainwater. A cascading water feature running alongside the planting troughs is designed to provide a 'calming ambience' while performing as a cooling agent through evaporation. The vegetation, or 'green eco infrastructure', is placed centrally within an inclined entrance lobby; it then steps gradually upwards via a densely foliaged inclined planter that extends all the way to a rooftop garden, accessed by a wide, straight flight of stairs.

'This inclined foliaged garden serves as an internal lung, scrubbing the air of the building's interiors clean while providing biophilic benefits for the building's users', says Yeang.

TOKYO-NARA TOWER, JAPAN

Tokyo-Nara Tower is a conceptual project, prepared for the World Architecture Exposition in Nara, Japan, to exemplify ideas for a climatically responsive skyscraper. The tower physically realises many of the theoretical ideas expounded by Yeang and represents a significant stage in the ongoing research into the nature and evolution of tall buildings. In this tower, vertical landscaping elements perform many important functions:

- The verdant foliage acts to cool the building by both shading and chemical photo-cooling
- The fringing of floors and atrial spaces allows careful planting to control air movements within the built structure
- The mass of planting relative to the built structure is favourable and comparable, thereby ensuring that bio-systems act symbiotically with mechanical systems to provide a balanced built environment

The maintenance of the vertical landscaping, as well as the upkeep of external fixtures, glazing and cladding panels, is ensured by specialised mechanical devices. These devices are constructed in the form of multi-purpose 'robot arms', cherry pickers on moveable trellises that travel along an external track that spirals around the tower.

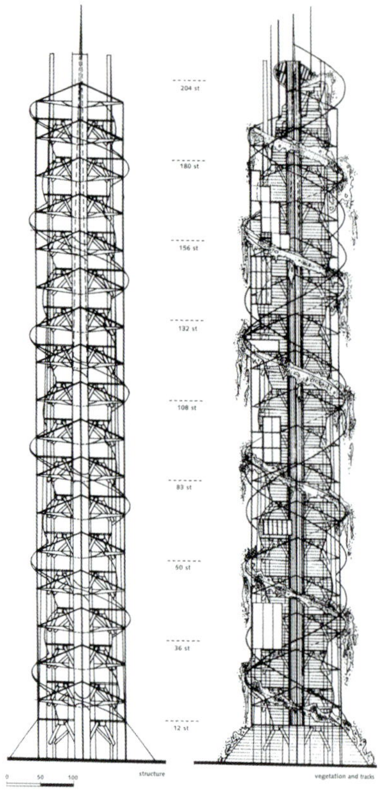

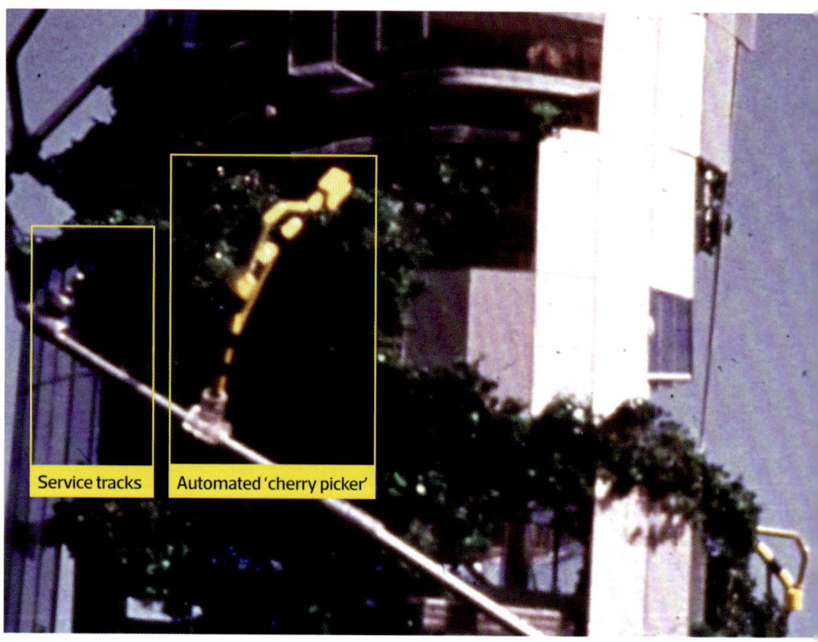

ABOVE LEFT
Elevation showing vegetation and tracks

ABOVE RIGHT
View of 'spiralling vertical landscape'

RIGHT
Service tracks that spiral up the building to carry mobile 'cherry pickers'

ABOVE
Vertical landscaping on C-College

C-COLLEGE OF HIGHER EDUCATION

C-College is a new development for higher education to create a model campus that promotes openness, interactiveness and green concepts. The design starts by giving the staff and students a luxuriant, well-landscaped environment that makes their academic life pleasurable, one that enhances the quality of their education and teaching.

A unique feature of the design is the central, vertical forested park, which acts as vertical landscaping and is the heart of the scheme. It provides a pleasurable park-like environment for study, play and convivial activities. Besides this, there is a variety of high-quality indoor spaces and green external spaces for students, staff and visitors to enjoy throughout their day at school.

This vertical greenery and landscaping not only encourage visual comfort to neighbourhoods but also reduce solar heat gain to the building. Greenery provides an insulating effect to the building structure, helping to lower urban air temperature and alleviate the urban heat-island effect. These not only bring natural life into the building and its surroundings but also help to create a healthier, friendlier and softer atmosphere for students, staff and visitors.

Diagonal Light Shaft

DESIGN IDEA

Developments in daylighting and high-performance glazing technologies have given rise to light-directing and refocusing methods such as heliostats and holographic glazing. The common strategy of redirecting sunlight is to reflect it off of ceilings or external shading devices to bring light deep into a building's layout. In multi-storey buildings in tropical regions, such technologies may present high-cost implications due to its availability, hence the idea of a diagonal light shaft allows the possibility of light being either directed inside through the implementation of reflective devices or filtered indoors through a more staggered concept of a typical vertical atrium. The aim of the diagonal light shaft is to cut through a building to allow daylight to penetrate deep into the interior. Internal lighting operates on a system of sensors that reduces energy use by automatically turning off lights when adequate daylighting is available. The diagonal light shaft can be viewed as a variation of a conventional light well. Typically a conventional light well is inserted vertically into a building mass with the aim of bringing daylight deep into its spaces. This is particularly needed for deep-plan buildings or buildings with underground levels. In a tropical climate, solar radiation can exceed 700-800 kw/m^2 during the day. Daylight has to be introduced, yet the accompanying solar gain must be controlled. It is imperative to find innovative ways to bring in daylight without the accompanying heat gain. The diagonal light shaft is an alternative strategy to bring daylight deep into a building's floor plate. Landscaped planter boxes within the solar shaft improve the interior quality of adjacent spaces and enhance views up into the building from the street below.

THIS PAGE
Conceptual sketch

NEXT PAGE
Central atrium of Solaris showing the uppermost opening of the light shaft

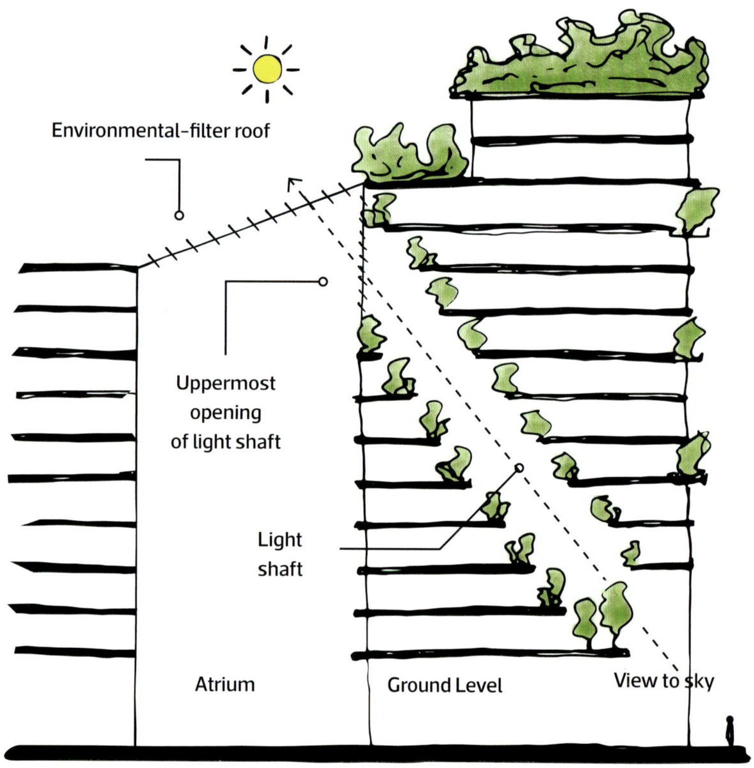

Environmental-filter roof
Uppermost opening
of light shaft

BELOW

Study for employing diagonal light shaft at Lot 2C5 Putrajaya (Initial Design)

ABOVE
Lot 2C5 Putrajaya

LOT 2C5 PUTRAJAYA

Lot 2C5 Putrajaya is a mixed commercial development comprised of 2 commercial components, including retail at the ground floor level and part of Level 1 with offices on levels 2 through 13. The overall development is divided into two blocks, a 7-storey podium block and a 7-storey tower block on top of the podium, resulting in a 14-storey building with both Block A and Block B. All ground-level retail areas are facing the Central Promenade, Dataran Wawasan, Putrajaya Boulevard and the drop-off areas. Due to the nature of the sloping site, from Dataran Wawasan into the P2 Road that makes up the Central Promenade, a number of retail areas facing the Central Promenade have higher floor heights, allowing for a future mezzanine floor.

The roof over the podium above Level 7 commercial and office areas is a multi-faceted surface, both structurally pleasing with metal decking and visually pleasing to its surroundings, and also able to conceal the M&E rooms, exhaust ducts and other utility facilities at the roof level. The roof garden incorporates BMU maintenance tracks, allowing for uninterrupted access by the BMU system to be subject and approved of by the employer's representative..

Level One Plan

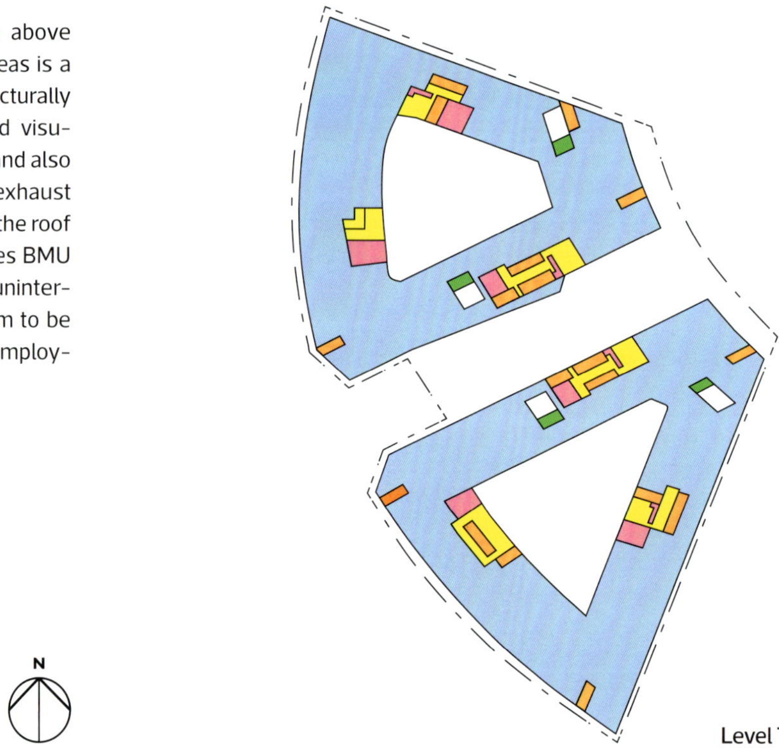

Level Two Plan

FIGURE 1

Simulation undertaken by the advanced Simulation Daylighting tool RADIANCE under CIE 10k overcast conditions to represent the worst external daylight scenario in Malaysia (Jahnkassim, 2014)

SIMULATIONS

Selected portions of the building layout were evaluated through the use of the advanced daylight simulation tool RADIANCE in order to evaluate both the effectiveness of the massing and façade, including the diagonal light shaft, in terms of increasing the total floor area of the daylight zone on a typical building floor plate. The simulation occurred under CIE 10k overcast conditions to present the worst external daylighting scenario in Malaysia (as shown in Figure 1).

The results demonstrate how daylight illuminance distribution and contours are increased, compared to a conventional layout, due to the introduction of a diagonal light shaft and central atrium (referring to a shaft located in the core areas of the building floor plate). These, together with the daylight contribution of façades, allow the illumination of areas that receive perimeter daylight to increase by 30% to 40%. As external daylight conditions in Malaysia may range from 5,000 lux on an overcast day up to 10,000 lux on an extremely sunny day, the absolute figures in lux must be understood against a bright overcast/cloudy day in Malaysia. Although the daylight contribution from façades far exceeds the contribution from a light well, the light shaft itself contributes significantly to ensure that daylight (without conventional heat gain and glare) can reach the core areas of the floor plate or the floor layout. The simulations demonstrate that a light shaft is able to bring 300 to 400 lux of daylight into the centrally located core areas of an office floor plate. In the absence of a light shaft, only the perimeter areas of the office layout receive adequate daylight.

SOLARIS, FUSIONOPOLIS, SINGAPORE

In the Solaris building, energy load is reduced through the deployment of an innovative passive-energy device called a 'light shaft'. A diagonal shaft that cuts through the upper floors of Tower A brings daylight deep into the building through an angle. The sunshades (up to 1 metre in width) also serve as light shelves, which deflect daylight into the building's interiors. Internal lighting operates on a system of sensors, which reduces energy use by automatically turning off lights when adequate daylighting is available. Landscaped terraces within the solar shaft bring added quality to adjacent spaces. The shaft enables pedestrians to see up into the building from the street below. These horizontal shades, which fold upwards when the ramped park opens out into corner terraces, are a distinguishing element of the building's overall aesthetic.

RIGHT
Internal view of solar light shaft bringing daylight into the building interior

BOTTOM
View of light shaft looking down

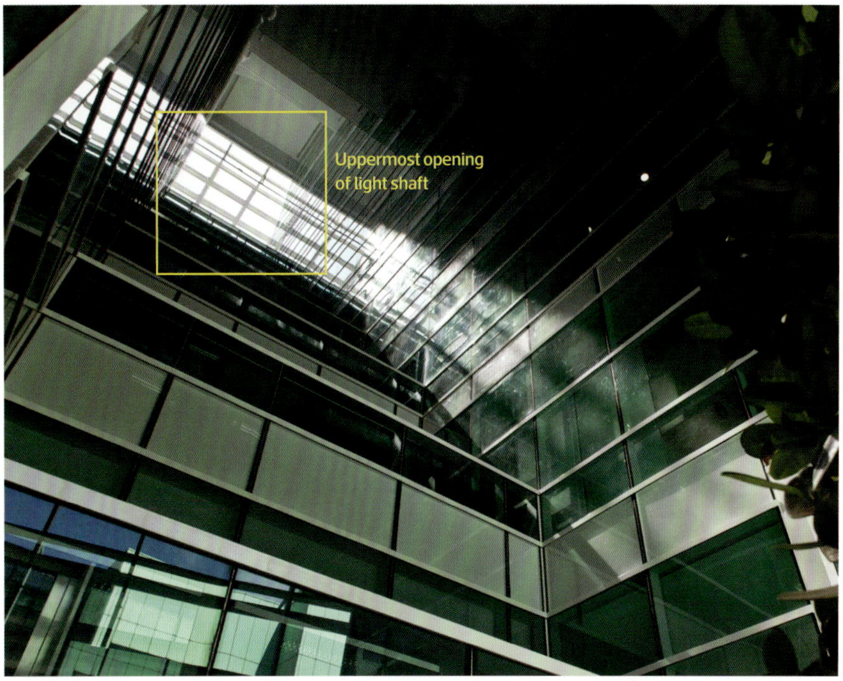

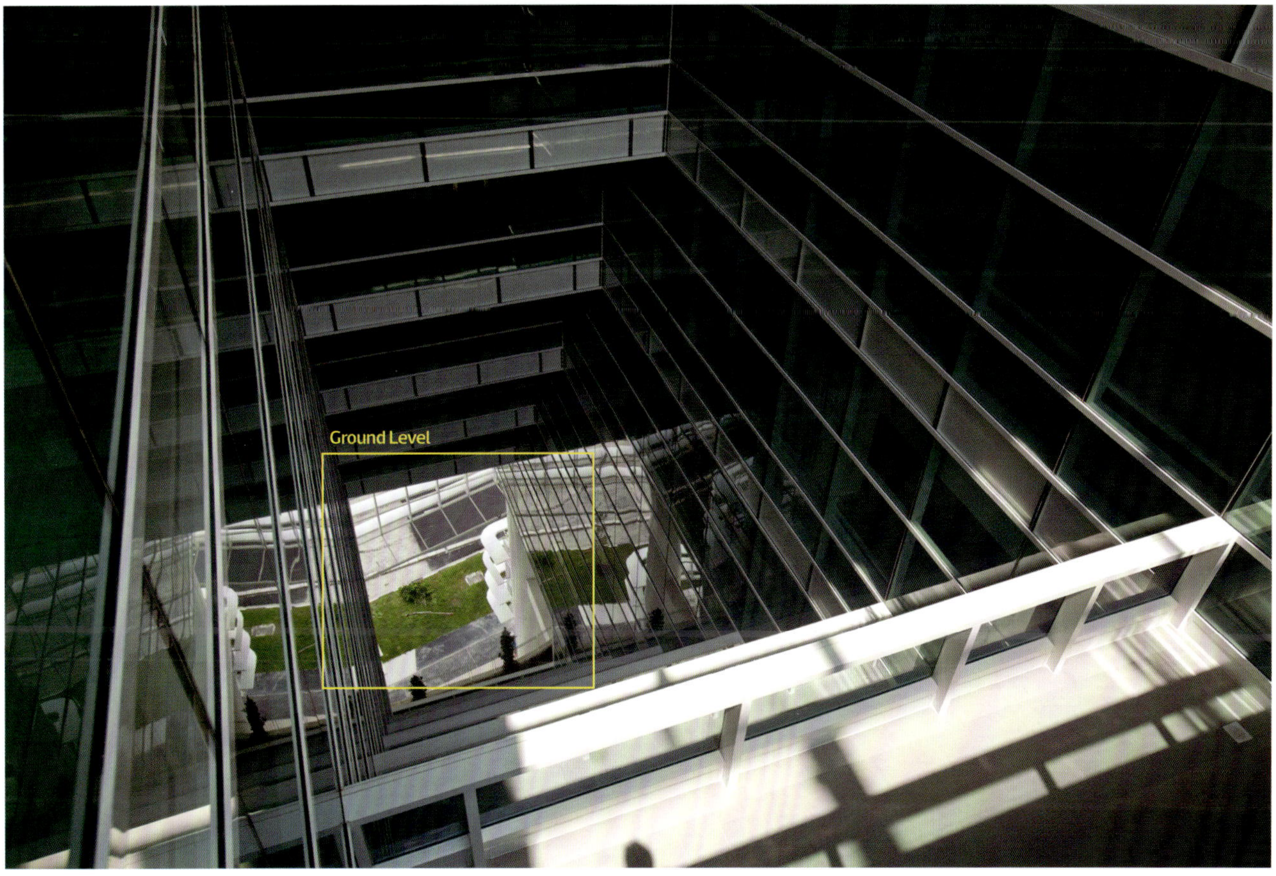

Mixed-mode Cooling System

DESIGN IDEA

Mixed-mode cooling is a hybrid approach that combines natural ventilation and low-energy mechanical systems, including air distribution mechanisms. The basic mixed-mode strategy is to encourage natural ventilation when the outside temperature is conducive and to minimise energy loss by changing over to a mechanically assisted ventilation system when the outside temperature exceeds practical limits. In mixed-mode systems, only the best-performing, least-consuming and most-appropriate technologies should be utilised. Examples include ceiling fans, demister fans, double façades, flue atriums and Trombe walls. The effectiveness of a mixed-mode design is dependent on the benign interaction between the interior of the built form and exterior ambient forces. Mixed-mode built forms usually have greater transparency and complexity because they admit and control ambient energy sources. The development of a mixed mode in a built form is dependent on the cost-effective exploitation of ambient energy sources without the incurment of any penalties in terms of discomfort. In more temperate climates, this is usually associated with these buildings' use of solar gain for warmth, natural lighting and ventilation. In principle, mixed-mode use aims to create as natural of an environment as possible, and building occupants have control over their environment for their thermal comfort via opening windows and drawing blinds.

BELOW
Example of mixed-mode cooling using extractor fans

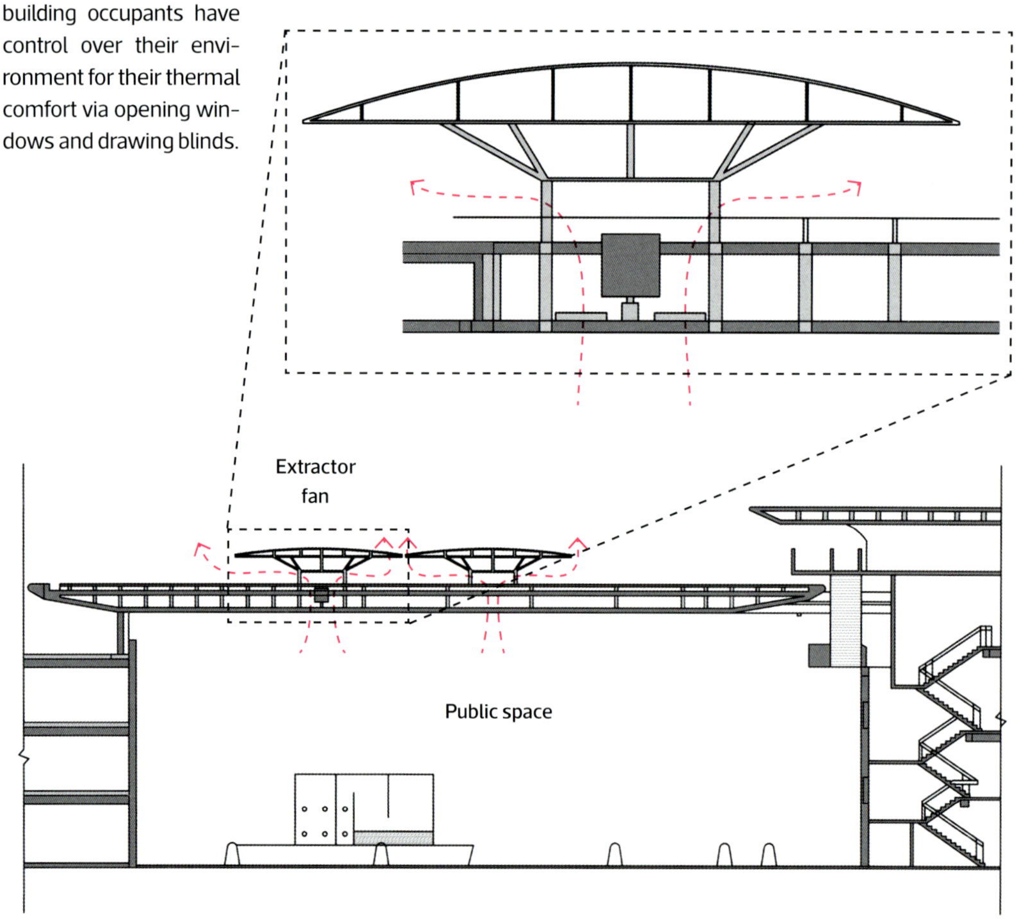

TTDI Plaza

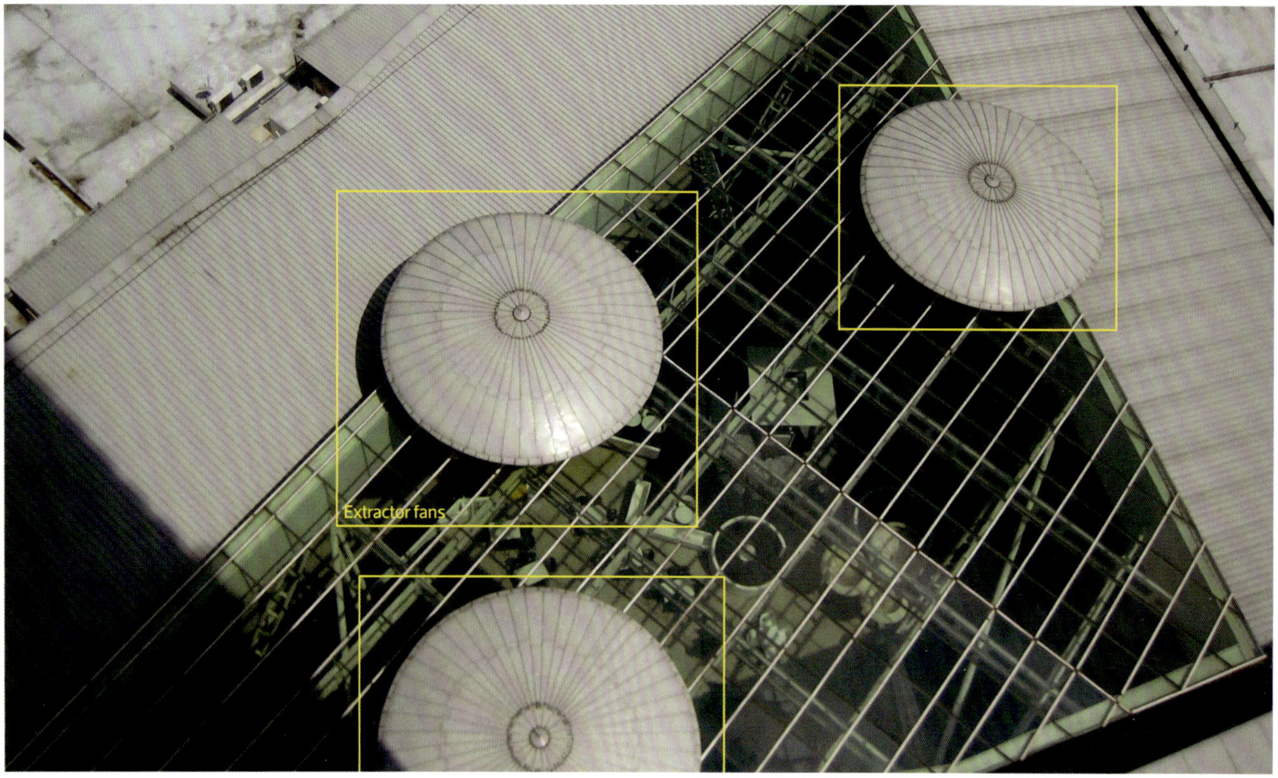

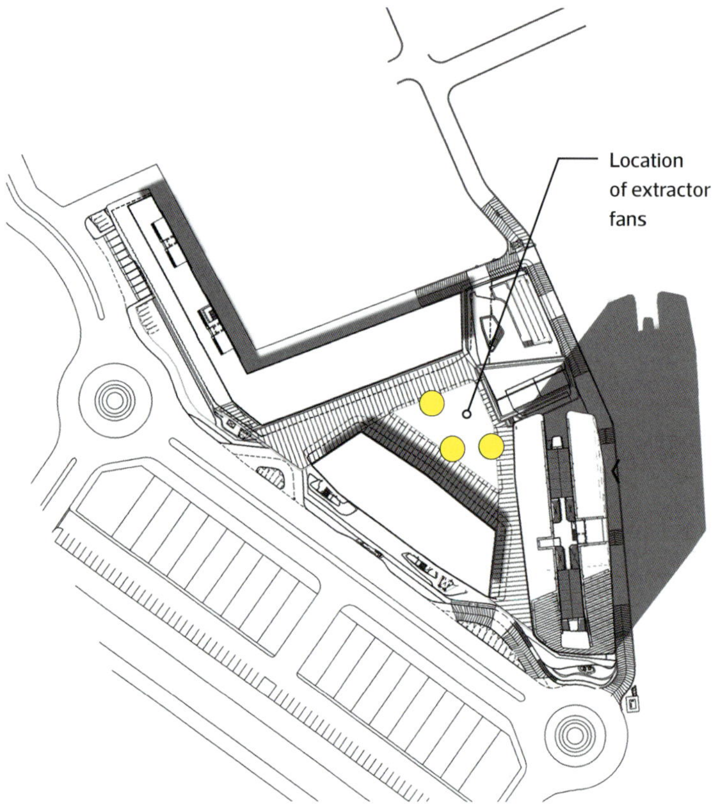

TOP
Rooftop view

ABOVE
View of the Plaza TTDI,
Taman Tun Dr. Ismail

RIGHT
Site plan

LEFT
View of the atrium

BELOW
Section through TTDI Plaza

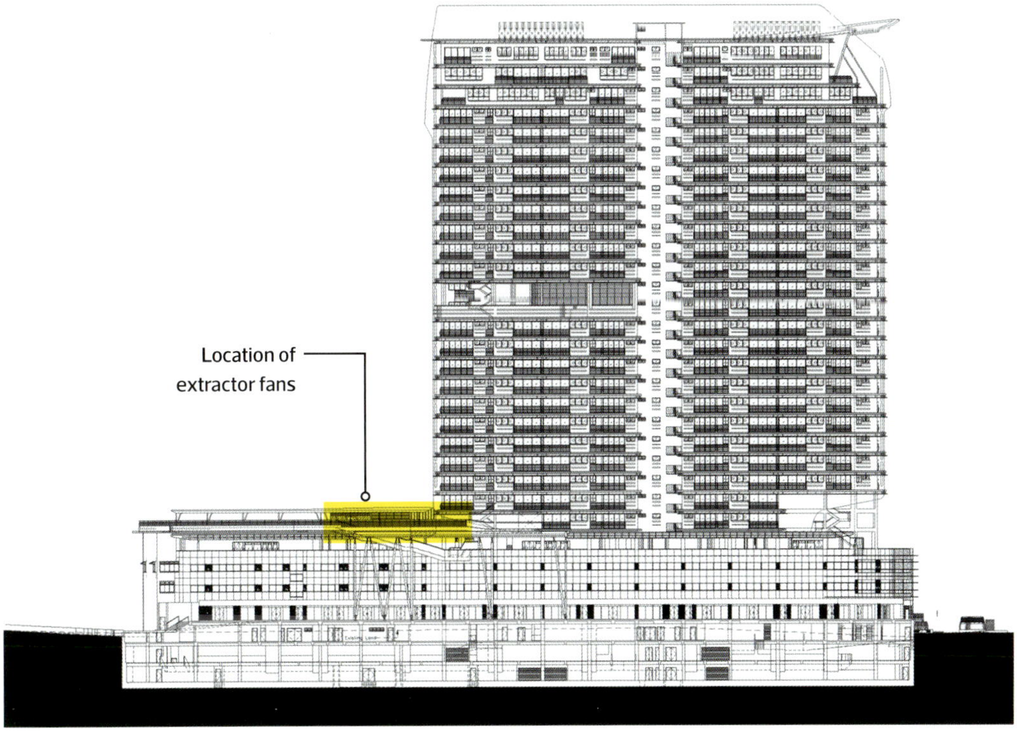

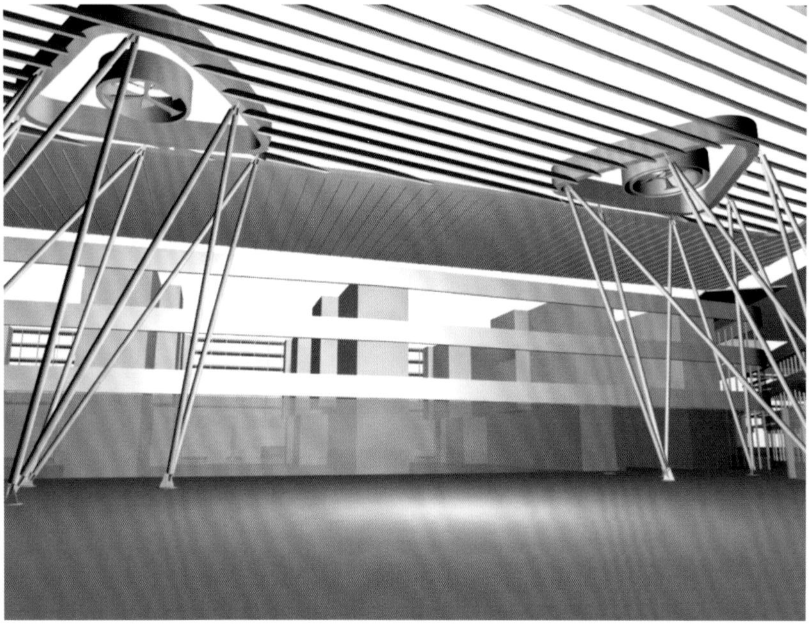

FIGURE 1
Original concept of atrium roof for TTDI Plaza

TTDI PLAZA

The TTDI Plaza contains a large, covered, day-lit courtyard space - a central court within a large mixed residential complex, the TTDI Residence. It is an accessible area for residents as well as a commercial hub for visitors of this development.

Mixed-mode cooling is a combination of natural wind-induced and stack-effect passive means assisted by low-energy mechanical systems in periods of calm or still air as an alternative to resorting to air-conditioning systems. In tropical cities, there is a growing trend of building residential suburbs to attach an outdoor plaza. In light of its popularity, it is imperative to ensure that these spaces do not consume lifetimes of high energy. For instance, a covered space may be designed with daylight admission and natural ventilation to create a semi-outdoor space from a typically large atrium-like space. Yet the roof can be the largest source of heat gain, particularly through radiation and conduction in an equatorial climate. A more in-depth understanding is required to assess parameters for tropical urban design, particularly when thermal comfort in outdoor urban areas is more extended and varied than in indoor climates.

The feature acts like an external atrium or a courtyard, which often serves as a commercial or social hub in new urban developments. Air-conditioning this 70,000-square-metre plaza would have committed the developer to a lifetime of high-energy wastage. While a glass-covered atrium is beneficial in countries of a more temperate climate, in the tropics it must be designed with a 'bioclimatic awareness' to filter and sieve the positive and negative elements of the climate. Constructed as either an opened semi-opened, or covered space, the courtyard often houses commercial activities like outdoor bazaars and food courts. Variable daylight can produce a bright and cheerful atmosphere that can enhance marketing of goods and services.

INITIAL CONCEPT DESIGN

Initially, external roof louvres were integrated to protect the plaza from overhead solar radiation and improve comfort conditions underneath. Unfortunately, these external louvres, part of the initial roof design, had to be taken out due to project budget constraints (original design of TTDI

Plaza as shown in Figure 1). An alternative passive system was required – one which would effect a degree of reduced heat gain while bringing in adequate levels of daylight. The TTDI Plaza was developed in its final design as a space with a 'mixed-mode' combination of high-performance glass and mechanical exhaust fans that exhaust hot air upwards while functioning as an aesthetic feature of the development.

SIMULATIONS

Optimising the design and profile of the roof was the focus of the simulation process. There was also consideration of cost effectiveness and client preferences. Initially, the team wanted to integrate a series of internal louvres to control direct solar gain. However, due to budget constraints, the louvres were not included and exhaust fans were introduced. Simulation studies were used to predict the performance of the plaza area with exhaust fans to further explore the possibilities of introducing additional roof elements and fine-tuning glass specifications to promote balance between daylight and heat gain. Integration was required between natural and mechanical means of ventilation.

Wind and sunlight are strong directional factors that can influence the microclimate around and inside a building.

Computational Fluid Dynamics (CFD) simulations are concerned with the numerical simulation of airflow and heat transfer, and multi-zonal methods give time-based results via graphical data. Multi-zonal analysis is a method for analysing infiltration and natural ventilation in buildings. A zonal airflow model can calculate bulk air movement in and through a building. Driven by wind and pressure induced by buoyancy, CFD simulations can give instantaneous, detailed predictions of airflow and heat transfer processes in and around building spaces by taking into account boundary conditions such as the effects of climate, internal energy sources and MVAC systems.

As per Figure 5, showing the predicted temperature stratification inside the plaza, the thermal model was split into four stacked zones (three floors and the roof zone). The mixing of outside air with interior air in the lower parts of the atrium was a critical factor in determining overall thermal comfort. Assumptions in the modelling process included:

- All interior adjoining spaces were held at constant temperatures of surrounding air-conditioned shop lots
- The outward 'arms' of the plaza were modelled with boundary conditions representing external weather conditions
- The exhaust system of the plaza was considered in establishing the airflow pattern

Assumptions for the CFD simulation are as follows:

Parameter	Assumption
Average Wind Flow	1.32 m/s (average for 23 years, 1969 - 2002)*
Wind Exposure	Suburban conditions

* Records from Petaling Jaya Meteorological Department

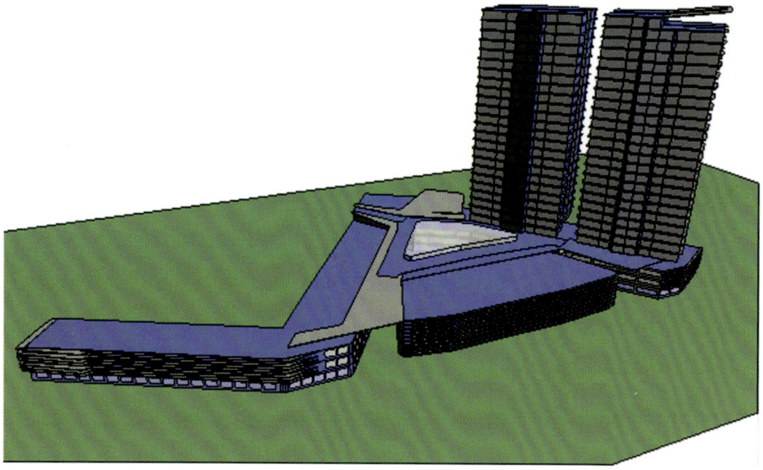

FIGURE 2

Simulation model use (final design) of TTDI Residence Towers

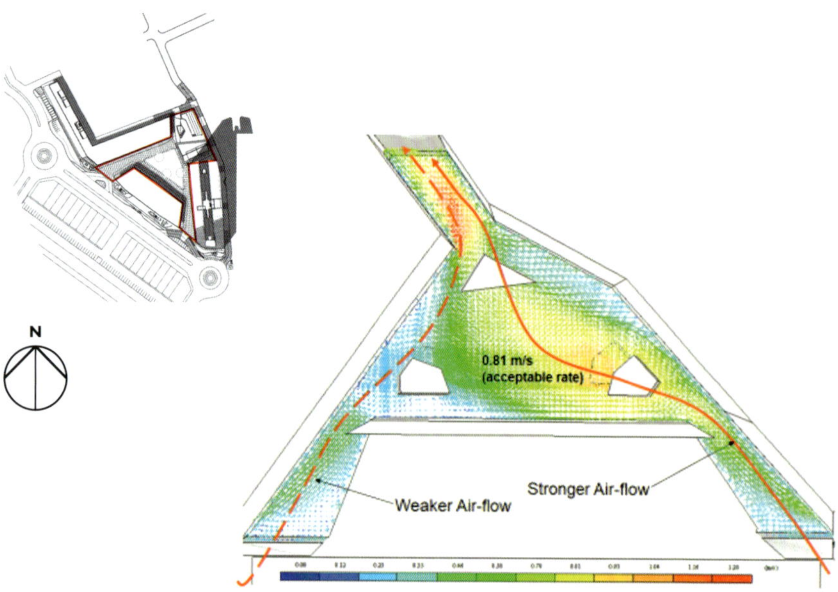

FIGURE 3

Simulation using internal CFD – airflow through the plaza (plan view)

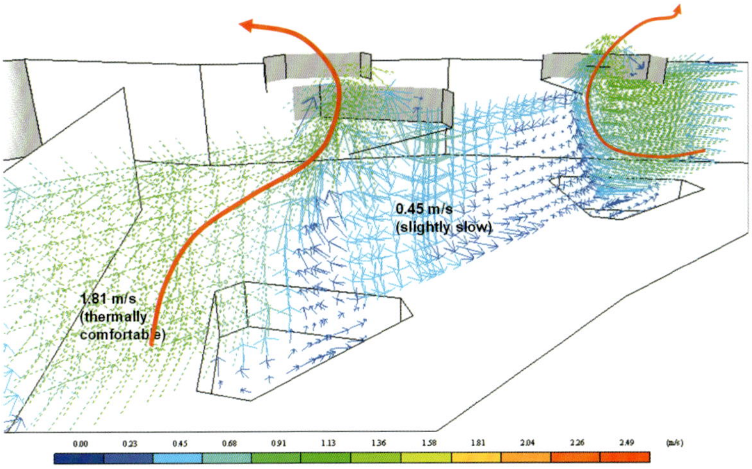

FIGURE 4

Predictions in the direction and flow of air in terms of velocity within the plaza – Vertical View A

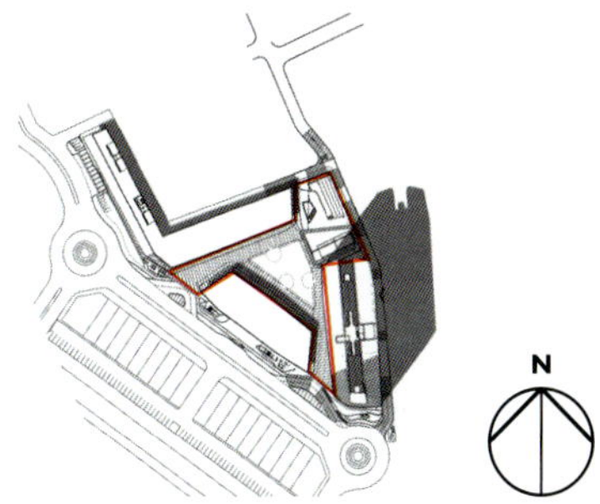

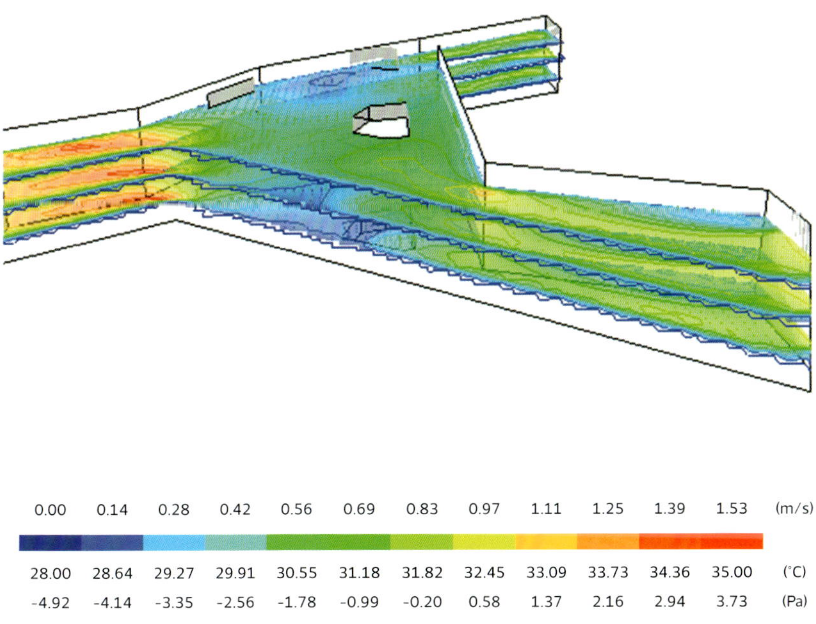

FIGURE 5

Temperature distribution / air velocity at body level – Horizontal Distribution

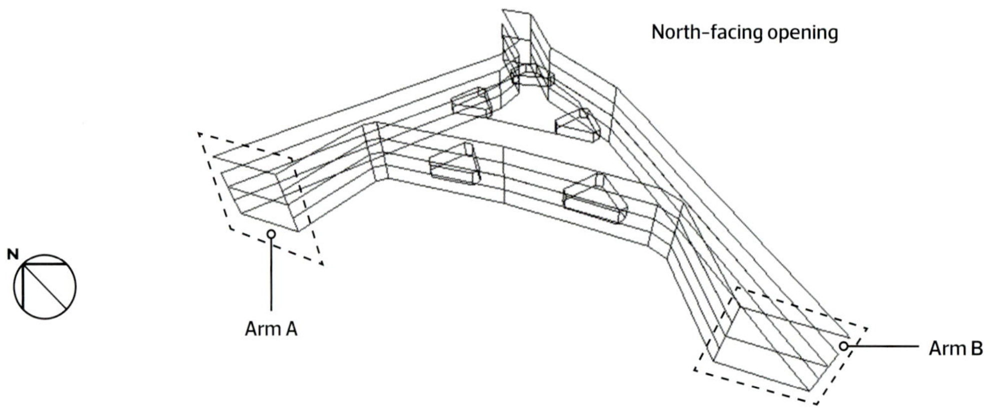

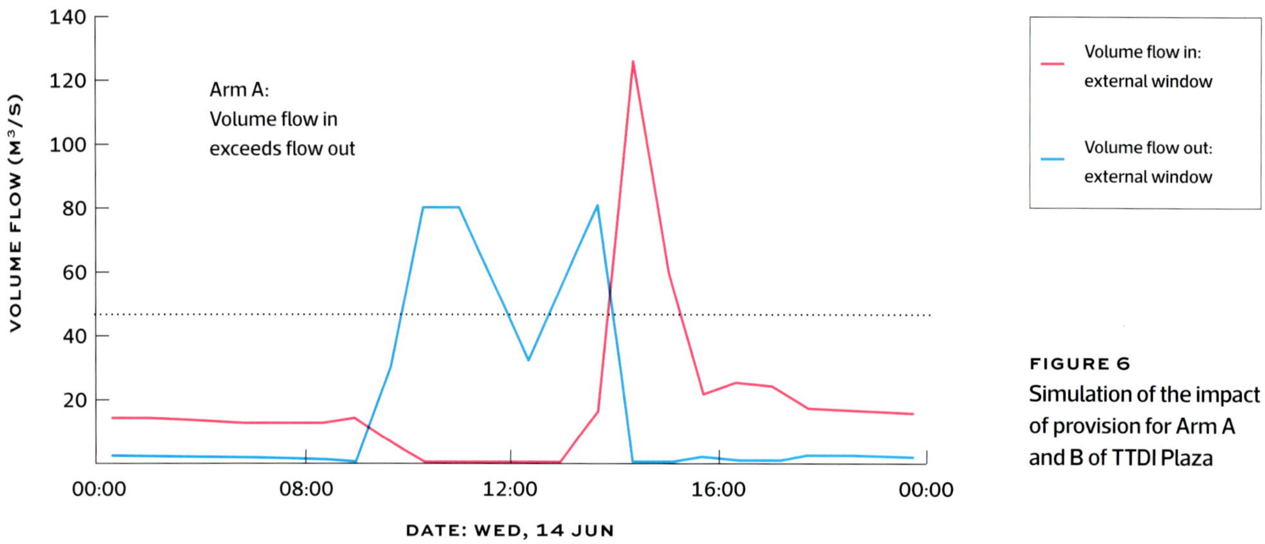

FIGURE 6
Simulation of the impact of provision for Arm A and B of TTDI Plaza

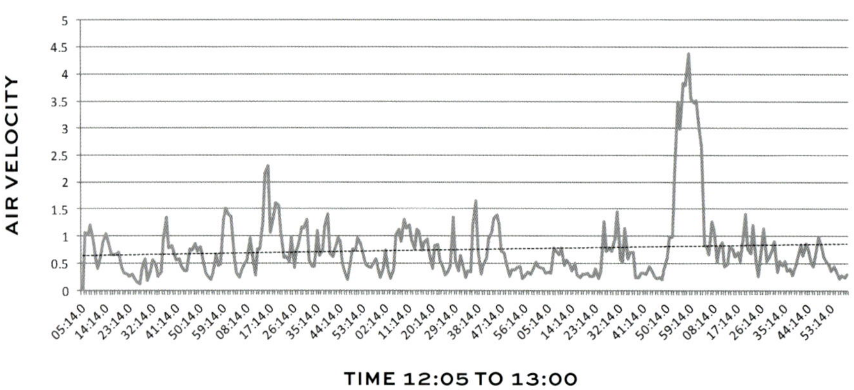

FIGURE 8
Results of a post-occupancy study in 2007 - Air velocity reading from 15/03/07

RESULTS

Overall results demonstrated that comfort conditions inside the plaza will remain at an acceptable level of 28°C–31°C even without the exhaust fan operating. An exhaust fan in the plaza would further help to remove excessive heat by aiding natural wind forces. Further vertical sectioning of CFD results displayed vertical temperature profiles as outcomes of thermal stratification at certain points in time. There is an average of up to 4°C of temperature difference between the floor and the apex of the plaza. Average wind speeds of 1.1–1.5 m/s were found within the plaza itself at human height (Figure 3).

Tested improvements included increasing the height of the glass canopy above the exhaust fans. This would then be integrated with mechanical ventilation. Both the roof profile and mechanical devices were simulated together to assess the updraft of air through the vertical cross-section of the plaza and improve cooling through thermal stratification via stack effect. Openings along the length of the steel roof of the plaza also help the removal of excess heat via stack effect.

Due to incident solar gain, any overhead glazing normally elevates internal air temperatures and causes a large vertical temperature gradient. Therefore, mechanical ventilation by extractor fans functioned to remove excess heat. CFD simulations were used to visualise and analyse these changes and verify the upward displacement due to combined forces of mechanical airflow and natural driving forces of stack and wind effects.

Multi-zonal analysis simulation tools were used to further investigate the potential impact of various placements and dimensions of openings at the apex of the plaza. These would allow removal of excess heat by cross-ventilation, heat that is trapped in the upper area of the plaza. Selected results are shown in Figure 6 and Figure 7.

IN-USE PERFORMANCE

A post-occupancy study was undertaken in 2007, and the field data in use closely matched the predicted simulation temperatures. However, the plaza did suffer from incoming solar penetration during periods of intense sun due to the absence of louvres, resulting in hotspots within the plaza. Otherwise, on most days, acceptable comfort was achieved.

Due to the eventual construction of shop houses on the south side of the plaza, the passage of wind induced airflow was eventually blocked in. However, most of the airflow originated from the north side, which features a large, green park. These results reinforce that it is not possible to predict the outcome of surrounding developments, which would ultimately affect the bioclimatic performance of this plaza space. However, this also points to the need for large, open landscape areas around the airflow inlet and outlet to ensure that cool air enters the plaza.

The average temperature from the field data was found to be between 28 and 31°C, closely matching the simulation results. As seen in Figure 8 and Figure 9, the overall average air velocity at the podium was between 0.7 m/s and 4.7 m/s.

JABAL OMAR TOWERS, MECCA, SAUDI ARABIA

A major feature of Jabal Omar Towers are roof-level wind scoops that draw air into evaporative cooling towers. The cooling towers through the centre of the high-rises are integral to the design of the development. This design brings warm air to the top of a tower, where a fine mist cools and humidifies the air. This cool, moist air then drops down the tower, cooling the corridors and providing a fresh air supply to all rooms and apartments. The cool air then exits the tower at the level of a roof garden, cooling the garden and prayer areas. The ramps that extend through the cooling towers continue into retail areas, bringing in the air from above. Planting and water ponds are placed on the tower roofs to further cool the intake air and to reduce the amount of airborne dust. The roof garden on top of the concourse is cooled by this series of towers along its length.

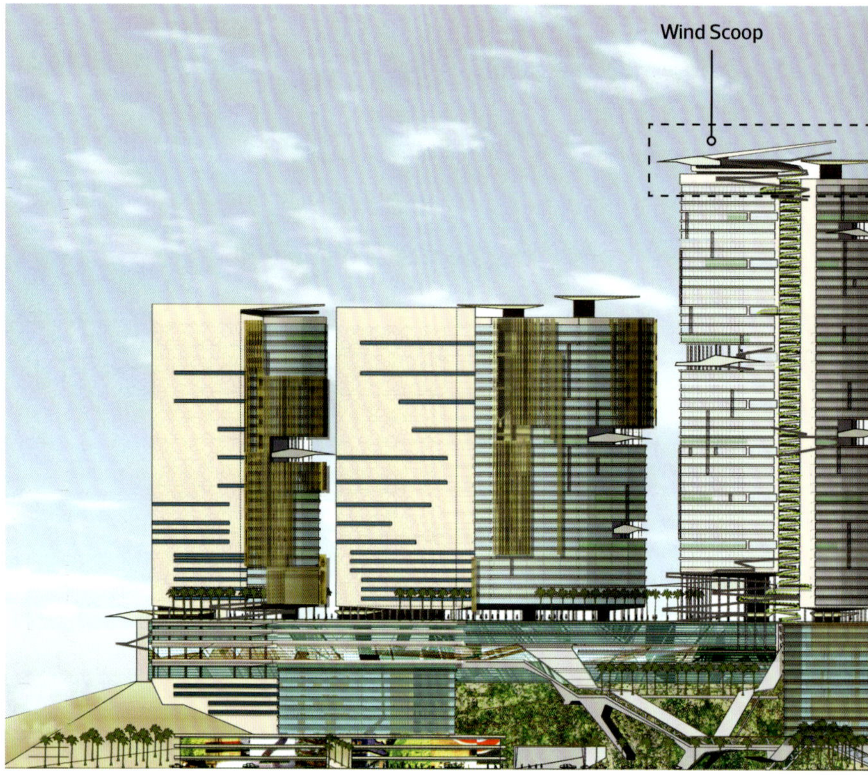

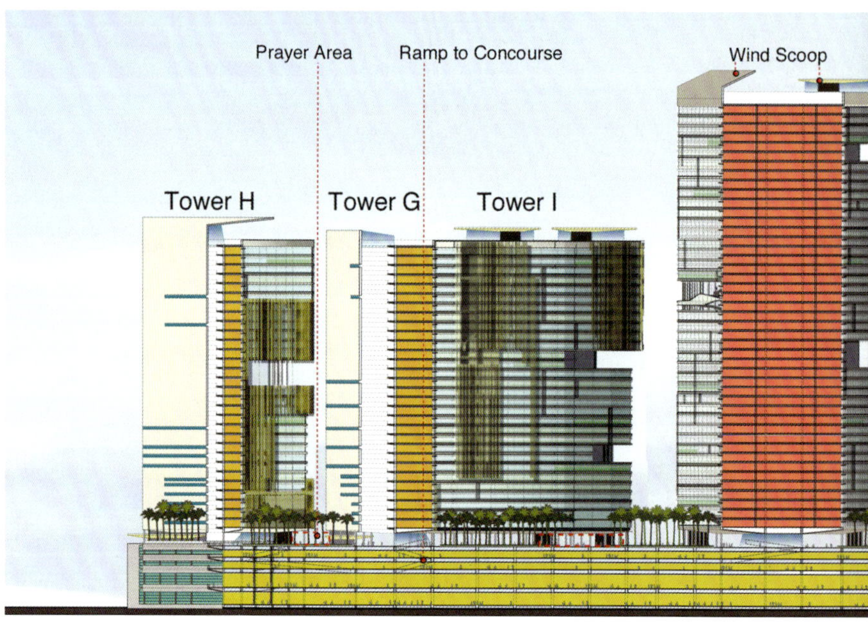

ABOVE

Elevation showing the roof-level wind scoop and evaporative cooling tower

BELOW

Overall section of the cooling tower through the centre of the high-rise

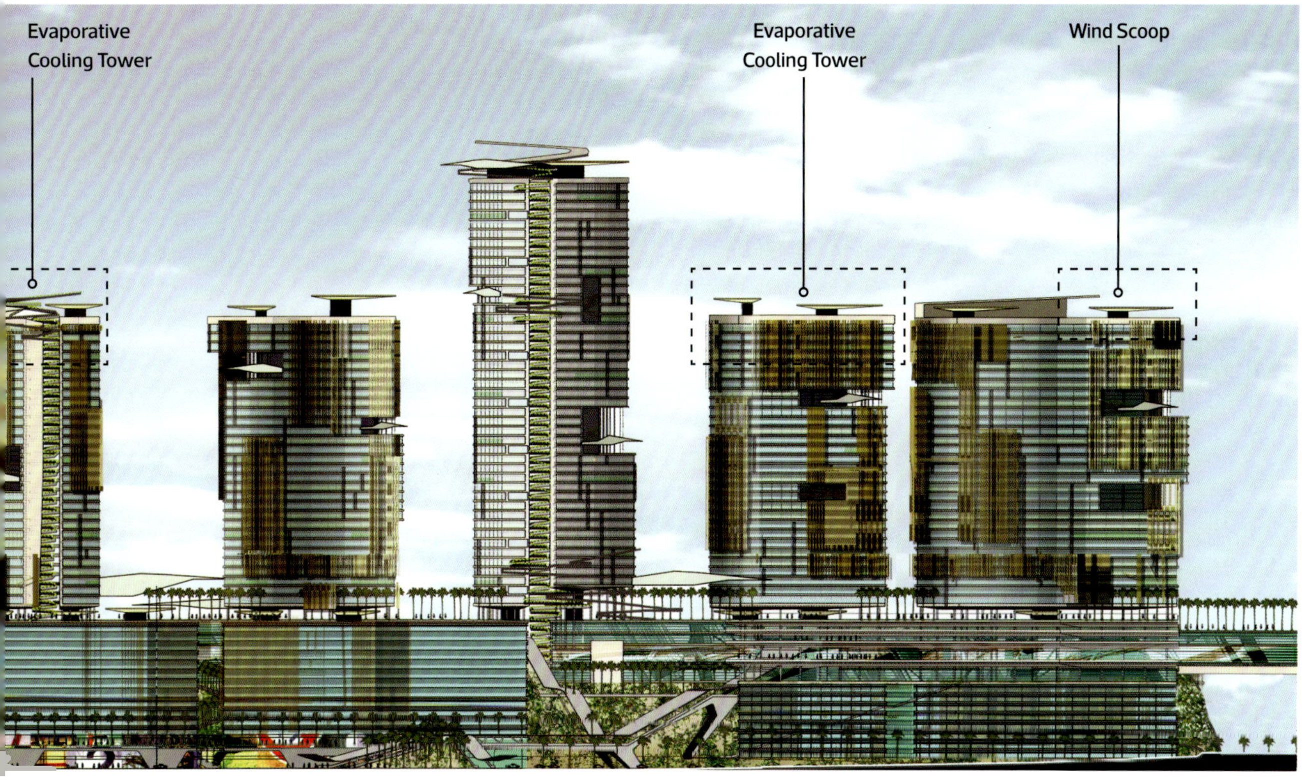
Evaporative
Cooling Tower
Evaporative
Cooling Tower
Wind Scoop

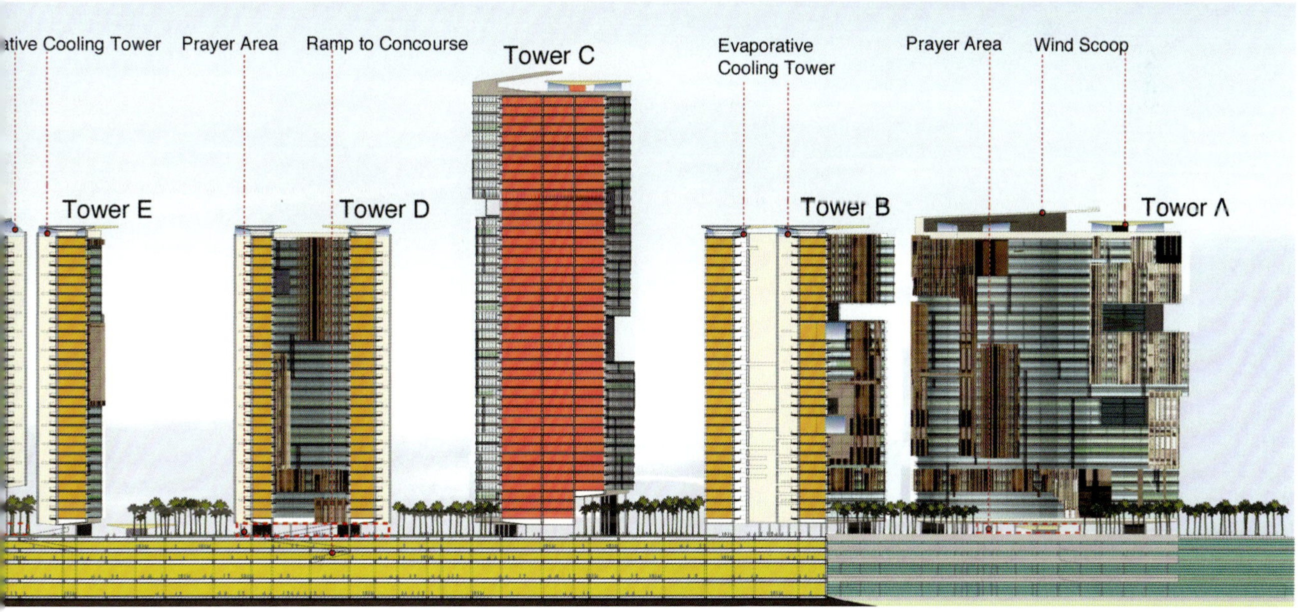
ative Cooling Tower
Prayer Area
Ramp to Concourse
Tower C
Evaporative
Cooling Tower
Prayer Area
Wind Scoop
Tower E
Tower D
Tower B
Tower A

BELOW
Environmental section of evaporative cooling shaft

FACING PAGE
Sketch perspective of the Jabal Omar scheme

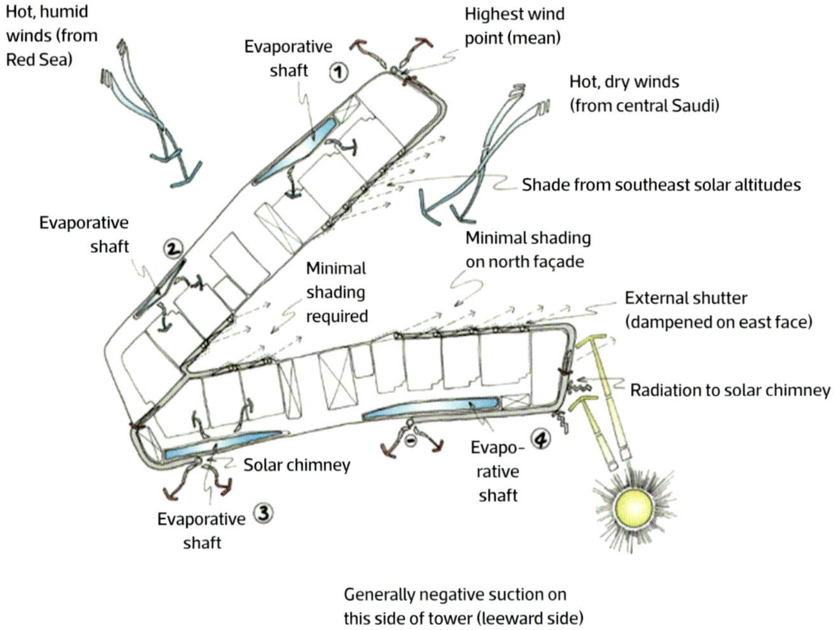

Typical environmental principles of Tower D (see previous spread)

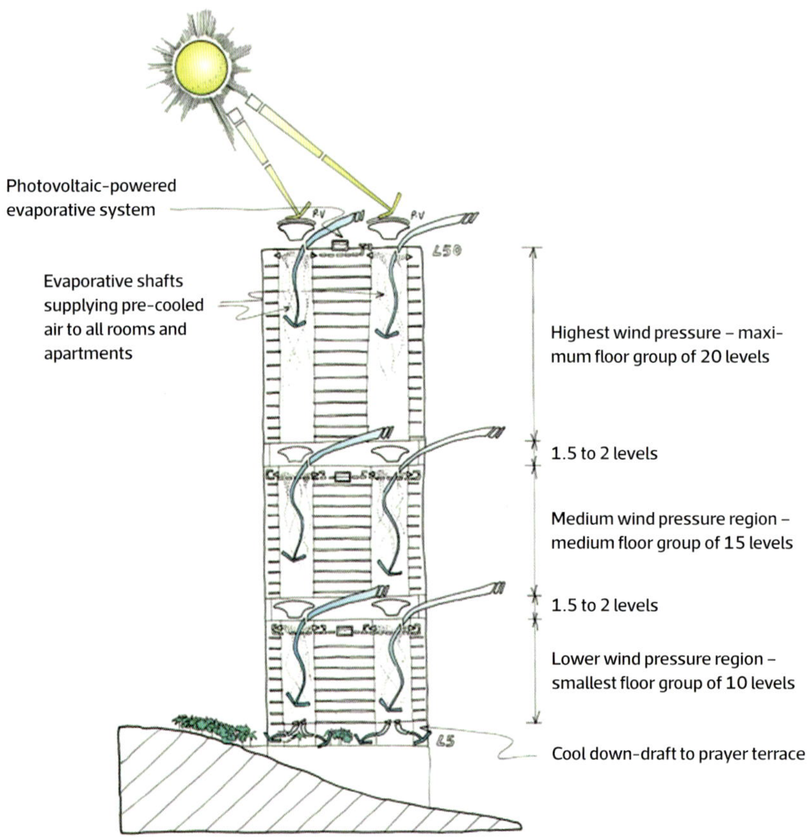

Typical vertical tower

Evaporative Water Cloud Device

DESIGN IDEA

Cities in hot climates are zones that are exposed to the long-term impacts of an urban heat island. As areas of hardscape and pavement and plazas increase, pockets of cool air must be provided to enable public activity and interaction under near-comfort conditions. Evaporative water-cooling systems are the combination of an air curtain and a water diffuser, which creates cool, refreshing zones in an environment where air-conditioning is typically the only way to escape the heat. A jet of cool air is paired with a fine mist of water, forming a cool and misty zone in the hot, humid tropics. This combination forms an artificial cloud which, in a tropical environment, provides welcome relief for passersby and therefore operates as an attractive lure.

BELOW
Section A-A of Standard Chartered Bank Pavilion

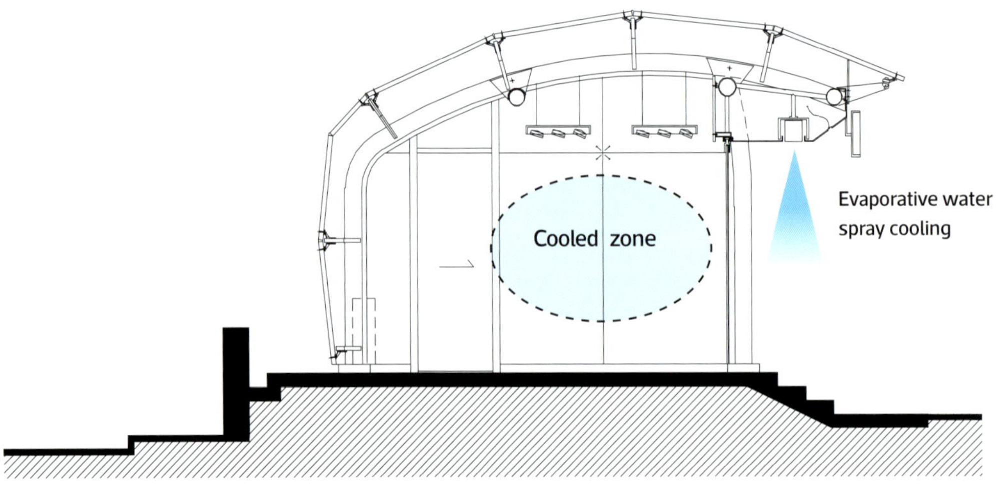

Section A-A

Standard Chartered
Bank Pavilion

Mixed-mode cooling device 2:
Evaporative water spray
Solutions Financial Kiosk
Credit Cards
SMI OneAccount
Credit Cards

STANDARD CHARTERED BANK PAVILION

Standard Chartered Bank Pavilion is located in Kuala Lumpur, Malaysia. This 1-storey building was completed in 2004, with a site area of 50 square metres. Its visually prominent design, makes it a landmark for the well-known shopping boulevard at Jalan Bukit Bintang. Its design details can be easily appreciated at an intimate distance. The pavilion is for a financial institute, essentially a customer service area for credit card applications, home loans and other transaction facilities. The overall shape and design of the pavilion is blended with the surrounding landscape, filling the urban void with a structure of human scale. The pavilion is divided into two parts: one is a small, semi-enclosed discussion area and another is a fully enclosed booth with a glass roof. Sliding glass doors are used to enclose the pavilion and glass partitions are used to subdivide the discussion areas. This optimizes the use and efficiency of the space. This also gives the spaces clear definition without cutting away the relationship with the exterior.

BIOCLIMATIC FUNCTION

An evaporative water cloud device is a combination of an air curtain and a water jet or demister, spraying a fine stream of pure water through the blower of the air curtain to create a zone of cool air in semi-outdoor structures. It reflects similar devices of passive technology in the Middle East. An example of this principle is the evaporative cooling tower designed by renowned professor Baruch Givoni as an outdoor device to cool spaces in hot, arid environments.

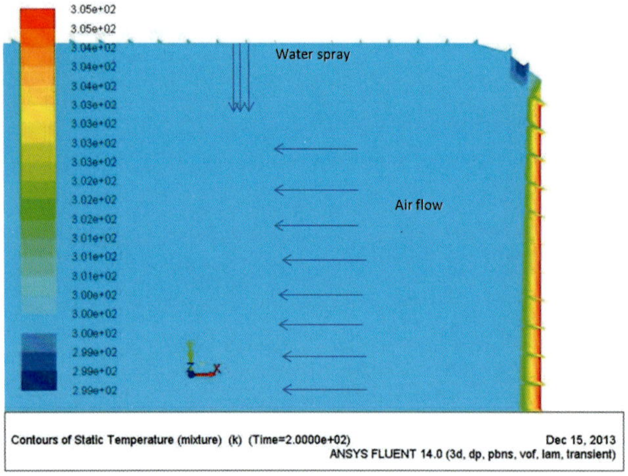

FIGURE 1
Simulate model of the spraying system – Contours of Static Temperature

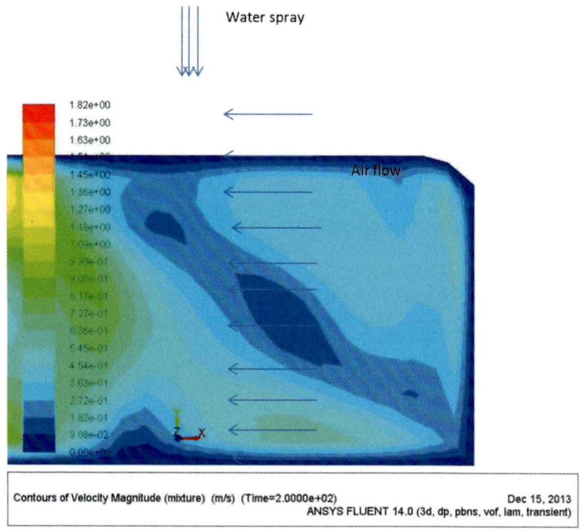

FIGURE 2
Simulation of spraying system – Contours of Velocity Magnitude

Urban environments consist not only of buildings (internal spaces) and external spaces between buildings; the experience of a city is a combination of semi-outdoor spaces and internal spaces. While internal spaces can benefit from air-conditioning in the tropics, semi-outdoor spaces need more passive means, which can be implemented even with a high degree of infiltration of hot air.

Maintaining a comfortable environment within an open system or space relies on reducing the rate of heat gain and encouraging the removal of excess heat. To prevent heat from entering a building and to remove heat once it has entered are the underlying principles for accomplishing cooling in passive cooling concepts. This depends on two conditions: the availability of a heat sink, which is at a lower temperature than the indoor air, and the promotion of heat transfer towards the sink.

PRINCIPLES

Evaporative cooling is a passive-cooling technique in which outdoor air is cooled by evaporating water before it is introduced to building spaces. The heat of the air evaporates water, which cools the air, which in turn cools the space in the building. The ceiling is thus transformed into a cooling element that cools the space below via convection and radiation without raising levels of indoor humidity. Via the evaporative mister, the water (heat transfer by evaporation inside and/or outside the building envelope) in the mist is also a source of heat sink, as heat is absorbed while water is converted into vapour. 1 kilogram of water evaporation provides the same cooling effect as melting 7 kilograms of ice, and hence provides a considerable effect. The cloud mister converts ordinary water into billions of micron-sized water particles. An example is when water is forced at 1,000 psi (or greater) through a fog nozzle, which generates 10 to 15 micron-sized water droplets and results in rapid evaporation, achieving total evaporative cooling even in highly humid climates.

SIMULATIONS

ANSYS FLUENT was used to investigate and verify the cooling impact of the device under the tropical conditions of the site. The aim was to model a series of water droplets that represents the minute spray of the cloud mister. There was also an estimation of the time needed to completely evaporate the drops. The modelling of water droplet evaporation is similar to models studying shower towers and passive down-draft evaporative cooling. Spray -cooling processes yield high heat transfer coefficients due to latent heat absorption during phase transitions from liquid to vapor.

The spraying system was a simplified version of the modelled within a room that

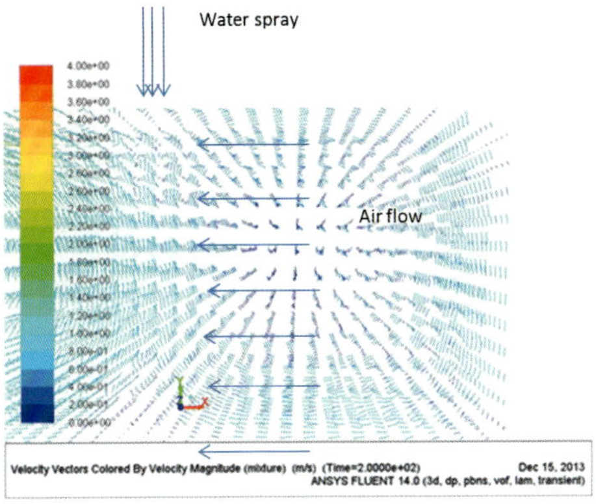

FIGURE 3

Simulation of spraying system – Velocity Vectors

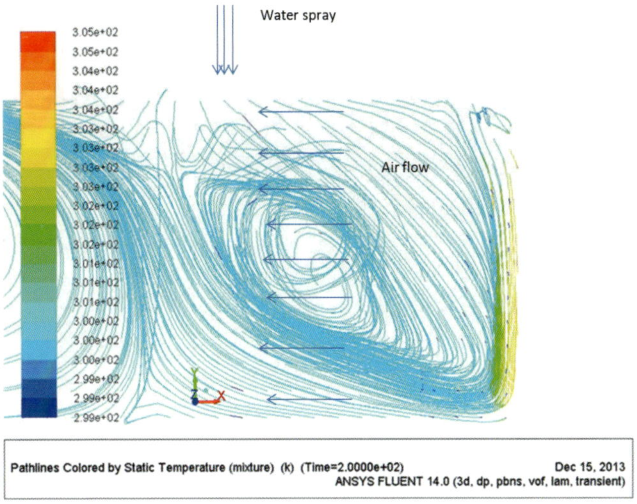

FIGURE 4

Simulation of spraying system – Static Temperature

represented the actual design. The airflow velocity was averaged at 2 m/s, with a spray rate of 0.01 kg/s (along the length of a 4-metre inlet, with chilled water temperature at about 5 °C). Results suggest a reduction in temperature within the region coupled with a slight increase in airflow, hence achieving comfort conditions. The humidity levels were acceptable but within the upper range. The studies demonstrate that evaporative cooling using demisters has the potential to maintain sufficient ventilation with indoor air velocities of 0.4 to 0.6 m/s, and when coupled with the delivery of conditioned air the comfort zone can be further extended, considering the physiological effects of cooling. Climatic acclimatization coupled with physiological cooling effects could provide thermally comfortable conditions over a wider range of temperatures during the hot period of the day.

Evaporative cooling, typically used for warm, dry climates, can also be used for passive cooling when implemented using certain combinations of features under warm, humid conditions. The resultant environmental performance, coupled with the physiological cooling effect of misters, can achieve conditions within the range of comfort neutrality under these conditions. The evaporative cloud cooler can provide a reasonable drop in temperature with a marginal rise in humidity, since people are generally tolerant to high humidity (up to 75%) when the physiological effect of cooled airflow is also achievable.

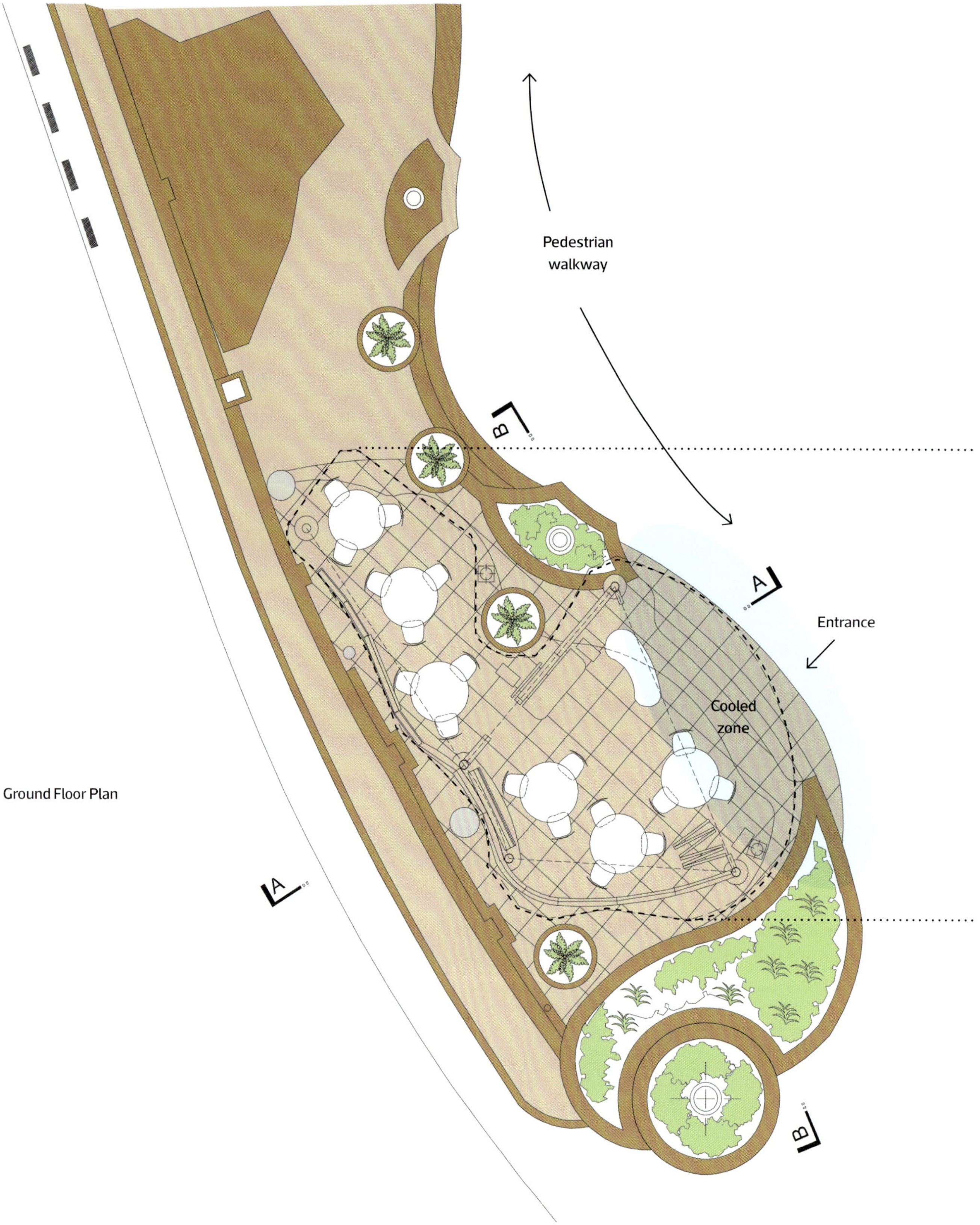

Ground Floor Plan

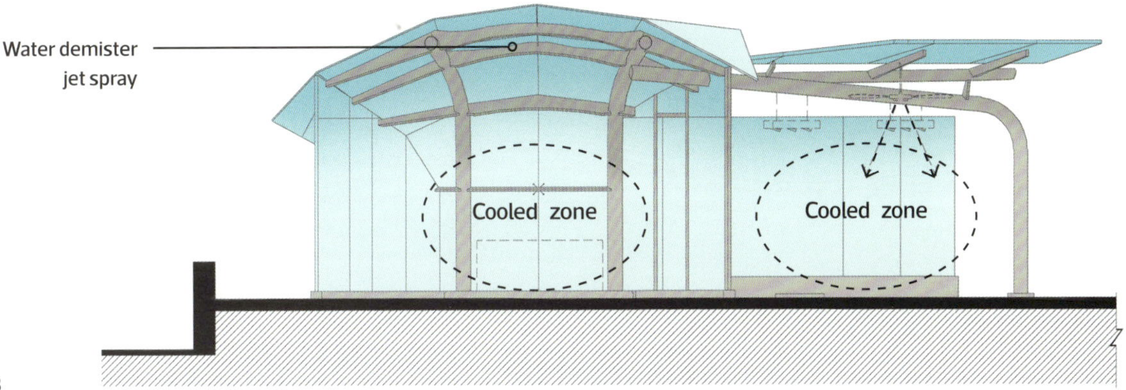

Section B-B

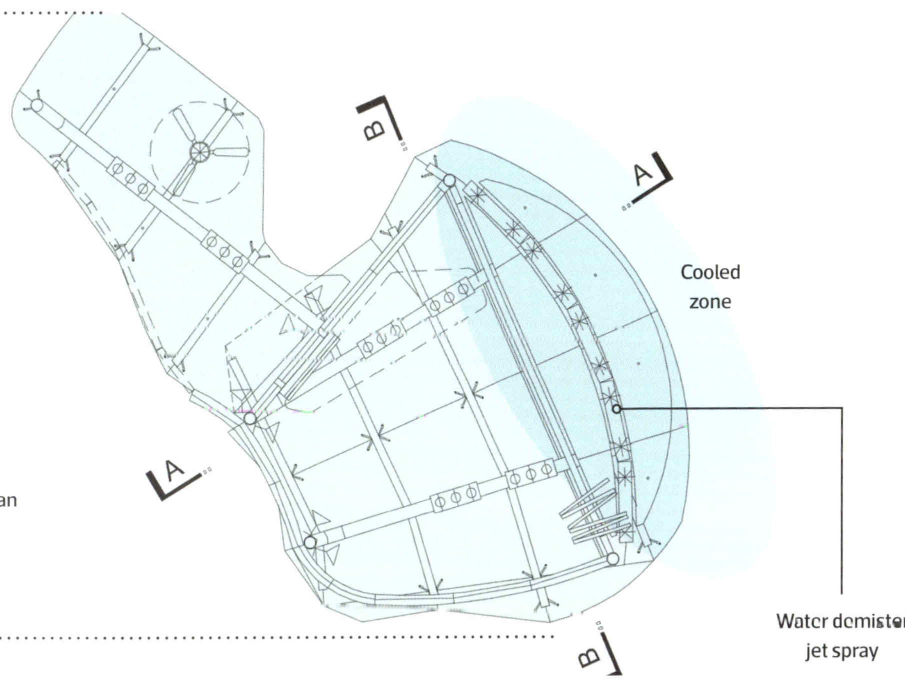

Ceiling Plan

Rain-check Wall

DESIGN IDEA

A bioclimatic approach to design enables a building envelope to filter between the positive and negative aspects of a climate, including daylight and heat gain. Particularly in hot, humid, tropical zones, monsoonal, seasonal and daily events such as wind-driven rain must be filtered by the building envelope, yet the envelope must allow natural winds into internal environments. A rain-check wall is an innovative device that integrates with naturally ventilated or mixed-mode common spaces, like an atrium or a multi-volume lobby, in order to admit prevailing winds for comfort and cooling while protecting the interior from the impact of wind-driven rain. It allows wind to cross-ventilate the atrium while keeping out the rain via a series of glazing panels separated by perforated panels.

BELOW
Concept diagram

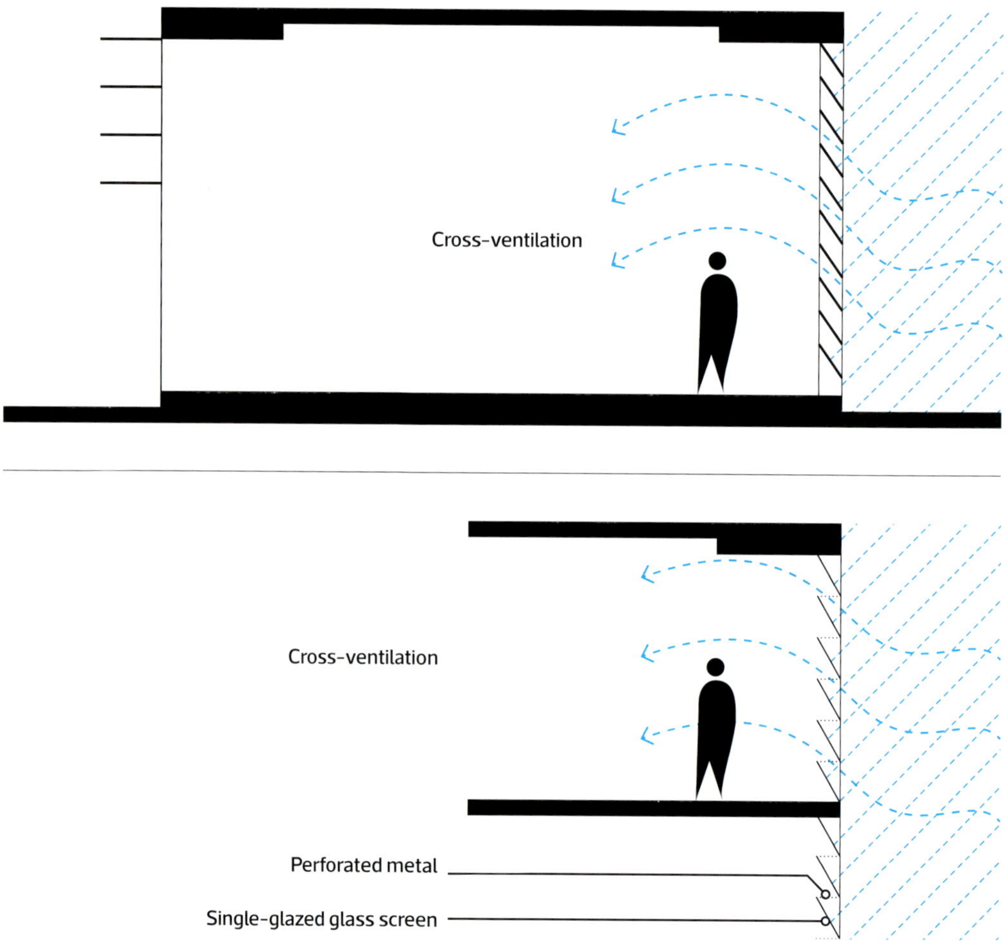

Solaris, Singapore

SOLARIS, SINGAPORE

Solaris is located in the research and business park in central Singapore's One North community, and is a flagship project in its second phase. The masterplan for the visionary mixed-use development was prepared by Zaha Hadid Architects.

Solaris has been certified as BCA Green Mark Platinum, the highest possible green certification granted by Singapore's sustainable building benchmark system (similar to LEED, GBI, GreenStar, BREEAM, etc.). The building's overall energy consumption represents a reduction of over 36% compared to local precedents and the high-performance façade has an External Thermal Transfer Value (ETTV) of less than 39 w/m^2. With over 8,000 m^2 of landscaping, Solaris also introduces vegetation that exceeds the area of the building's original site.

The rain-check wall is used in the Solaris building for the naturally ventilated ground floor in tandem with the central atrium's operable glass-louvred glazing. This innovative device allows wind to cross-ventilate the atrium while keeping out the rain. It is a glazed façade, a series of angled glass panels separated by horizontal perforated metal strips between each panel (as shown in Figure 3), letting in wind to naturally ventilate but keeping out rain. Since it is glazed, it enables the occupants to visually see out. Further development might make all the components operable and automated via sensors in order to enhance its environmental filtering functions.

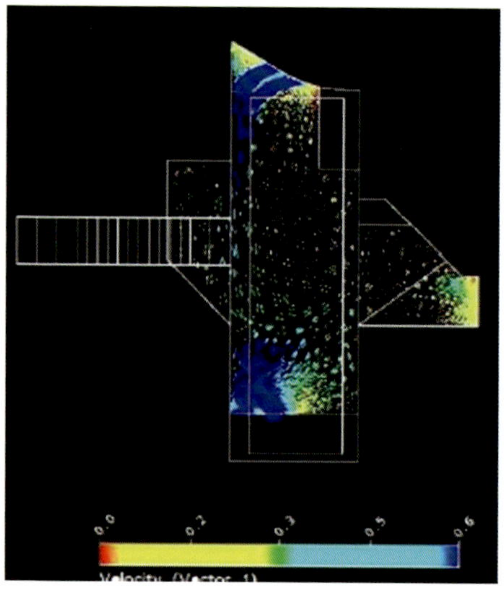

FIGURE 1
Natural ventilation to atrium ground floor with North prevailing wind at 2m/s. Wind velocity at 1.6m above the ground – Plan View.

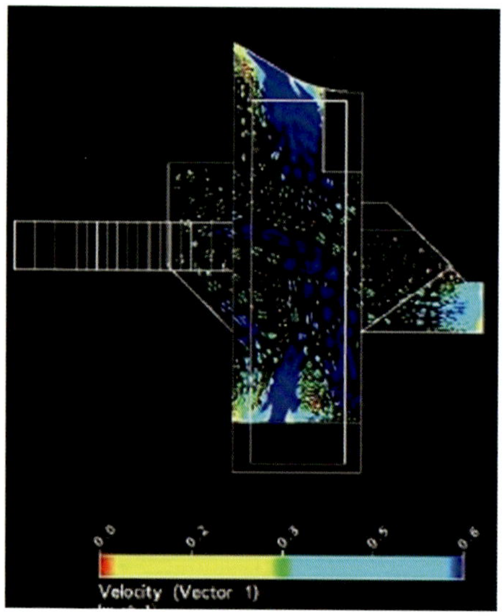

FIGURE 2
Natural ventilation to atrium ground floor with South prevailing wind at 2m/s. Wind velocity at 1.6m above the ground – Plan View.

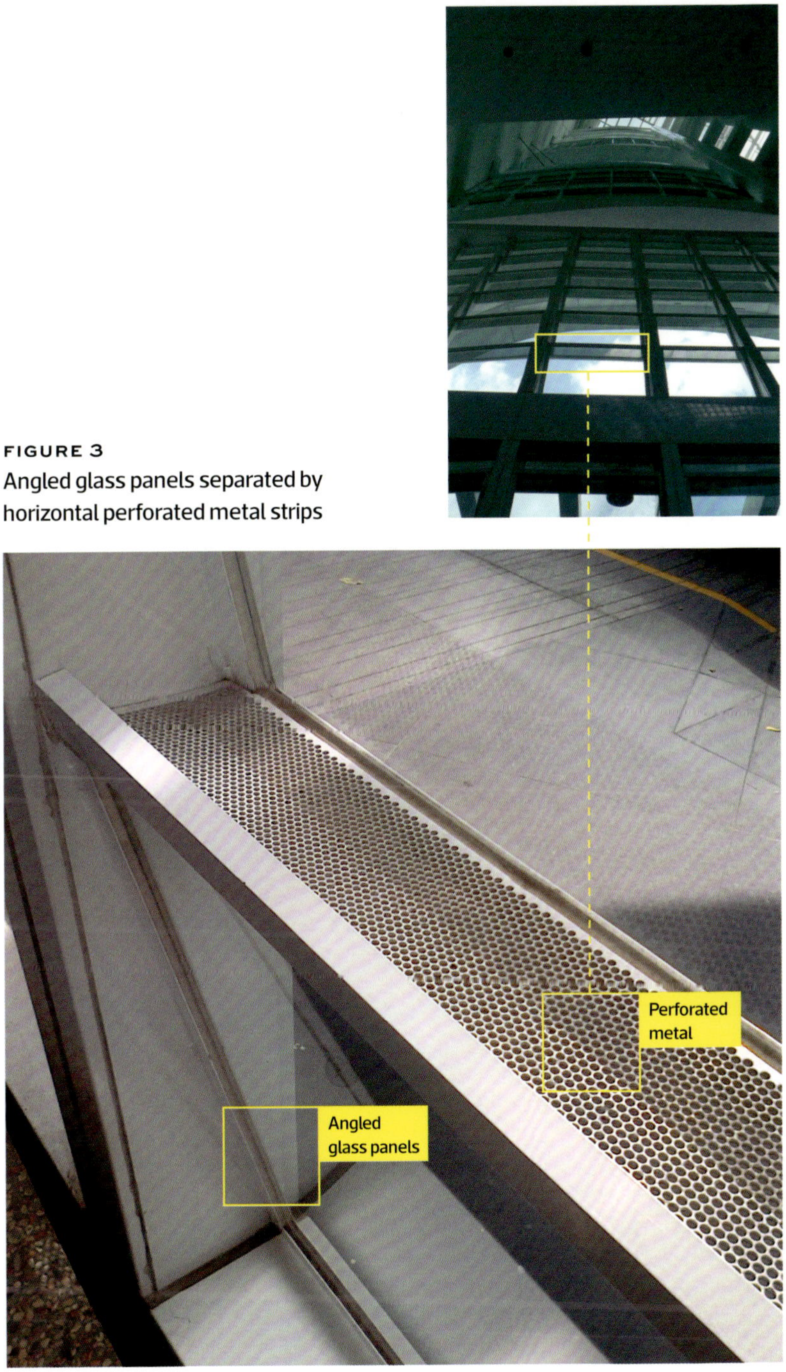

FIGURE 3

Angled glass panels separated by horizontal perforated metal strips

ANALYTICAL PRINCIPLES

The simulation of wind-driven rain is typically extrapolated from the simulation of external windflow. Typically, CFD analysis is conducted as in Figure 2 and additional factors that represent the phenomena of a rain droplet falling under the action and effects of gravity are factored in manually. Under these conditions, an equilibrium is quickly established between two forces – gravity (downwards) and aerodynamic drag (upwards). The resulting velocity is called terminal velocity, or simply fall speed (Vt). The gravitational force is proportional to the drop mass (m), the 3rd power of its diameter (D), while frictional force is proportional to the cross-sectional area (A) of the drop, the 2nd power of its diameter (D). The force balance is as follows:

$$m g = Cd\ r\ Vt2\ A,$$

where:

- g is gravitational acceleration
- r is air density
- and Cd is the drag coefficient

The problem is that Cd is not constant; rather, it is a function of diameter (D), fall speed (Vt) and the kinematic viscosity of the air.

It is a common practice to assume in analytical modelling and simulation that the freezing rain droplets' horizontal speed (Vh) and the horizontal wind speed (VW) are identical. Hence, the former can be estimated from the latter (e.g., Vh=Vw).

Perforated metal to admit wind but keep out rain

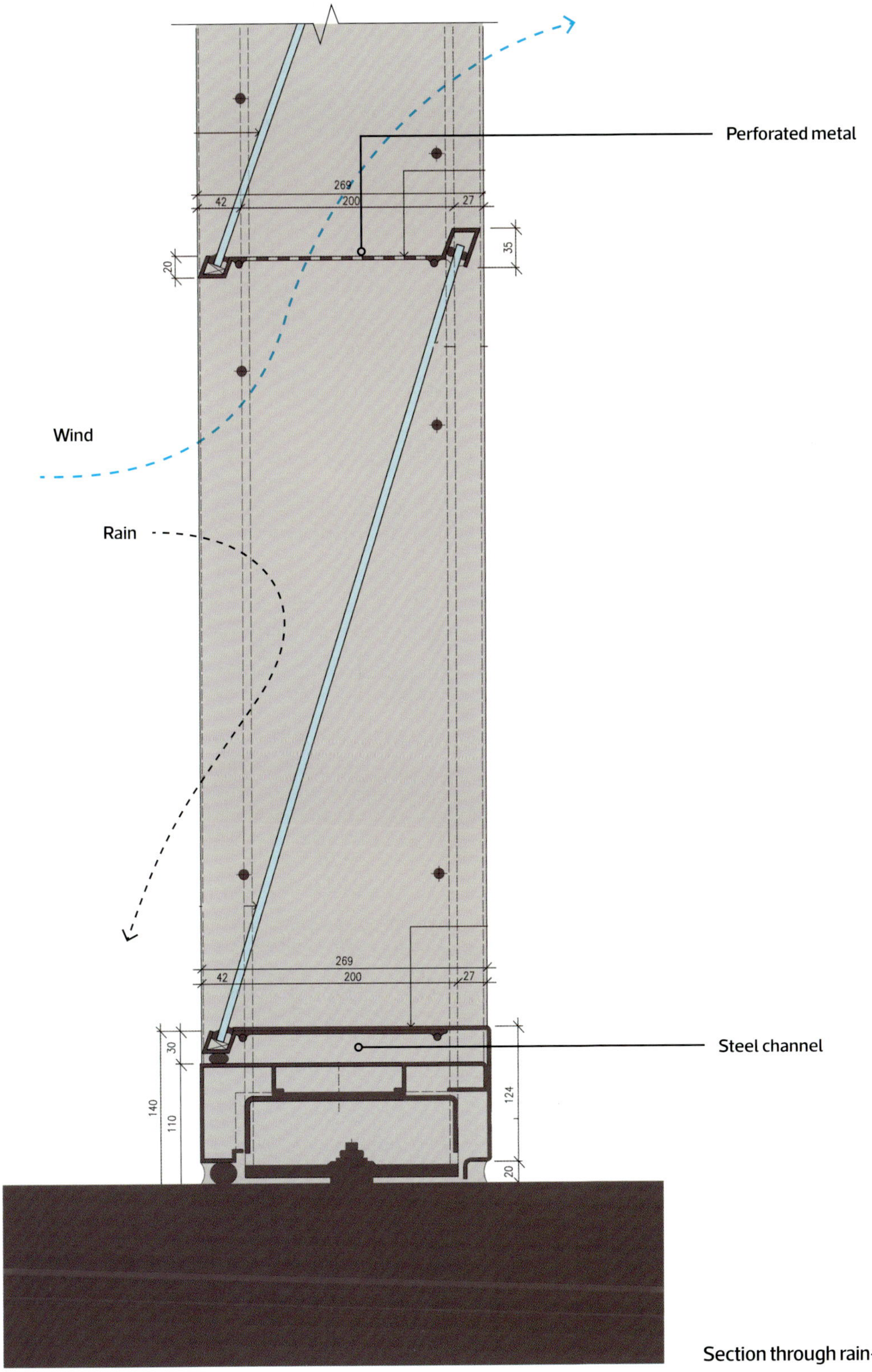

Section through rain-check wall

Environmental-filter Roof

DESIGN IDEA

Working in conjunction with the low-energy strategies of mixed-mode systems and naturally ventilated multivolume spaces and common areas, this device complements the vertical nature of the rain-check wall. The environmental-filter roof is a horizontal or sloped automatic roof with operable parts (either via sensors or manual operation) that can be opened to allow natural ventilation into internal spaces and closed to keep out rain during inclement weather. It allows a more dynamic performance of the roof of an atrium or a multilevel space to respond to the uncertainties of climate. The operable nature of the roof allows it to react when necessary, to exhaust the buildup of hot air in a hot climate or to close in times of rain.

BELOW
Concept sketch

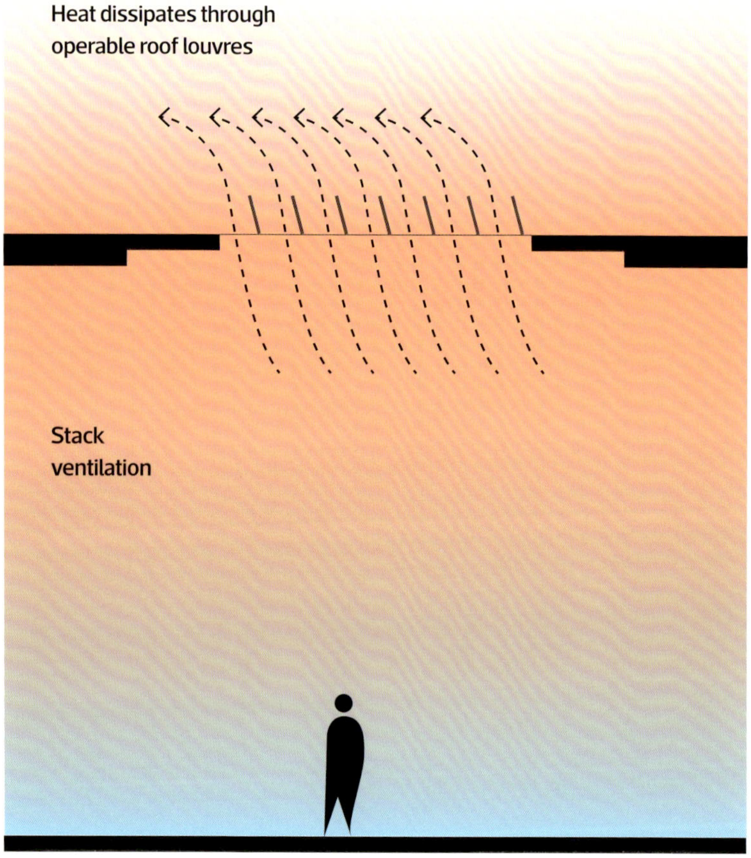

Solaris, Singapore
Roof planting
Automated environmental-filter roof over atrium

THIS SPREAD
Operable Glazed Skylight Louvre Detail Drawing

THIS PAGE
Operable louvres atop the glazed Solaris atrium roof shown in closed position

FACING PAGE
Operable louvres in open position

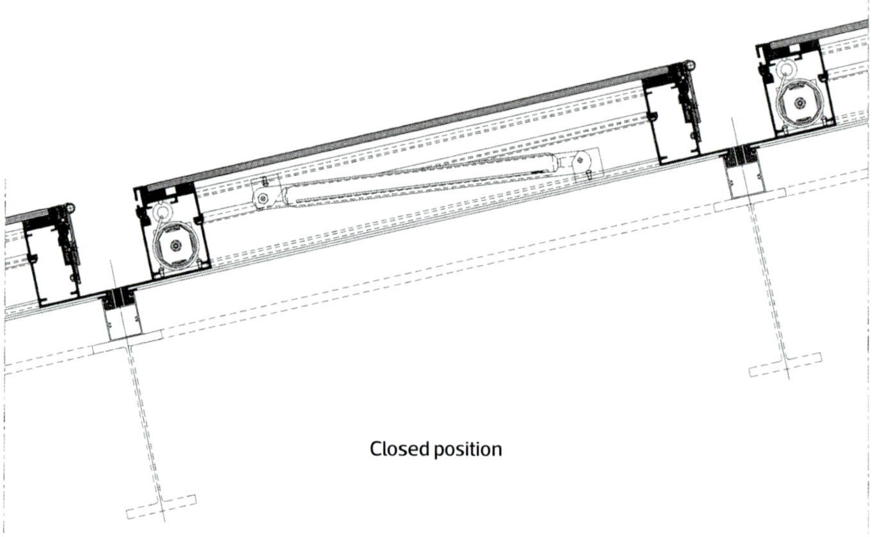

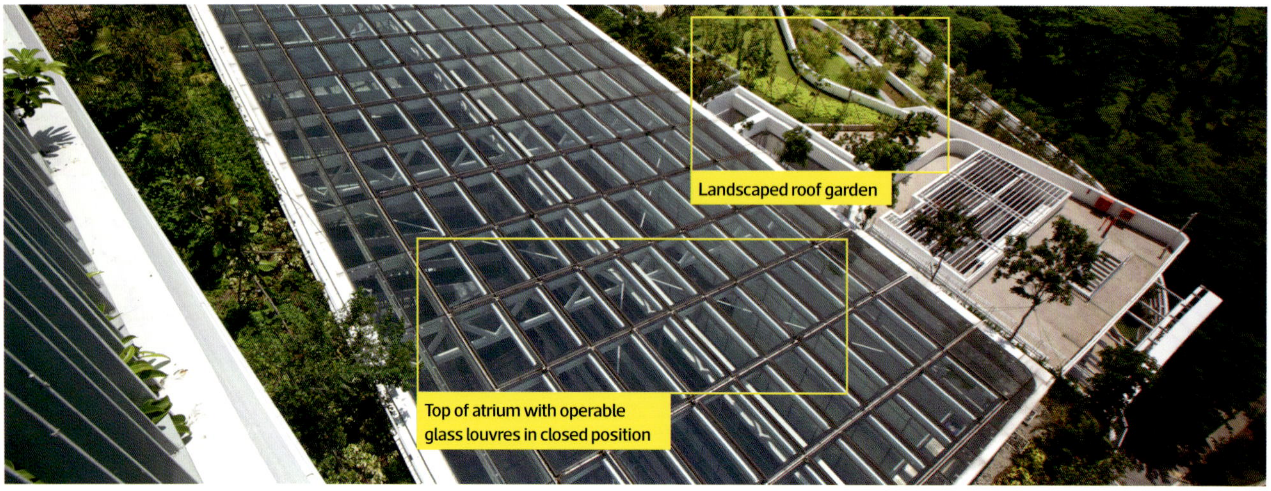

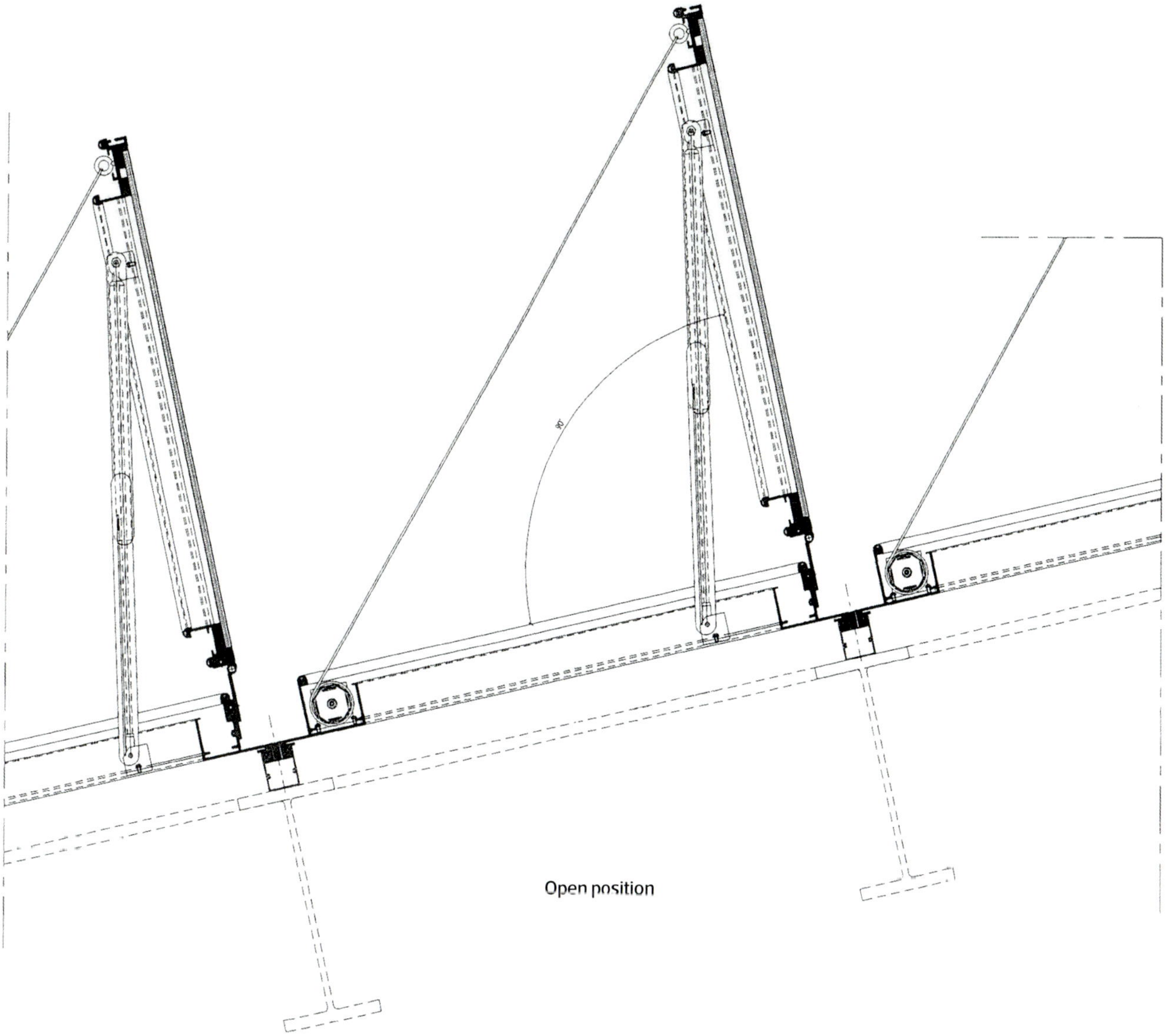

Open position

SOLARIS, SINGAPORE

The environmental-filter roof of the Solaris building is a common multivolume space where natural wind forces and daylight are harvested in order to create acceptable comfort conditions without air-conditioning. These utilise dynamically controlled and operable louvres at the apex of the atrium, which allow thermal stratification to occur and hot air to be exhausted from the higher levels of the multivolume space.

FUNCTIONS & INTENTIONS

In general, designing for natural ventilation in the tropics necessitates an 'open system' to encourage maximum air movement, thereby achieving acceptable indoor comfort under hot, humid conditions. As opposed to office environments, transitional areas such as lobbies and multistorey atriums represent areas where the expectation for thermal comfort in a hot, humid climate is lowered. Hence, in view of significantly reducing energy consumption for air-conditioning, there should be a strategy where natural ventilation and stack forces are utilised where the need for a cool, dry environment is less acute. Therefore, transitional areas such as atriums and lobbies should be naturally ventilated and day-lit.

The use of daylight would allow electric lights to remain secondary, and be able to be switched off throughout the day. These areas – particularly on the ground floor – are commonly used as reception areas (i.e., spaces which 'greet' the occupant or visitor as they enter the building).

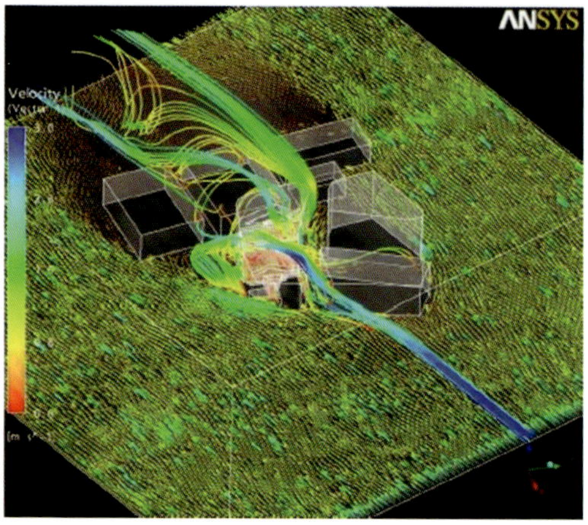

FIGURE 1
Streamline plots of north prevailing wind at 2 m/s (Aurecon, 2011)

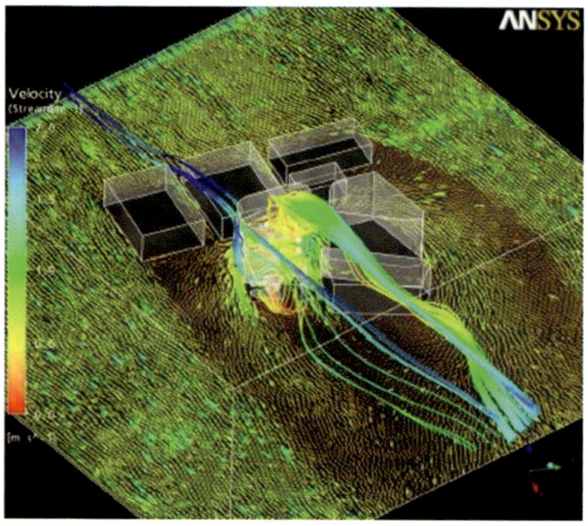

FIGURE 2
Streamline plots of south prevailing wind at 2 m/s (Aurecon, 2011)

SIMULATIONS

CFD analysis and simulations were used to assess the feasibility and opportunity of providing natural ventilation to the Solaris atrium. CFD analysis was undertaken to demonstrate whether wind velocity within the atrium space could achieve the desired velocity of 0.6 m/s. This is a requirement borrowed from Singapore Green Mark criteria (Residential and Non-Residential Version 3), as there is no other reference available on natural ventilation in Singapore. The assumed external wind from the north and south is 2 m/s, which is also borrowed from Green Mark criteria.

A series of options were tested to improve wind velocity. In each option, the general size and location of openings (inlets and outlets) were altered; resulting differences in air velocity, flow patterns, dead zones and buoyancy impacts were analysed.

RESULTS

The studies demonstrate that average wind velocities within the atrium space almost achieve the desired velocity of 0.6 m/s. The average wind velocities at the

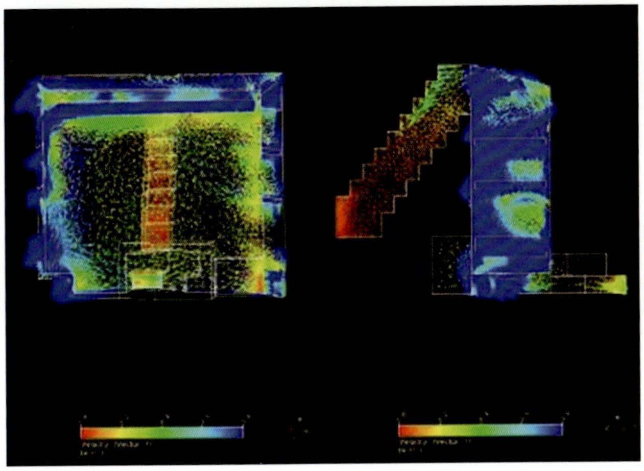

FIGURE 3
North and east elevation showing wind velocity vectors in atrium (Aurecon, 2011)

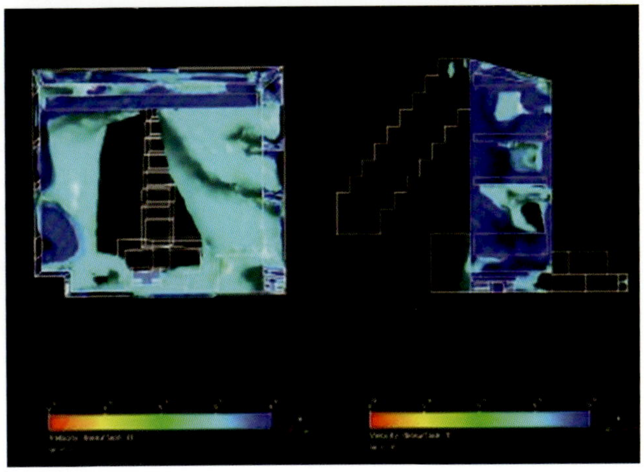

FIGURE 4
North and east elevation – Isothermal plot showing wind velocity in atrium (Aurecon, 2011)

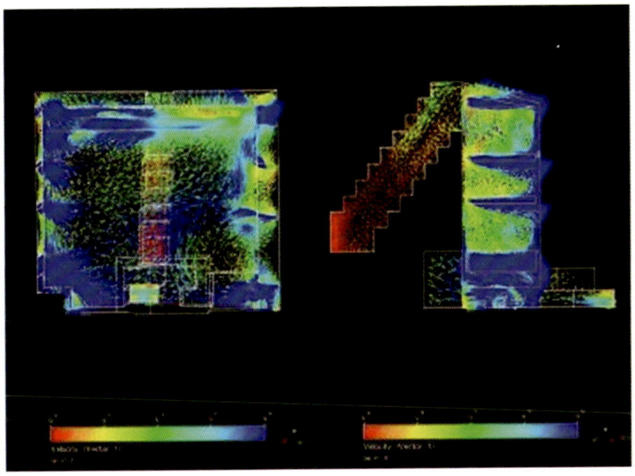

FIGURE 5
North and east elevation showing wind velocity vectors in atrium (Aurecon, 2011)

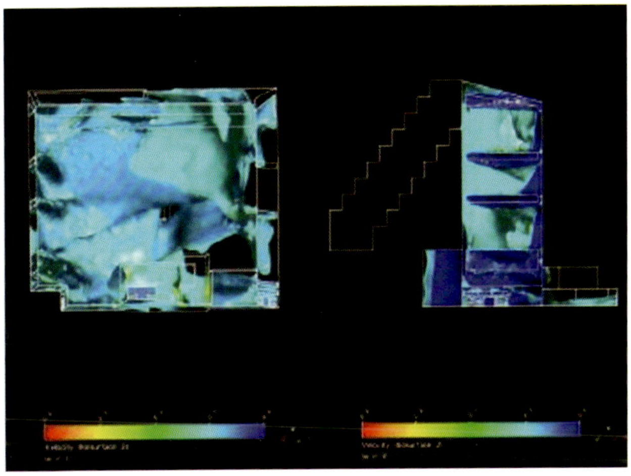

FIGURE 6
North and east elevation – Isothermal plot showing wind velocity in atrium (Aurecon, 2011)

atrium's ground floor (measured at 1.6 metres above the ground) are as follows:

At the:

- Skylight louvre opened with north prevailing wind at 2m/s = 0.49 m/s
- Skylight louvre opened with south prevailing wind at 2m/s = 0.53 m/s

The simulation results highlighted the potentials of either increasing various façade openings to catch more wind or adding and implementing mechanical aids in the form of jet fans. These could be good suggestions for future development of surrounding buildings, which could obstruct any incoming wind.

Upper opening of diagonal light shaft
Operable louvred skylight
Skybridge

FACING PAGE
Central atrium

THIS PAGE
Glazed atrium roof with operable louvres in open position

Skycourts: Places-in-the-sky

DESIGN IDEA

Skycourts are incisions in a built form for users to experience a more humane environment as an, open-to-the-sky zone for them to step out onto from enclosed floors. Skycourts can act as thermal buffers and create event spaces and areas for relaxation. These extensive gardens allow for interaction between the building's occupants and nature, offering the occupants opportunities to experience the external environment and enjoy the views. Skycourts can contain lush environments so people can view greenery from inside the building. Under hot climatic conditions, these deep recesses significantly shade internal spaces from direct sunlight and help reduce glare. Integrated landscaping reduces the ambient temperature of the building, increasing thermal comfort and the efficiency of engineering systems. Plants also act as visual screens and sound diffusers. A court can have full-height glazed doors that open out from internal areas to the terrace space. Besides providing shading, these skycourts can serve as emergency evacuation zones, as areas for planting and landscaping, as flexible interstitial zones for future expansion (e.g., in the event of a future increase in the permissible plot ratio) or as bases for the future spatial addition of ancillary areas such as executive washrooms, kitchenettes and other extensions.

BELOW
Menara Mesiniaga skycourt diagrams

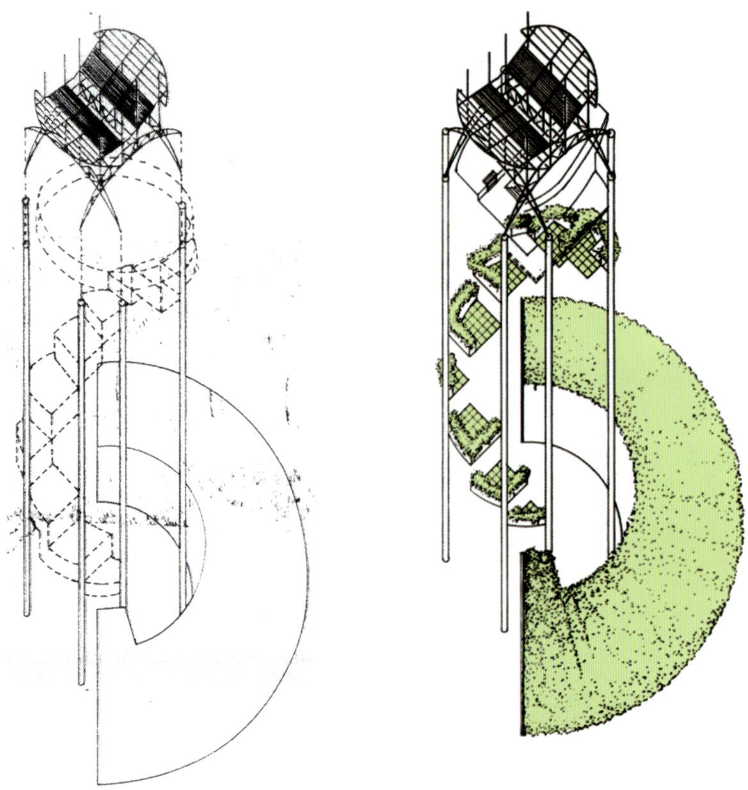

UMNO Tower (skycourt boxed)

ABOVE
Sky terraces in Menara Mesiniaga

BELOW
Mezzanine terraces that double as break-out spaces in Menara Mesiniaga

Future photovoltaic solar receptacle
Rooftop plaza
Aluminium fins and louvres for sunshading
Triple-storey skycourt
Garden terrace
Triple-volume entrance lobby
Three-storey planted mound

MENARA MESINIAGA & MENARA UMNO

Mesiniaga Sdn. Bhd. (IBM Sole Agent in Malaysia) is the client for Menara Mesiniaga, located in Subang Jaya, Selangor, Malaysia. This 14½-storey building (including one basement) was completed in August 1992, with a total net area of 12,345.69 square metres and comprised of an office, gym, café, circulation & toilets, mechanical rooms, carpark, skycourts, balconies and a pool deck. With a plot ratio of 1:1.6, this building was built on a site area of 6,503 square metres. The building brings together the principles of the bioclimatic approach to the design of tall buildings developed over the previous decade by the firm.

Menara UMNO is located in Jalan Macalister, Penang, Malaysia. It was completed in March 1998, with a site area of 1,920 square metres and a plot ratio of 1:5.5. The proposed tower on this site is 21 storeys and contains spaces for a banking hall at the ground floor and level 1 as well as an auditorium for meetings and assemblies at level 6. The auditorium is also accessible by a separate external staircase. Above this are 14 floors of office space.

BIOCLIMATIC FUNCTION AND INTENTIONS

Yeang highlights that the skycourts not only 'protect the hot sides of the building' and 'frame an important view' but also 'enable users to experience a more humane environment' within the high-rises.

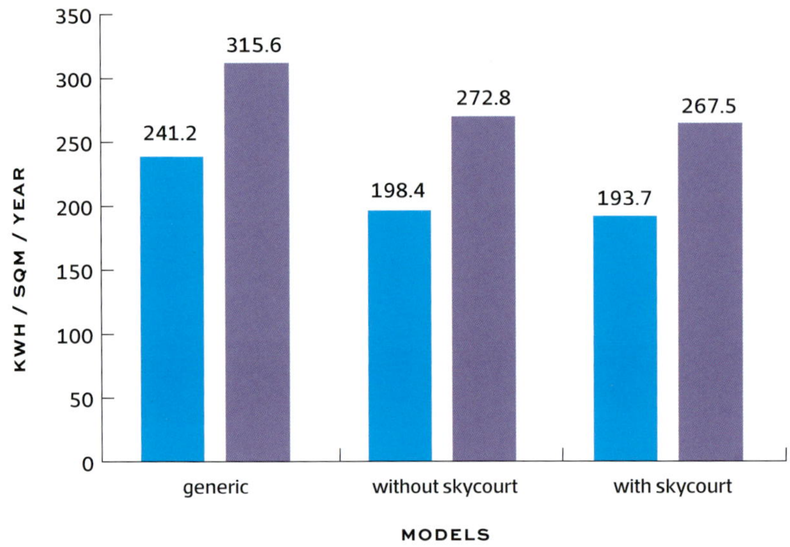

FIGURE 1 Menara UMNO – The impact of skycourts (bioclimatic)

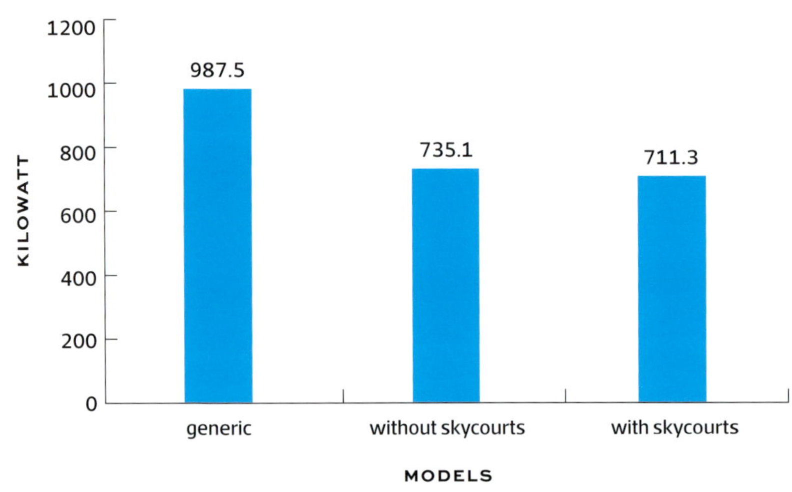

FIGURE 2 Menara UMNO – Peak cooling impact of skycourts (bioclimatic)

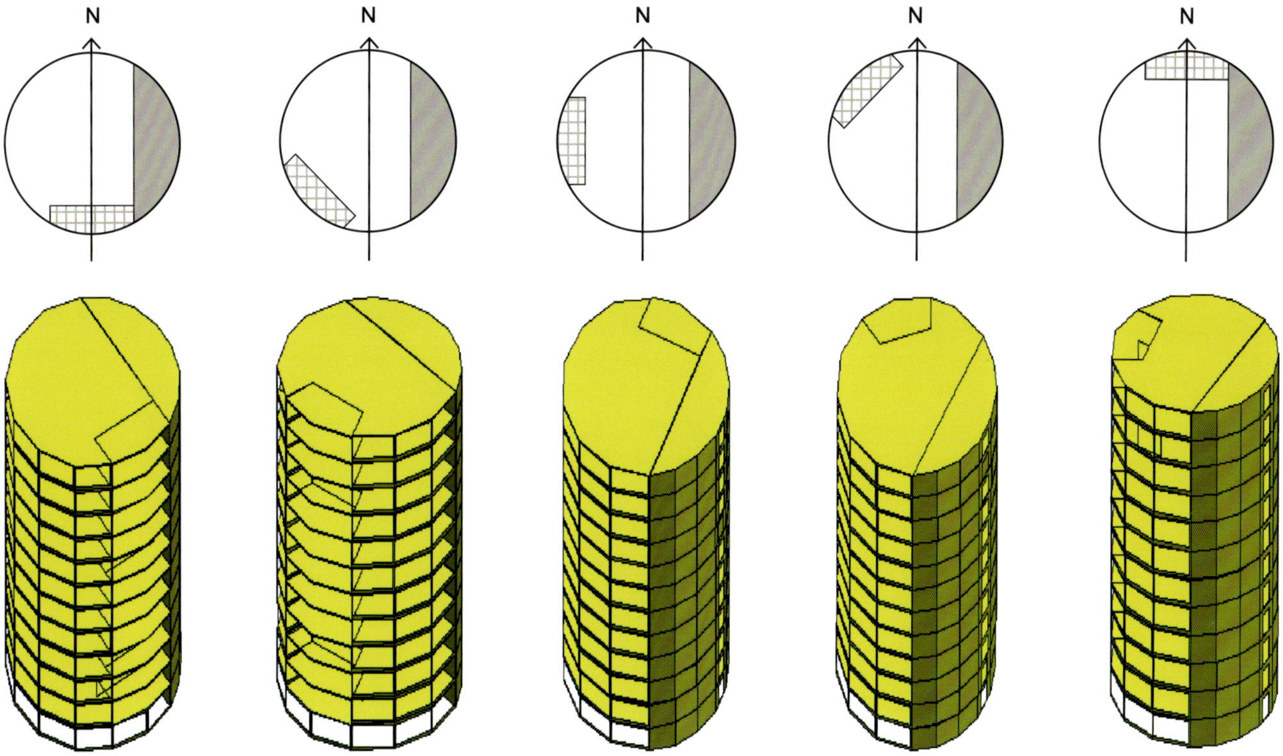

FIGURE 3 Mesiniaga – Variation in skycourt orientation

Yeang defines 'skycourts' as:

Deep recesses placed on the building's hot sides to give shading. Placing balconies at the hot elevations permit the glazing to these areas to be full-height clear panels. These can be sliding, openable panels to give access to these balcony spaces. These balcony spaces can serve as evacuation spaces in case of emergencies, as large terraces for planting and landscaping, as a flexible zone for the addition of future executive wash-rooms or kitchenette facilities.

These serve as in-between zones located between the insides and the outsides of the building. It functions in a similar way to the traditional 'verandah-way' in old shop-houses and masonry houses in the tropics. The tops should be shielded by a louvred roof to encourage wind flow into the inner areas of the building. These may also function as wind scoops in apartment buildings.

SIMULATION STUDIES: SKYCOURTS

Simulation studies were undertaken after the building had been occupied to evaluate the impact of skycourts compared to a generic high-rise. The aim was to evaluate theories to serve as guidelines and 'lessons learnt' for future work. In Menara UMNO, skycourts were modelled at 5.5 m wide and located on every third floor on the western side of the tower. A solar sun path analysis was conducted and hourly results were fed into a dynamic energy simulation tool in order to assess the impact with and without skycourts.

MESINIAGA: IMPACT OF SKYCOURT ORIENTATION

In Mesiniaga, a series of parametric runs were undertaken to evaluate the thermal impact of the orientation of skycourts and which options could achieve further reductions in cooling loads and energy use. Simulation tools were used to investigate the energy impacts of alternative placements of skycourts in Mesiniaga.

A series of skycourt options was modelled by aligning the skycourts vertically on different orientations. The aim was to analyze the impact on cooling load, peak cooling demand and annual energy performance according to the various orientations. In each case the skycourts are aligned vertically, in contrast to the original design that has a spiralling feature. The orientations tested included southwest, west, northwest, north and northeast.

Each skycourt is constructed with identical floor areas. As far as possible, these floor areas are equal to the total areas of the skycourts in the original design of Mesiniaga. The results of the impact of different skycourt orientations in terms of total energy and cooling load performance under the Malaysian climate are presented in Figure 4.

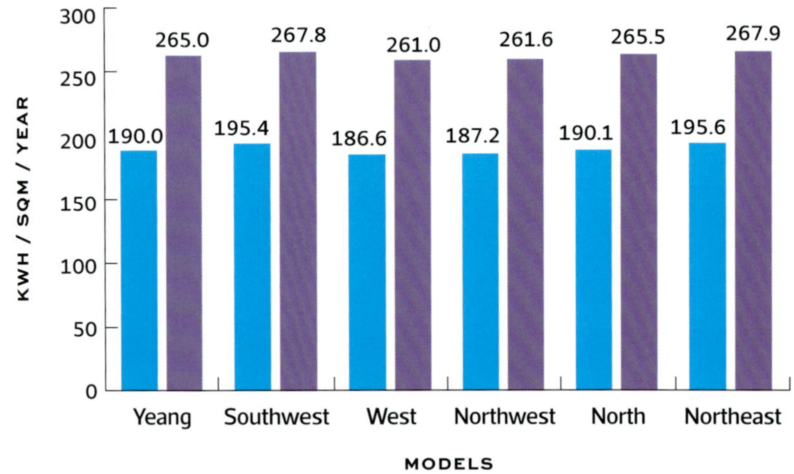

FIGURE 4 Menara Mesiniaga – Impact of skycourt orientation on cooling and total energy use

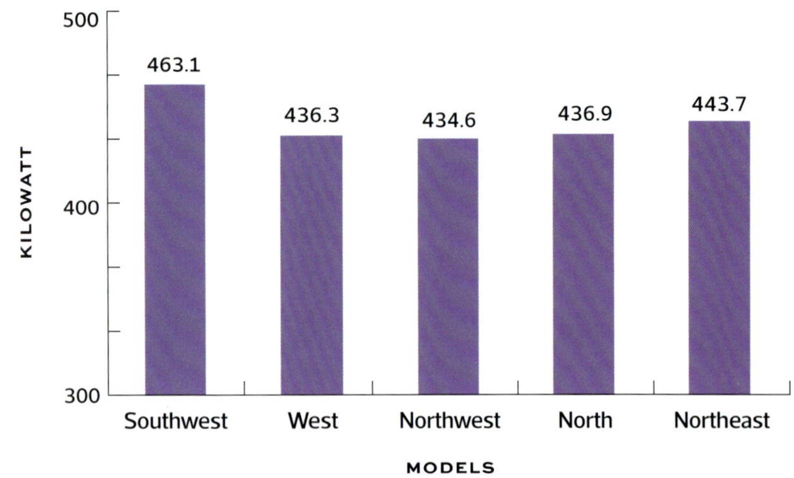

FIGURE 5 Menara Mesiniaga – Skycourt orientation variation in peak cooling demand

Cooling Total

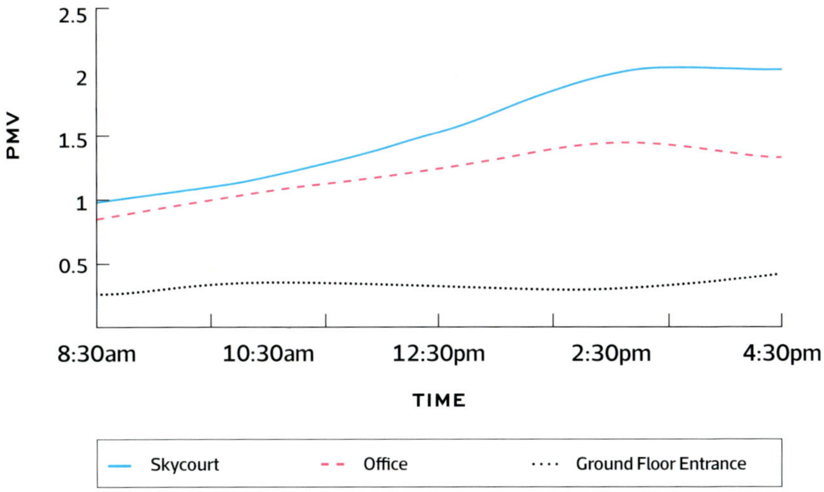

FIGURE 6 Menara Mesiniaga – PMV readings for offices (A/C), skycourts and fire escape for Level 6

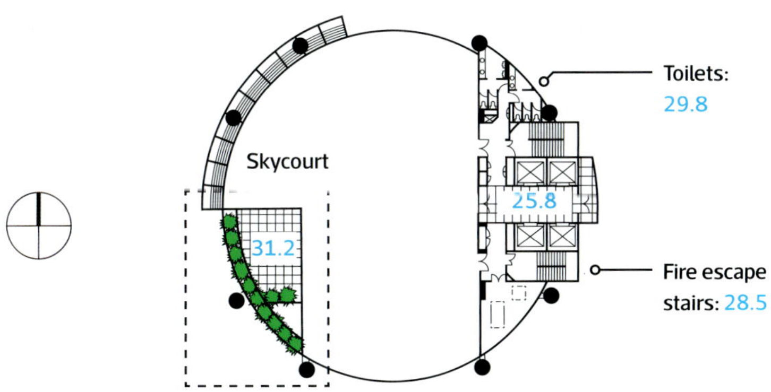

FIGURE 7 Menara Mesiniaga – Plan of office floor showing differences in temperature readings (in °C) throughout different spaces within Level 3 (Time: 2:00 pm)

PERFORMANCE IN USE – THERMAL COMFORT STUDIES OF SKYCOURTS IN MENARA MESINIAGA

Figure 6 shows that although the conditions in the fire escape areas are slightly warmer compared to the skycourts in the morning (between 8 and 11 am), they progressively become cooler. The skycourt conditions are a reflection of high temperatures in the late morning and afternoon.

Figure 7 shows the differences in dry-bulb temperature readings of major spaces on a typical floor of Mesiniaga – the naturally ventilated toilets and fire escape areas are warm while the skycourt is the warmest in the afternoon.

The use of these fully glazed sliding doors in conjunction with skycourts allows occupants to enjoy the greenery provided within the skycourts from inside the building. A majority of users indicated that the extensive landscaping significantly improved the overall atmosphere experienced within the offices. The advantages of the skycourts are thus related to this provision of external gardens, as they give the occupants the opportunity – if they choose to – to step out into a different environment. They provide elements of visual interest and a view into a landscaped balcony.

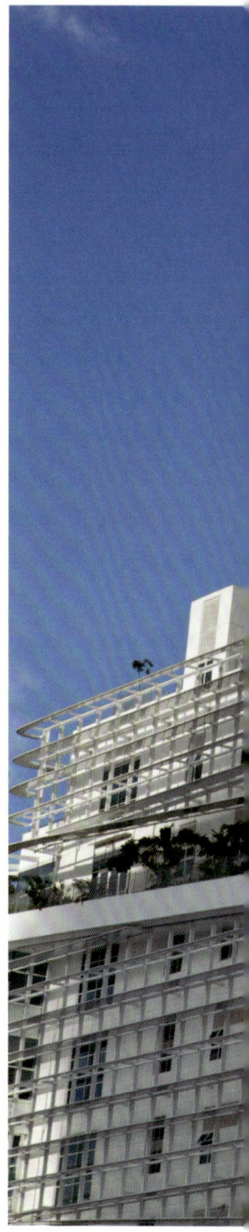

SOLARIS, SINGAPORE

The most prominent ecological feature of the Solaris building is the 1.5-km-long linear park that begins within a basement-level ecocell and rises upwards, wrapping itself around the building in a continuous fashion that makes it the world's longest vertically spiralling vegetated ramp. Here, though, unlike the ramp within the EDITT project, the landscaped planters are accompanied by a parallel path, turning the ramp into an accessible park and facilitating servicing of the greenery. Recessed into the façade, the ramp, fulfils a number of functions: it shades, cools, and insulates the building while providing a social amenity and enhancing biodiversity. Where the ramp meets a building corner, it opens out to become a terrace, while sun-shades above lift up to enable the growth of larger trees and admit extra sunlight. These skycourts as vegetated spaces therefore provide social space for inhabitants while performing very real sustainable functions.

FACING PAGE
Outdoor seating area in skycourt

ABOVE
Landscaped terraces as 'places-in the sky'

RIGHT
A visualisation of sky terraces

NATIONAL LIBRARY, SINGAPORE

More than 6,300 square metres of this building are devoted to green space in the form of urban skycourts, constituting more than 60 percent of the building's footprint. The northeast façade contains a pair of 40-metre-high skycourts planted with 3-metre-high trees. These skycourts are protected by windbreakers, which reduce the impact of high-speed winds that can occur at higher levels of this 120-metre-tall building – gusts can reach more than 35 m/s. The windbreakers baffle the wind and break it into smaller, weaker eddies before it enters the skycourts. Post-occupancy evaluation has shown that over 90 percent of library users and staff are satisfied with the building, and studies show that the environmental impact of the National Library is lower than that of a typical office building of similar size. The Energy Efficiency Index of the building is around 172 kwh/sqm/year, compared to the index of a typical office building in Singapore, which consumes around 250 kwh/sqm/year. The building received several prizes, including an award from the World Association of Chinese Architects.

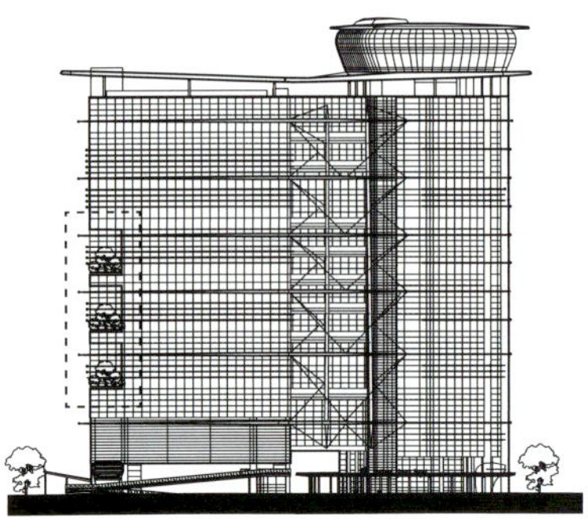

LEFT
North Bridge Road Elevation (skycourts highlighted)

ABOVE
Plants also act as visual screens and sound diffusers

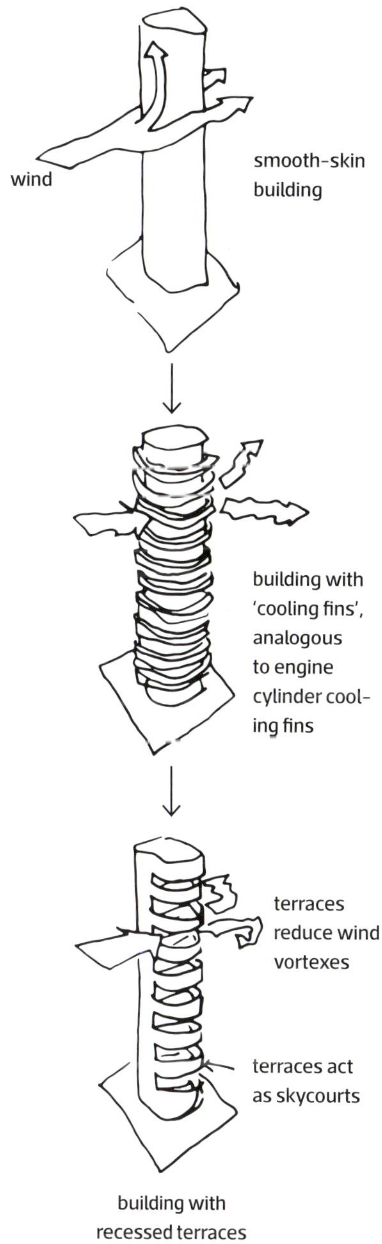

MENARA BOUSTEAD, KUALA LUMPUR, MALAYSIA

This project includes several important innovations that reoccur in Yeang's works – principally the introduction of skycourts. The objective was to design the office building to be more than just a series of enclosed concrete trays stacked in the air. The plan-form is based on a square with protrusions and is encircled in part by an outer layer. This formation allows the introduction of both skycourts and terraces in the outer corners of the plan, and characteristically marks the overall form of the tower throughout its height. These terraces are located at all corners all the way up the building. These skycourt terraces also provide flexible zones for additional services such as supplementary air-conditioning units. The skycourt, as a device, is an element that is developed significantly in Yeang's more-recent designs, but the basic combined principles of deep façade recesses, balcony terraces, planters, heat-sink cladding and overall solar configuration are all grounded in Boustead.

MBF TOWER, PENANG, MALAYSIA

The predominantly residential apartment content of the MBF Tower, and the potential for separation and openness that this affords, has resulted in a singular statement that evokes Yeang's thematic idea of 'places-in-the-sky'. The tower is developed from tropical high-rise ideals, where the upper parts of the tower have large, two-storey-high skycourts (the building's key feature) that provide ventilation and deck space for planting and terraces. The triple-banded plan has four apartments on each floor level, on the north and south edges. These are separated by a central area of access galleries, elevator cores and staircases. In turn, all these elements are further separated with floor slots and gaps, both horizontal and vertical. In addition, the upper levels of the tower have generous, two-storey skycourt 'cut-out' openings, which penetrate the entire section. Taken together, this intensification of the articulation of elements in both plan and section creates a flowing, three-dimensional inner volume that is laced with cool, cross-ventilated channels, lowering the thermal load of both circulation sapces and apartments alike. This is supported by a vertical landscape that festoons skycourts, terraces and planters with a profusion of nature and natural shading.

Views of the MBF Tower

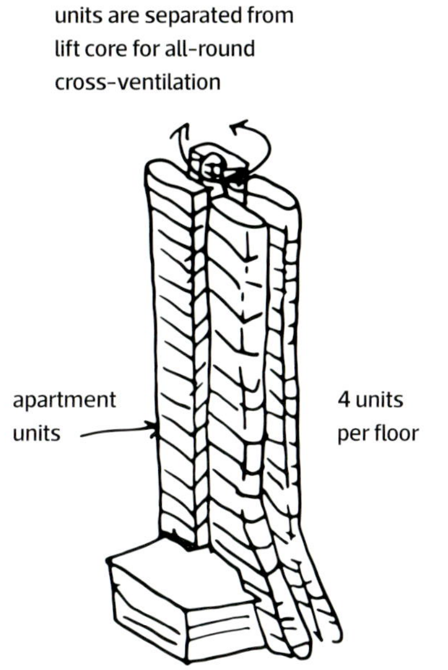

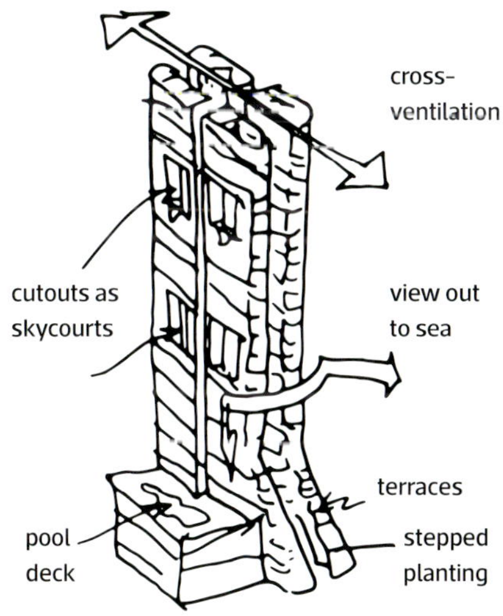

ABOVE
Cutouts were used to create skycourts

Double-Layer Façade

DESIGN IDEA

A double-layer façade is an extra skin on an external building envelope, providing additional thermal insulation in hot, temperate and cold climates. In certain contexts and cases, it is a high-tech construction system composed of two layers of skins that are placed in such a way so that there is a cavity between them that allows airflow; these layers also act as a screening device. The cavity between the two skins may be filled with naturally or mechanically ventilated air. These double-skin façades can also act as windbreakers and as insulators to reduce the energy use of buildings.

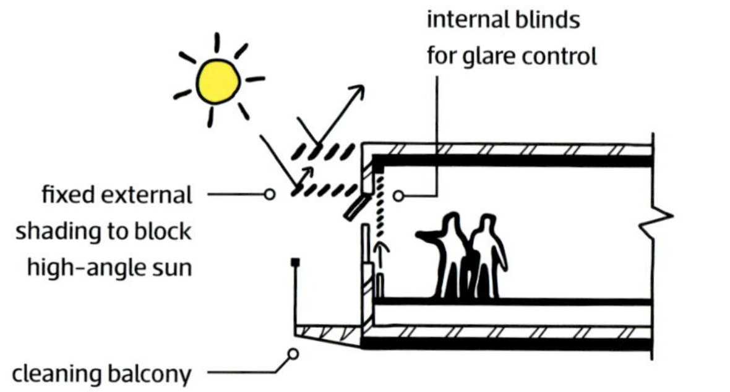

South Façade

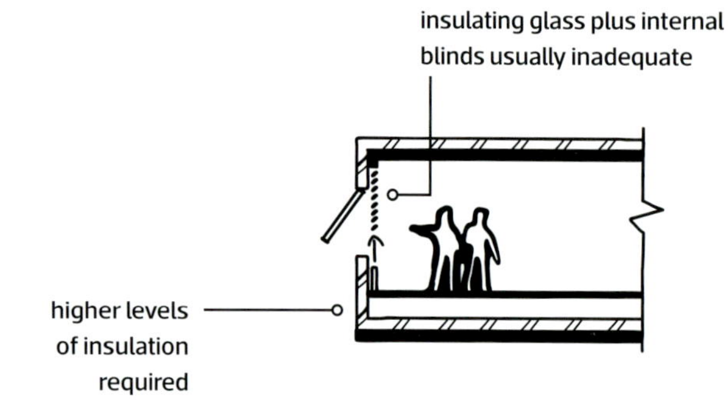

North Façade

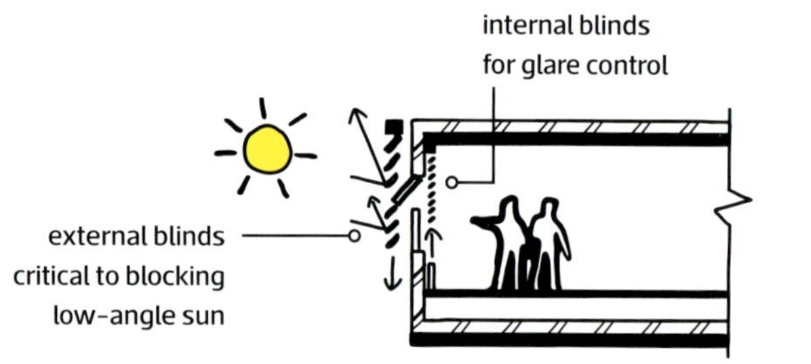

West/East Option 1

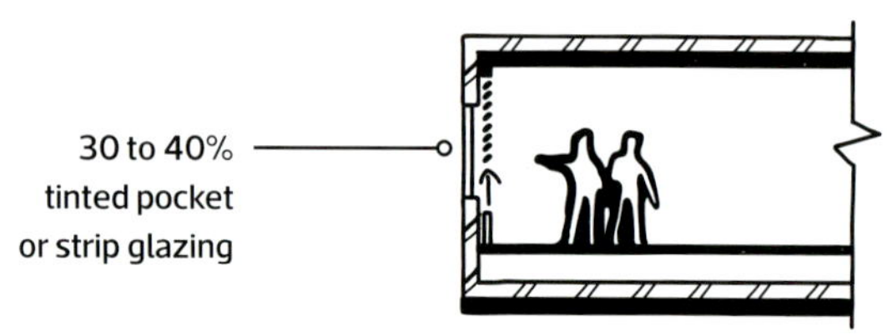

West/East Option 2

RIGHT
Concepts for façades

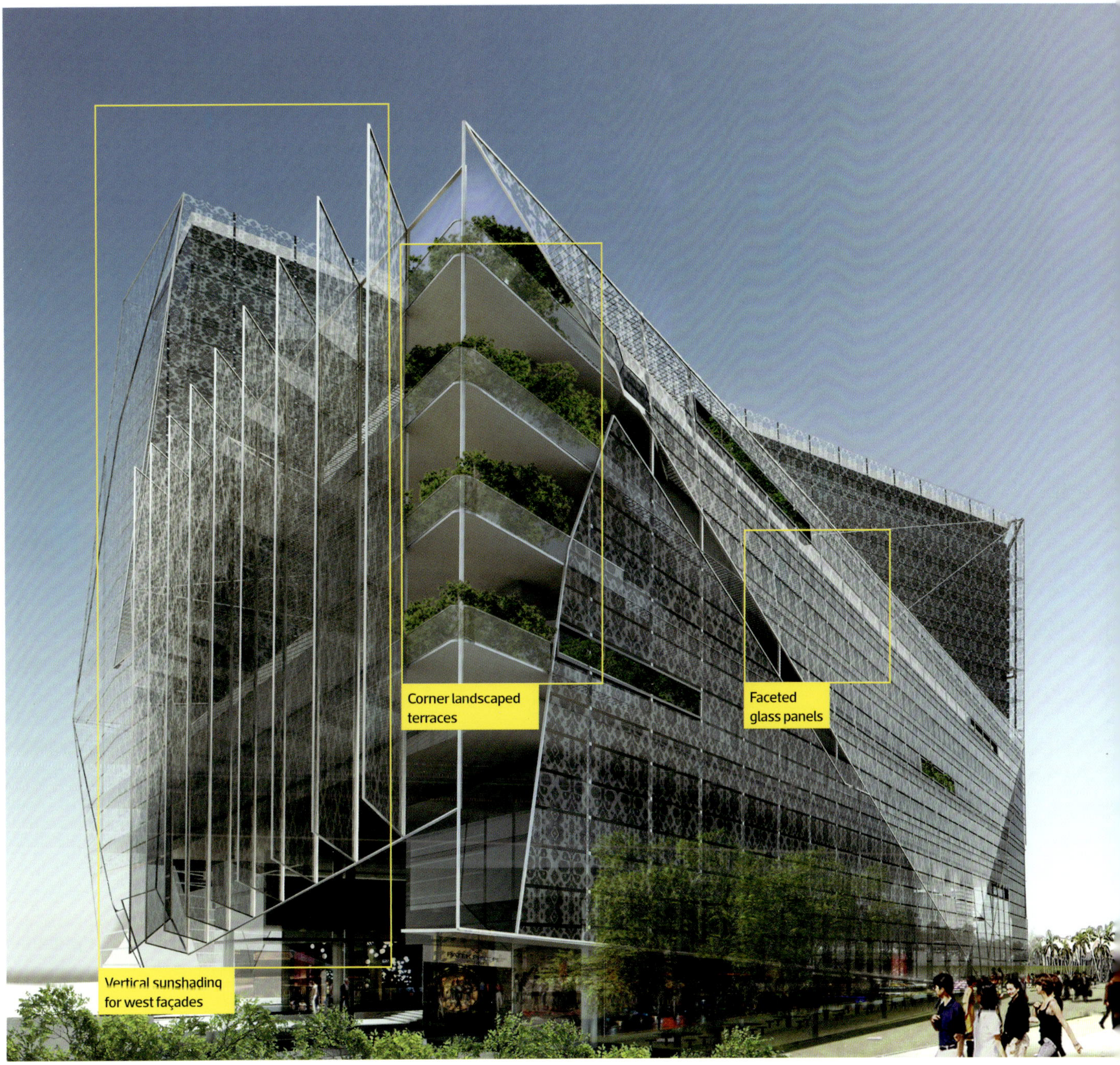

Lot 2C5 Putrajaya, Malaysia

ABOVE
Faceted glass panels

RIGHT
Double Layer Façade

RIGHT
Section of façade elements

BELOW LEFT
Axonometric cutaway of fritted glass

BELOW RIGHT
Fritted 'songket' patterns

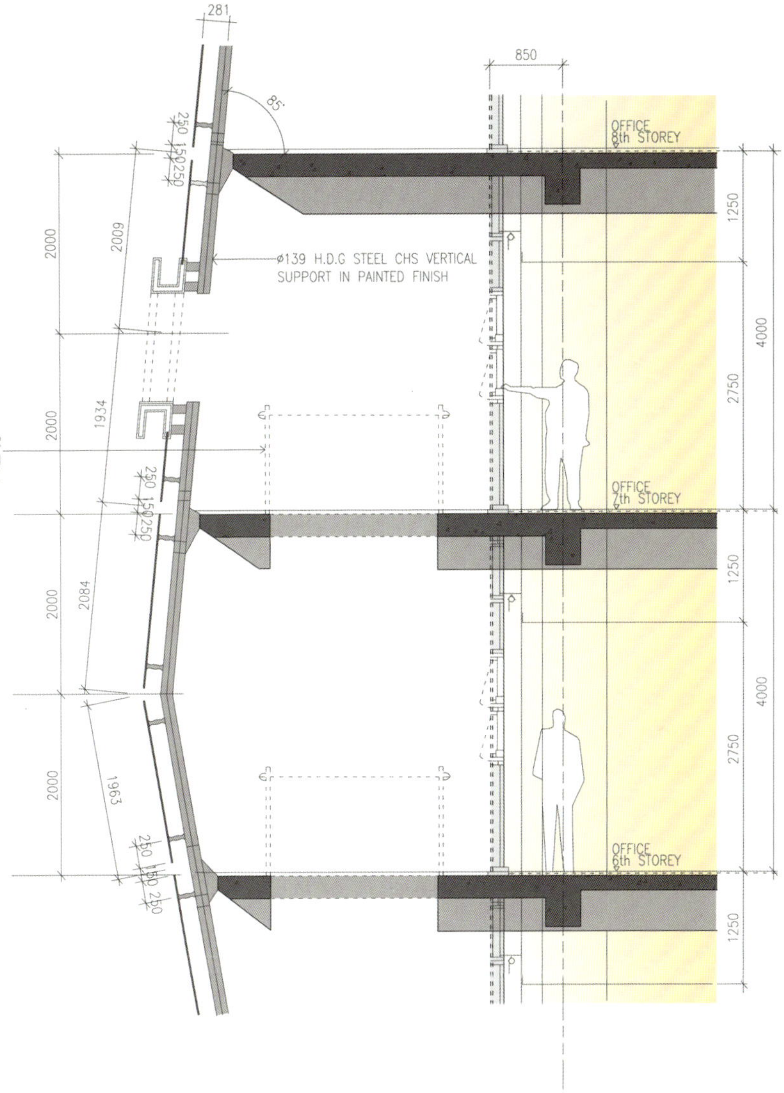

BIOCLIMATIC FUNCTION AND INTENTIONS

An ideal shading system under hot climatic conditions is that which prevents direct solar radiation from entering interior spaces while providing sufficient natural light for occupants.

As Steemers (1989) summarises the main criteria in any assessment of building shading systems:

> *To assess the performance of a shading device, one could argue that maximum shade from direct solar radiation should be balanced with minimum reduction of diffuse radiation while still providing a reasonable view.*

Under hot conditions, the principle issue is protection from direct solar radiation. The featured shading system has some of the highest impact in terms of reducing cooling load and total energy use under the tropical climate.

However, there is always the demand from clients to have large areas of glass and façade treatment in multi-storey buildings, which is synonymous with a more global image of architecture. In these cases, too, there is a limitation to the extent of any horizontal projection due to external shading on a high-rise façade. In order to maximise lettable floor areas in a commercial office tower, glazing systems are typically placed at the outermost edges of a building. This reduces possibilities for incorporating external shading as filtering devices. Additionally, shading is normally a feature added onto the 'main' body of the high-rise tower, requiring additional construction detailing and an increase in maintenance costs.

Hence, solar hybrid shading systems are forms of external shading designed as integrated parts of the 'body' of a building rather than add-on components. These external shading systems were designed as 'loose clothing' – made of double-glazing construction such as patterned or fritted glass – and made an integral part of the building design. It recalls Yeang's perforated shading armoury in the UMNO Tower, Shanghai Tower and Hitechniaga Tower.

SIMULATIONS

A solar penetration analysis was conducted using an hourly solar analysis tool in order to assess the performance of the solar shading device. Results show that solar penetration was minimal in most perimeter zones. Where the penetration of direct sun was found to be significant and of concern, alternative dimensions and projection widths of the shading device were optimised. Results are shown in Figure 1 and Figure 2.

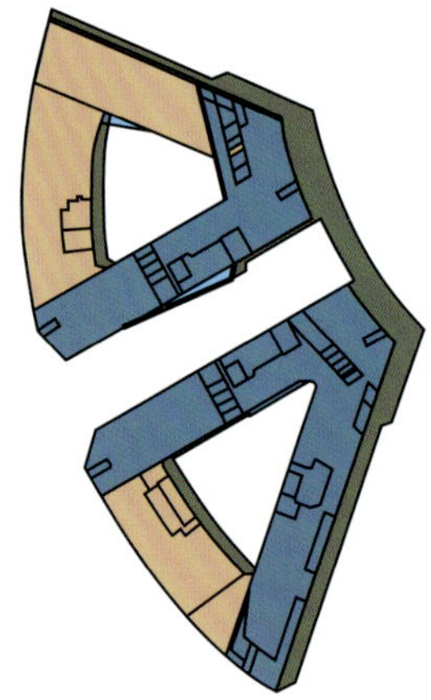

Suncast Image	
View time	21 March, 2:00 pm
Site latitude	3.12
Longitude diff.	18.45
Model bearing	0.00
Sun	azi = 249.96 alt = 79.79
Eye	azi = 140.00 alt = 90.00

FIGURE 1
Solar shading analysis shows no significant penetration of direct solar radiation

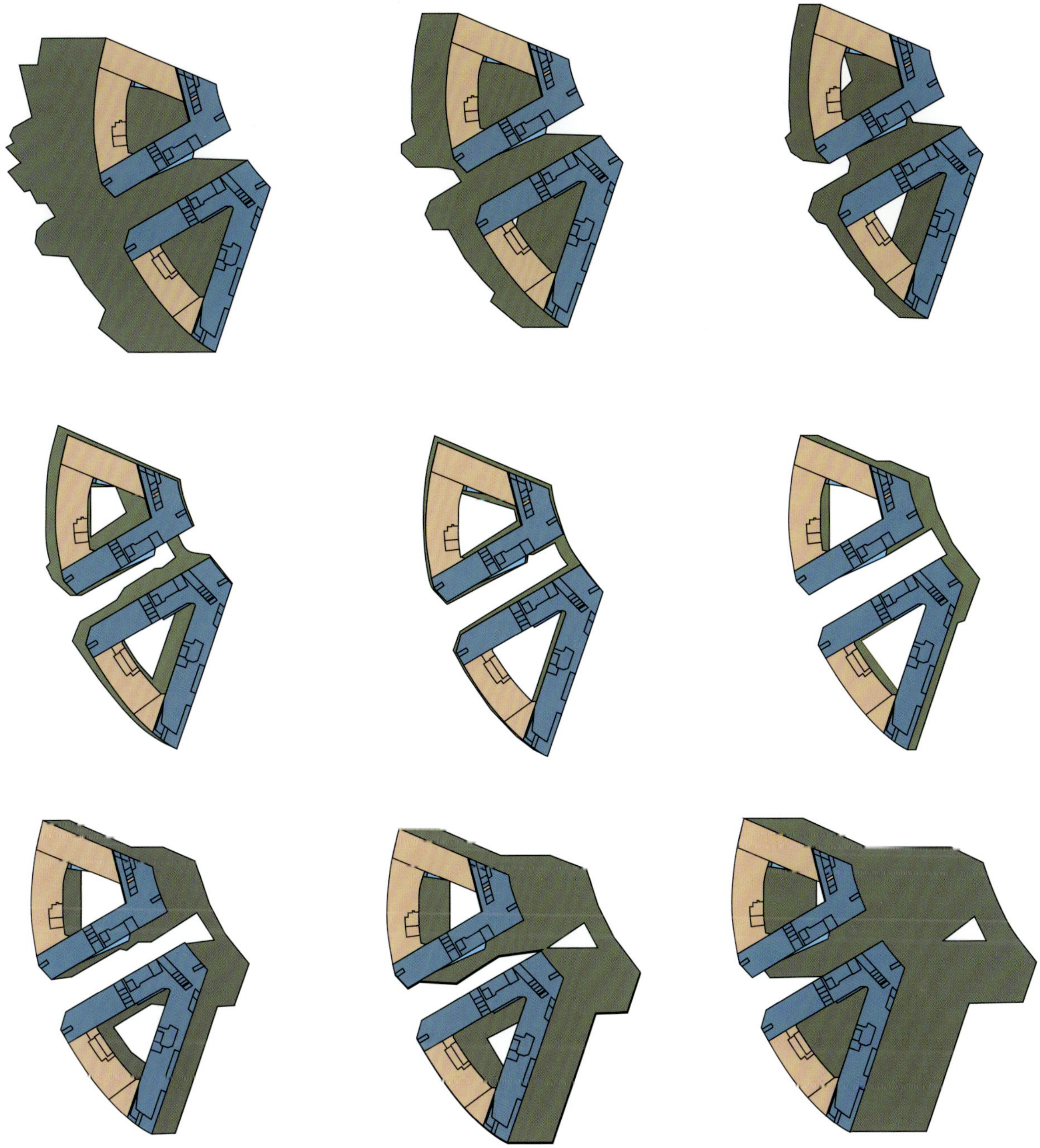

FIGURE 2
Hourly analysis shows some penetration at 5 pm. However, by this time, external temperatures and solar radiation had decreased significantly.

Lot 2C5 Putrajaya

HITECHNIAGA TOWER, KUALA LUMPUR, MALAYSIA

Here, a series of perforated metal 'shields' are used as outriggers on the main form to shade the building. However, in this case, both the scale and curvilinear scallop shaping of these elements extend far beyond mere function, marking a point in Yeang's formal articulation of the bioclimatic tower aesthetic. At the same time, these mechanisms are both solar-defensive and solar-demonstrative. Juxtaposed with the highly articulated form, the architecture assumes a 'warrior-like stance', crowned at the tower's summit by additional shielding devices developed from the earlier principles of Menara Mesiniaga.

Ecobridges and Ecoundercrofts

DESIGN IDEA

Ecobridges and ecoundercrofts are external devices that enable an uninterrupted ecological nexus and connectivity across landscapes, particularly over urban landscapes that have been bifurcated or fragmented by human intervention and structures such as roads, drains and impervious hardscape surfaces. The ecobridge (a wide, vegetated bridge) and ecoundercroft (wide, short, subterranean tunnels) enable 'fingers' or ribbons of vegetation to span across or go under these obstructions.

These reconnect partitioned vegetated areas, repairing and reuniting disparate landscapes and enabling these to become whole, thereby enabling greater species interaction and species migration between and across the reconnected landscape, whether for breeding, feeding, searching for water or refuge. The enhanced connection enables a greater pooling of natural resources within the habitat, thereby enhancing local biodiversity and enabling greater opportunities for ecological survival without the need for human intervention.

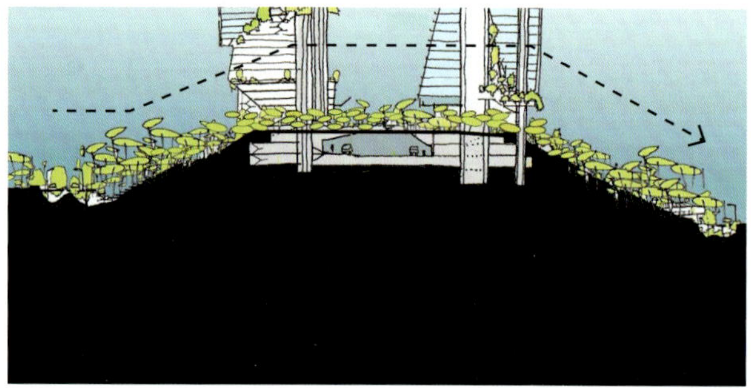

- improves ecosystem interaction between species
- engenders sharing of resources within ecosystem
- encourages increase in species diversity
- engenders a more stable ecosystem

Ecobridge

Ecoundercroft

RIGHT
Concept sketches

FACING PAGE
SOMA Masterplan showing ecological corridors

Ecobridge
Ecobridges
Detention pond
Detention ponds for sustainable drainage
Detention pond
Ecobridge
Ecoundercroft
Ecobridge
Detention pond
Ecoundercroft
Legend
Ecological Corridors (Big Trees)
Boulevard Trees
Secondary Vegetation
Ground Cover

BKE ROAD LEVEL
BKE ROAD LEVEL

FACING PAGE
Ecobridge in elevation
and aerial view

THIS PAGE
Ecoundercroft in elevation
and ground-level view

SOMA MASTERPLAN, BANGALORE, INDIA

The SOMA Masterplan in Raja-rajeshwari Nagar in Bangalore, India, is an iconic project designed to harmonize with Vashtu Shastra principles and successfully introduces an 'ecological corridor'. Located in the hot, humid tropics, this masterplan has a gross built-up area of 2,000,000 square metres and a site area of 867,500 square metres. The unique feature of the masterplan is a continuous ecological corridor that weaves across the 86.75 acres of Rajarajeshwari Nagar using ecobridges and ecoundercrofts, linking all green spaces within the site and seeking to link to adjoining sites. The green eco-infrastructure provides 'nature's utilities' to the project while enhancing the ecological biodiversity of the development. The design seeks to encourage a sustainable lifestyle for the users and enhance the community's access to green areas, social connectivity and a healthy lifestyle.

BIOCLIMATIC FUNCTION AND INTENTIONS

Crucial to ecological design and masterplanning is the maintenance of an ecological nexus and continuity across the landscape to enable species interaction and movement. Ecobridges and ecoundercrofts enable the fragmented landscape and isolated green areas to be 'stitched' together, creating a new network of green ecoinfrastructure to reconnect the entire terrain in a region that has been devastated by human intervention. This reconnected green ecoinfrastructure becomes a new wildlife 'corridor', linking several smaller habitats with larger ones, serving as a green route through existing urban areas and connecting existent green areas within urban areas. Creating new green ecoinfrastructure is one of the strategies for the green retrofitting of existing cities. In general, a fragmented landscape becomes ecologically simplified, with lowered opportunities for long-term survival.

These corridors can form new habitats in their own right. They connect existent wildlife corridors in the form of woodland belts or wetlands, vestigial agricultural land and vegetated strands or existing landscape features such as overgrown railway lines, hedges and green areas beside waterways. The green ecoinfrastructure does not have to lie just within a project's site but could be connected to other larger habitats external to the site, so that the entire region or locality becomes an expanded network of green ecoinfrastructures which further contributes to the region's overall biodiversity. A well-designed green infrastructure can heal landscapes, repairing their ruptures and reconnecting their parts.

Besides horizontal connectivity across landscapes, vertical connectivity of built forms both externally and within is also vital. The design of our built forms must extend ecological linkages upwards using green walls and other devices, extending from the lowest basements eco-cells to street-level greening to rooftop gardens, all linked through landscape at the ground plane to the hinterland. This vertical connectivity will further support the existing hierarchy and form of habitats and green spaces within communities.

Eco-design and eco-masterplanning can purposely employ this green ecoinfrastructure to integrate with other ecoinfrastructures, including the site's water management system (its 'blue' ecoinfrastructure), eco-engineering of road networks, drainage systems, utilities and carbon-neutral clean-tech systems ('grey' ecoinfrastructure) and the functions and activities of our human society, its built systems and myriad of activities on the landscape ('red' ecoinfrtastructure).

Further development of the ecobridge device, presently implemented at the ground plane, could extend upwards to become ecobridges-in-the-sky, linking to green skycourts on the upperparts of buildings.

Creating a network of new green eco-infrastructures in existing cities using ecobridges and ecoundercrofts enables the linking of existing parks and green areas together, and can be enhanced further via linkages to the city's green hinterland or surrounding greenbelt. This is among the key initial steps to take in the rehabilitation and retrofitting of our existing cities into 'ecocities'.

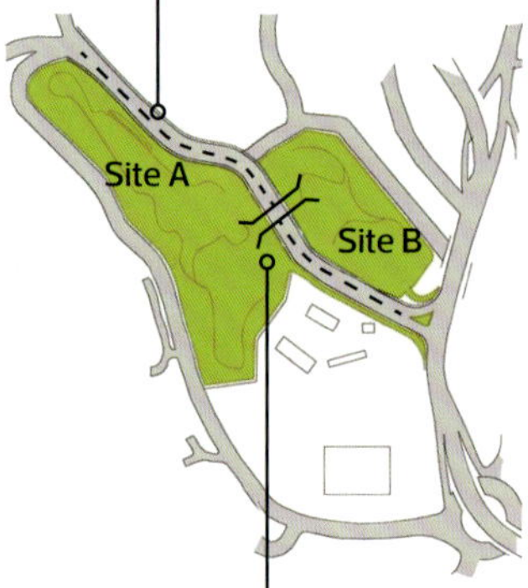

FACING PAGE
Concept

LEFT
SOMA Masterplan showing locations of ecobridges and ecoundercrofts

CAMBAIE OMEGA, LA REUNION

The masterplan for Cambaie is designed as a model ecocity. Although the design is tailored here to address this locality's and dweller specificities, the general principles for ecocity design proposed can be generically adopted for the development of sustainable, green, residential townships elsewhere. The objective of the design is to enhance the biodiversity of Cambaie through these ecological corridors. Having a 50:50 ratio between green and urban areas in Cambaie reduces heat build-up in typical urban localities. The green infrastructure becomes the physical green environment within and around our built environment as a network of multi-functional open spaces, including formal parks, gardens, woodlands, green corridors, waterways and street foliage. Crucial to ecological design and masterplanning is the maintenance of an ecological nexus and continuity across the landscape, enabling species interaction and movement. Ecobridges and ecoundercrofts are deployed to distribute vegetation across the masterplan, thereby allowing the fragmented landscape and isolated green areas to be 'stitched' together to create a new network of green ecoinfrastructure and reconnect the entire terrain in a region that has been devastated by human intervention. This reconnected green ecoinfrastructure becomes a new wildlife 'corridor', linking several smaller habitats with larger ones and serving as a green route through existing urban areas. These bridges assist in balancing what Yeang would call the abiotic and biotic content of a site.

FACING PAGE
Cultural plaza showing vertical connectivity within the built forms

RIGHT
Masterplan showing wildlife corridors as green routes through urban areas

Vertical Habitats: The Linked Green Wall

DESIGN IDEA

The linked green wall is a vertical ecoinfrastructure that establishes a continuous habitat on all façades of a building, thereby enhancing its ecological performance and contributing to the site's biodiversity. Conditions of this green armature are especially conducive to populations of butterflies and species of small birds. This idea of continuity is necessary to promote biodiversity. The green wall effectively acts as one large habitat, as opposed to a segmented design in which the biodiversity impact is less effective due to balkanization. The vegetated green wall provides ecological continuity, natural air filtration and enhanced thermal performance. It acts as a living, breathing, regenerative cladding as well as a living art installation and biological air filter. Green walls, both indoors and out, decrease local CO_2, help regulate humidity levels, trap dust, reduce noise and create habitats for urban wildlife. Exterior green wall installations reduce solar gain (the entrapment of heat on building surfaces) and, by extension, building energy costs, provide protection from the effects of UV radiation and acid rain and help lessen the building's contribution to the heat-island effect (resulting from vegetated land being replaced with concrete and asphalt).

BELOW

A close-up of DiGi Data Centre's façade reveals green walls that establish a continuous habitat.

DiGi Data Centre Building
Fresh air intake behind green wall

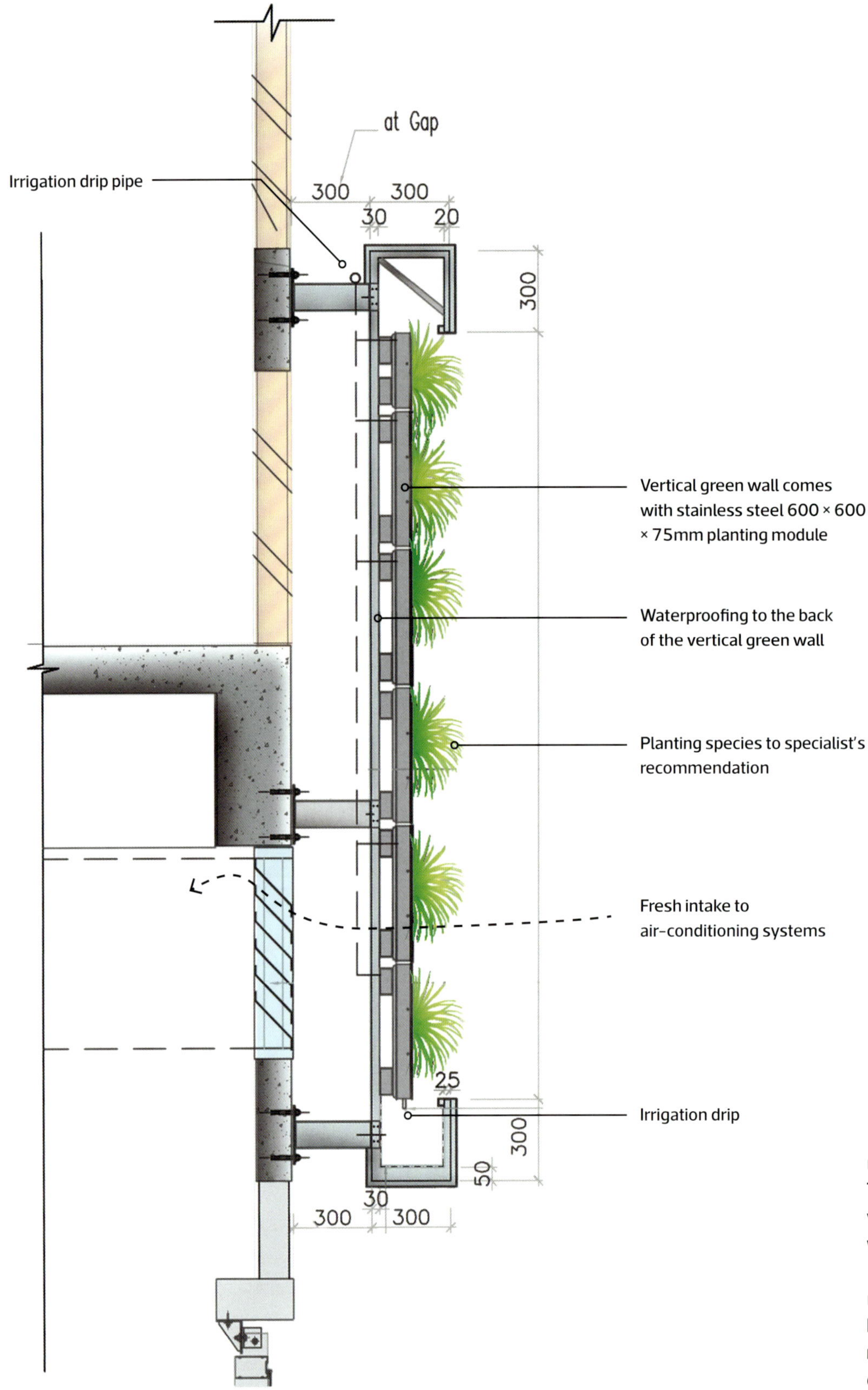

LEFT
Typical detail for vertical green wall

FACING PAGE
Linked green wall meets ground at one corner

DIGI DATA CENTRE BUILDING

An example of a vertical habitat is the linked green wall in the DiGi Data Centre building. The DiGi Technology Operation Centre is located at Subang High Tech Park, Shah Alam, Selangor, Malaysia. This 4-storey building (23.5 high) is a data centre with ancillary facilities (i.e., administration offices, a reception lobby, Telco Tower and a service management centre [Command Centre] for Digi Telecommunications Sdn. Bhd). The project has a total gross floor area (GFA) of 12,468 square metres and has been awarded a GBI Gold rating.

This green wall is linked across all façades of the built form and is linked at one corner to the vegetation on the ground. Placed behind some of the green walls are air-conditioning intake grills, so the green walls can 'scrub' the incoming air before it enters the building's air-conditioning system.

Further development of these vertical habitats can be achieved by designing the habitats with the guide of a 'biodiversity matrix' developed for the locality, creating a variety of different hardscape conditions on the built form's façade as a vertical complex of habitats.

FUNCTIONS & INTENTIONS

The vertical habitat is a continuous green infrastructure located vertically on the façade of the built form, linked not only over and within the building but to the vegetation and landscape at the ground plane, enhancing its ecological performance, contributing to the site's, and increasing the organic mass in an otherwise totally inorganic built form. This vertical ecoinfrastructure also becomes a green armature that is especially conducive to populations of small species (such as butterflies, dragonflies and small birds).

In addition to improving the project's conservation footprint via the addition of large areas of native vegetation, the vertical green wall contributes to the building's overall performance in the following manners:

1 Ecological Continuity – This vertical ecoinfrastructure establishes a continuous habitat on all façades of the building, thereby enhancing its ecological performance and contributing to the site's biodiversity. Conditions of this green armature are especially conducive to populations of butterflies and species of small birds. The continuity of the design further promotes biodiversity as the green wall effectively acts as one large habitat, as opposed to a segmented design in which the biodiversity impact is less effective due to balkanization;

2 Natural Air Filtration – The green walls have been developed in conjunction with the building's ventilation design to act as a biological air filtration system. 5 fresh air intakes are strategically located immediately behind the green wall trellis in order to capitalize on the particulate filtration and CO_2 sequestration afforded by their proximity to greenery.

3 Thermal Performance – The extensive 1,460m^2 green wall contributes to the overall thermal performance of the building envelope. This contribution is significant, as the project's green wall covers an area equal to approximately 32% of the total surface area of the building envelope. The enhanced thermal performance afforded by green walls as architectural cladding is documented by a growing body of academic research.

The vegetated green wall provides ecological continuity between the vertical plane in built forms and the landscape at the ground plane. It also provides natural biological air filtration and can enhance the thermal performance of a built form's façade. It acts as a living, breathing, regenerative biological habitat.

Green walls to act as a biological air filtration system

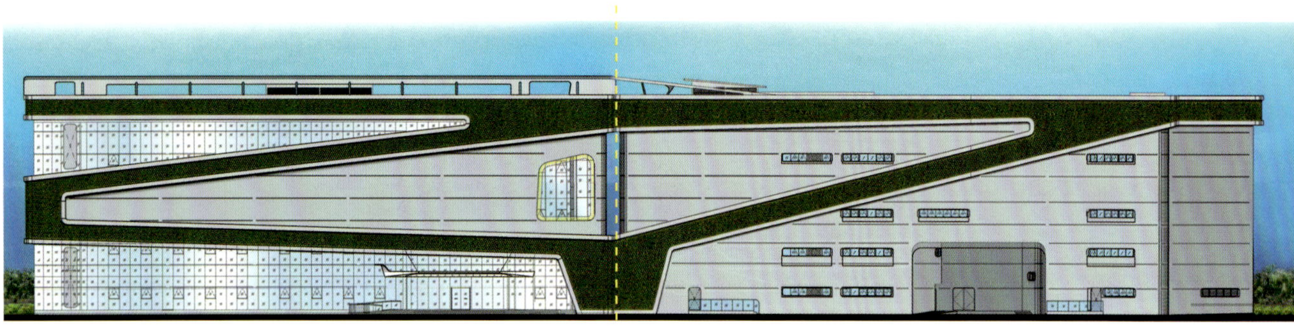

Northwest Elevation

Southwest Elevation

FACING PAGE
Southwest elevation

ABOVE
Southeast elevation

BELOW
The bifurcating system of vegetated walls that wraps itself around the building's façades.

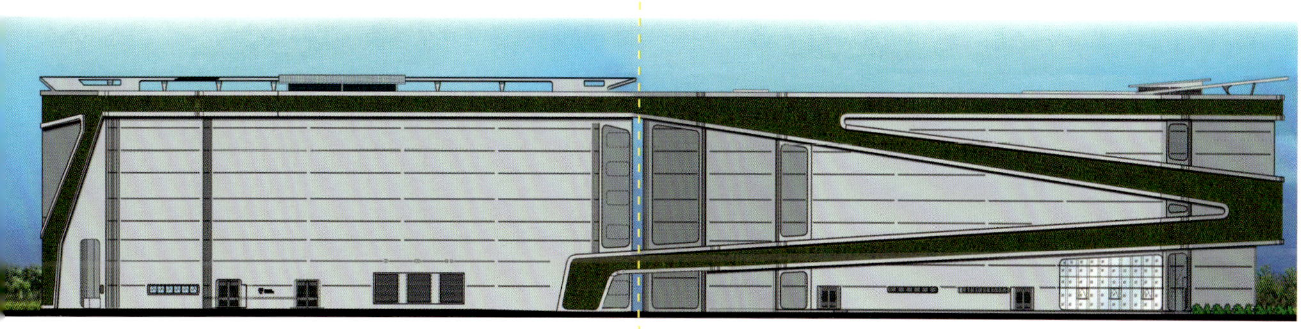

Southeast Elevation

Northeast Elevation

ZORLU ECOCITY, ISTANBUL, TURKEY

This competition entry combines a number of Yeang's ideas and translates them into a 'city within a city'. At Zorlu, Yeang's 'urban design intention was to rehabilitate the existent ecology of a locality that had been fragmented and devastated by human activities, agriculture, forestry, urban development and sprawl. The approach was to reconnect the ecological nexus of the site using a series of devices to give Istanbul a large, ring-shaped urban park. With a programme of social, cultural, retail and commercial activities spanning east-west across the entire park, the design recognised the need to make the venture financially viable'. Planted ramps bring Yeang's green ecoinfrastructure up the façades of the towers. South-facing green walls rise to green roofs, helping to create a landscaped continuum from the site's southern boundary. This continuous planted ramp helps remove warm, polluted air (and carbon monoxide) from subground levels, supplementing mechanical systems required to reduce ambient temperature in the summer.

FACING PAGE
Zorlu Masterplan

ABOVE AND RIGHT
Vertical linkage of land-scape from wall to roof

Linear Park-in-the-Sky

DESIGN IDEA

A large, vegetated, landscaped recreational space in a high-rise building recreates conditions on the ground and provides communal spaces for interaction in the tower. A linear park connection allows continuous linkages between plantings in the tower that engenders a healthier ecosystem.

The Linear Park-in-the-sky is a solution to provide a park in a high-rise built form, not as a series of landscaped skycourts but as a vegetated ramp that is a linear, continuous ecological armature at the built form's façade, connecting the greenery at the ground plane to greenery at the upper floors and roof gardens.

The linear park's connection enables a continuous ecological linkage between the plantings at the ground plane with those in the tower. The continuity of the landscaping is a key characteristic in ecological design, as it permits unrestricted movement of species between vegetated areas. This encourages an increase in overall biodiversity and contributes to the overall health of the habitat.

The linear park assists in balancing the biotic and abiotic content of a building. It is not just a singular linear strip, but can open out into a skycourt or terrace whenever the vegetated ramp reaches a corner of the building, enabling interaction with the users of internal spaces in the tower and functioning aesthetically as punctuation to its linearity.

The Linear Park-in-the-sky is an essential constituent in the endeavour to reconfigure the skyscraper's built form and to design high-rise typology as cities-in-the-sky. The conventional principles of urban design, essentially formulated for the horizontal plane, here are inverted in a vertical context and condition. This approach of designing the high-rise as a form of vertical urbanism provides a new and novel basis for redesigning the high-rise built form, thereby enabling new avenues to recreate the high-rise built form and make it into a more diverse, pleasurable and humane built environment for its occupants and inhabitants.

The Linear Park-in-the-sky concept, with its concentration of shading plants, is one part of a comprehensive strategy to cool a building's façade and thereby reduce its air-conditioning energy load. In temperate and cold climates, the linear park needs to be encased, whether partially or totally (e.g., via glazed walkways or casements), so that species can survive over extreme climatic periods.

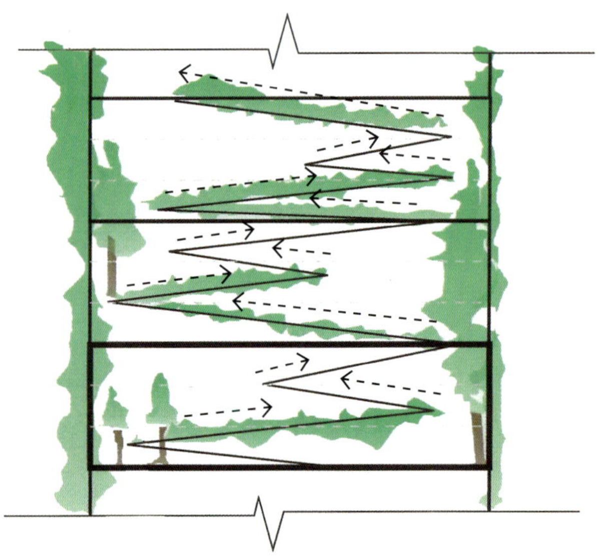

RIGHT
Concept sketch

EDITT Tower

Continuous landscaped ramp
'Sky forest'
Skybridge

Apartment
Office
Condominum
Condominum
Office tower elevations
Sections

FACING PAGE
Ecologically function, communal green spaces and parks and parks that create the experience of living within an 'urban forest'.

LEFT
Shenzhen Garden City

BELOW
Elevations and sections of Shenzhen Garden City

EDITT TOWER

The EDITT Tower was designed as the entry for a competition organised by the Urban Redevelopment Authority of Singapore and the National University of Singapore for a mixed-use, multi-storey cultural, leisure and multi-media complex in the city's entertainment district on a site near the National Library. With this tower, which won second place in the design competition, Yeang demonstrated his early approach to ecological tower design. This 26-storey tower has a site area of 838 square metres and a plot ratio of 1:7. Roughly half the surface of the EDITT tower was designed to be covered with a vegetative blanket. The passive architecture also allows for ample natural internal ventilation. Yeang sees the EDITT tower as a model for eco-friendly tower design in the tropics. 'EDITT Tower is a project where we wanted to exemplify all our ideas in a single building', Yeang told CNN in 2007. In EDITT Tower, street-level vegetation spirals upwards as a continuous ecosystem, facilitating species migration, engendering a more diverse ecosystem and greater ecosystem stability and facilitating ambient cooling of the façades.

FUNCTIONS & INTENTIONS

We need to reinvent the tall building type as a 'city-in-the-sky', a high-rise vertical structure analogous to a city's urbanism, complete with public realms in-the-sky and resplendent with the types of parks and gardens that we find in green cities and precincts. We need to recreate what we find biophilically and physically pleasurable and vital in green spaces in our urban life within the tall building's built form.

The idea of the vertical linear park is the provision of a parkland-in-the-sky placed within the skyscraper. This is in the form of a continuous, linear, walkable ramp, and adjoining it is a continuous landscaped zone that has an ecological nexus, with the greenery at the ground plane rising upwards on the façade and joining with all of its green skycourts and roof gardens, in aggregate becoming a park of interconnected green spaces.

Morphologically, the tall building is a huge volume of built-up space sited on a small land footprint. In many tall buildings the area of built-up space can exceed several hectares, yet most of these tall buildings today are nothing more than series of homogenous concrete floor plates repeated like trays stacked on top of each other, often for only a single use, although occasionally with alternate applications. It is this homogeneity that gives the high-rise its bad reputation, demeaning and monotonous structures for its users and dwellers.

In rethinking the tall building typology, we need to design for 'vertical urbanism'. Tall buildings will no longer be simply architectural designs dominated by expedient efficient structural engineering, but 'vertical urban designs'.

By this, we mean that we need to take all of those vital and pleasurable aspects of urban design that are conventionally crucial at the horizontal plane and transpose these onto the vertical dimension as a framework of urbanity 'in-the-sky'. Accompanying this vertical urbanism is the idea of 'vertical landscaping', which in its ideal condition brings greenery and landscaping that we find in the ground plane upwards in the skyscraper, biologically balancing the physical abiotic constituents of the human-made structure with organic biotic constituents, together working as a whole, as a 'constructed ecosystem'.

Besides creating parks and green spaces in the tall building's built form, all those essential aspects of urban design, such as place-making, creating of the public realm and figure-ground relationships, designing the 'spaces between buildings', creating communities, public and private accessibility systems, ecological landscaping, and vistas, will now need to be reconsidered vertically – the design challenge becomes place-making in the sky.

Take, for example, place-making. Vertically considered, the concept of place-making in the sky immediately conjures up new opportunities not previously considered when designing tall buildings. Thus, by looking at a tall building with a vertical urban design and vertical landscaping lens, what we see emerging are new ways for designing tall building typologies, new design opportunities within a vertical approach to urban design.

Why tall buildings? Well, there are only a few ways to accommodate urban growth – one way is to expand a city's limits sideways by extending city boundaries outwards, which sometimes means building on arable land, thereby reducing food production opportunities. If not arable land, this could mean building on greenfield or on forested or vegetated land. This could easily lead to a loss of biodiversity, an

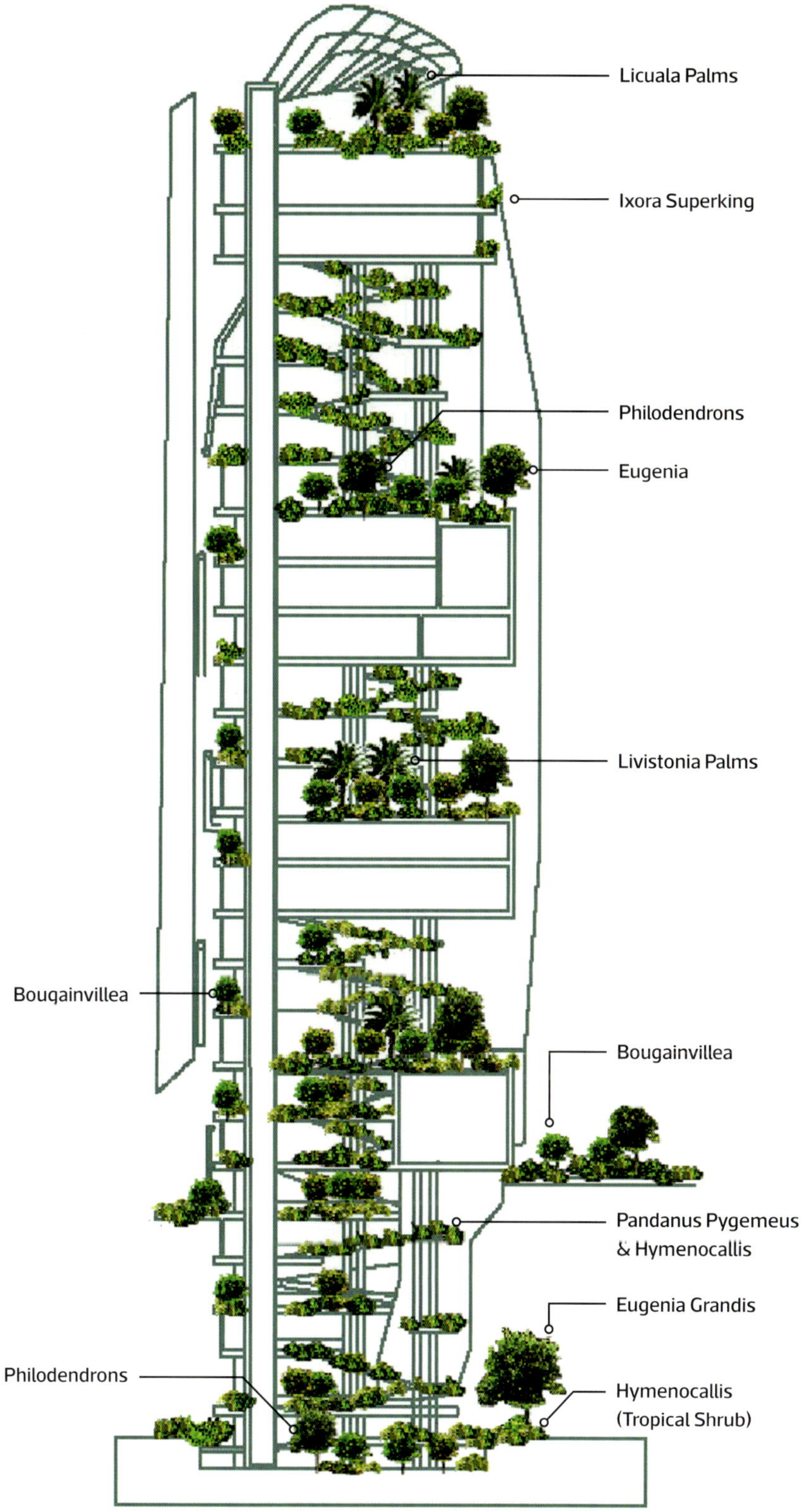

Usable area= 6,032.29 m^2
Planted area= 3,841.34 m^2
= 63% of surface
area vegetated

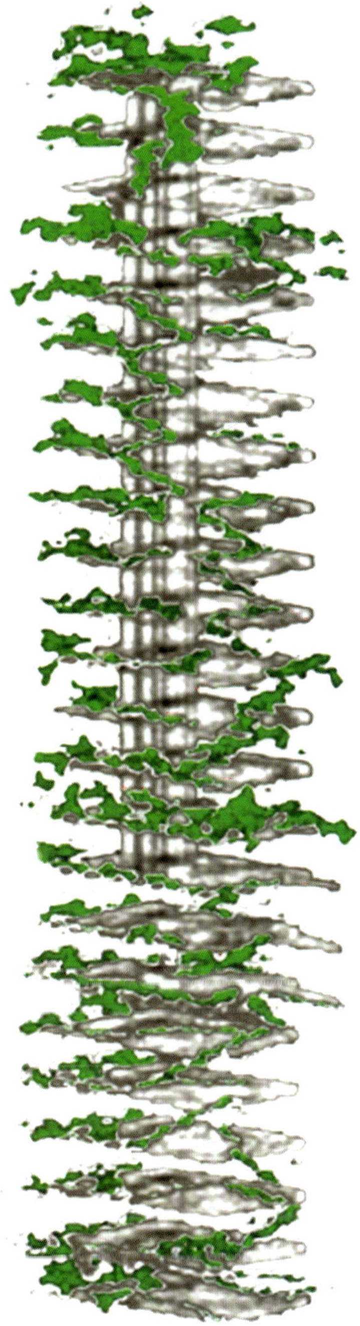

LEFT
Planting concept to reintroduce organic mass to an urban site to counterbalance the inorganic nature of the site.

ABOVE
Ecological connectivity

increase in the overall heat island effect, and an increase in urban temperature.

The second way to accommodate urban growth is by building new satellite cities away from metropolises. This option requires satellite cities to be linked to a metropolis via motorways or a rapid mass-transit system. This incurs high energy transporation costs, an increase in the use of energy resources (essentially fossil fuels), and attendant increases in carbon emissions.

The third approach, and by far the most commonly adopted as it does not entail high initial capital costs, is to optimise land use within a city's existent boundaries, building on brownfield sites within city limits and intensifying existing land use in areas that are found to be sustainably justifiable, such as above public transportation hubs.

In most instances, cities tend to opt for the third approach, which, via the process of intensification, leads to the tall building type. With continued city growth, high land prices, and owner egos, the tall building type is likely to be with us for a while.

To ensure that the intensification of urban land use remains a sustainable endeavor, intensification should occur over or near transportation hubs in order to reduce the energy costs of transportation, generally a significant consumer of energy and a large contributor to urban pollution and carbon emissions. Concurrent with land-use intensification must be a concerted effort to retrofit the city's existing built stock, utilities, and landscaping.

Moving these concepts to reality is not such a huge task, and one that would not be difficult for architects and planners to implement. It requires a change in both the design profession's mindset to rethink the tall building type as a vertical urban design, as opposed to previous conventional mehtods.

Designing tall buildings as vertical urban designs requires neither new construction or engineering technologies; these are already existent. Architects and engineers just need to rethink the way they engineer and construct in relation to the reconfigured design. What is crucial is to use the latest cleantech systems, eco-engineering systems that are low in embodied energy and are carbon neutral, and construction systems that facilitate disassembly for material reuse and recycling.

For cities that are already densely populated by skyscrapers and have a scarcity of hinterland, such as those in Singapore or Hong Kong, we should look at alternative ways of adapting existent vertical built forms, intensifying and linking them horizontally at upper levels, better utilizing the spaces between them, or utilizing air space over existent roads and motorways.

Of greater importance to designing sustainable and green buildings is the retrofitting of our huge existing stock of buildings to make our existing cites green and ecological. This does not mean widespread demolishing and rebuilding, but careful retrofitting and insertion.

Challenges in making tall buildings a part of the solution for sustainable urban growth has to do with finding efficient and rapid ways to make existing cites green, such as implementing green transportation systems, converting current systems into renewable energy systems, ensuring the efficiency of closed-cycle water management systems, implementing city-wide sustainable urban drainage, providing an ecological nexus of greenways across the city's urbanscape that links with the hinterland's natural landscape, developing a network of localised food production, the reduction of urban pollution and reduction of waste via city-wide recycling, etc. There are, of course, other physical design issues in the new intensive vertical city, such as multiple vertical land uses, enabling privacy in high-rises, the creation of liveable high-rise communities, and addressing adequate fire, health, and safety issues vertically. Concurrent with the aforementioned, we need new planning legislation to create new, compact ecocities, three-dimensional urban design matrices of multiple spaces, functions, and landscaping.

RIGHT
Ground-level view of EDITT Tower with skycourts clearly visible

SOLARIS, FUSIONOPOLIS, SINGAPORE

Designed in late 2008, the Solaris building is one of Yeang's greenest buildings to date, although some unbuilt schemes (and some in design at the time of this writing) promise to be greener still. What is especially significant, though, is that the client, the Assistant CEO of a landholding group, specified a very green building from the outset, reversing the conventional scenario in which the architect persuades the client to build a sustainable project. Yeang was actively sought out by the project's lead architect, CPG Consultants, to work as the 'architect of design'. The building lies within the 30-hectare Fusionopolis development, situated to the west of Singapore's Central Business District. The most prominent ecological feature of the Solaris building is the 1.5-km-long linear park that begins within a basement-level ecocell and rises upwards, wrapping itself around the building in a continuous fashion that makes it the world's longest vertically spiralling vegetated ramp. Here, though, unlike the ramp within the EDITT project, the landscaped planters are accompanied by a parallel path, turning the ramp into an accessible park and facilitating service of the greenery. Recessed into the façade, the ramp fulfils a number of functions: it shades, cools and insulates the building while providing a social amenity and enhancing biodiversity. Where the ramp meets a building corner, it opens out to become a terrace while sunshades above lift up to enable the growth of larger trees and admit extra sunlight. These vegetated spaces (ramp, terraces and roof gardens) therefore provide social space for inhabitants while performing very real sustainable functions.

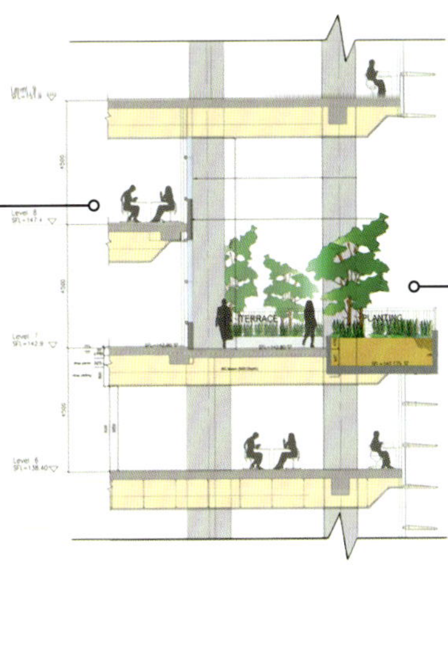

FACING PAGE
Sky terraces as social spaces

ABOVE
Corner landscaped terrace

LEFT
Typical cross-section

ABOVE
Shading plants is one part of a comprehensive strategy for cooling buildings

FACING PAGE
Ground-level view

GYEONG-GI COMPLEX, SEOUL, SOUTH KOREA

Yeang's competition entry for the Gyeong-Gi Complex, located outside of the city of Seoul, includes the design of a masterplan and a pair of two key buildings - a 58-storey tower for central government use and an 8-storey provincial headquarters building. The Architect of Record for this project was Beyond Space Partners. Design teams were asked to draw up proposals for a site that had been cleared of all flora, fauna and topsoil. 'There was nothing of the earlier ecology left on the land', says Yeang, who responded by re-imagining the site as hosting a rich and

View from interior
shown on facing page

LEFT
Masterplan showing habitats

FACING PAGE
Aerial view

diverse ecology, including a tower containing a 'vertical forest'. The site's ecology is recreated via a matrix of viable habitats and species, matching ecologies with the potential of green roofs, green walls, skycourts, ecobridges and a range of landscapes. The masterplan introduced forestry not only to the landscape but within the buildings themselves through the creation of extremely large skycourts embedded into the tower forms. This vegetation also sits atop the roof of the Provincial Council building and links to a park on the far side of an adjacent road via an ecobridge. Green areas within the built form comprise 47 percent of the total site area.

The forested Park-in-the-sky contains automated shutters that close over the colder months, turning these areas into heated winter gardens. These Parks-in-the-sky are partially opened during middle seasons (spring and autumn) and become fully exposed in summer months, echoing the façade treatment of the Plaza of Nations complex designed for Vancouver. 'This design is an advancement of my earlier vertical ecoinfrastructure concepts. Here, the design goes beyond the addition of indigenous landscaping and greenery', says Yeang. 'It sets out to create a variety of new natural habitats within the development and relates these habitats to endemic species, which were identified following research on the area's flora and fauna. Working with the ecological landscape firm Biodiversity by Design (UK), we have also set out biodiversity targets to be achieved over the life of the development, signifying a new level for green design.'

Central promenade as public space

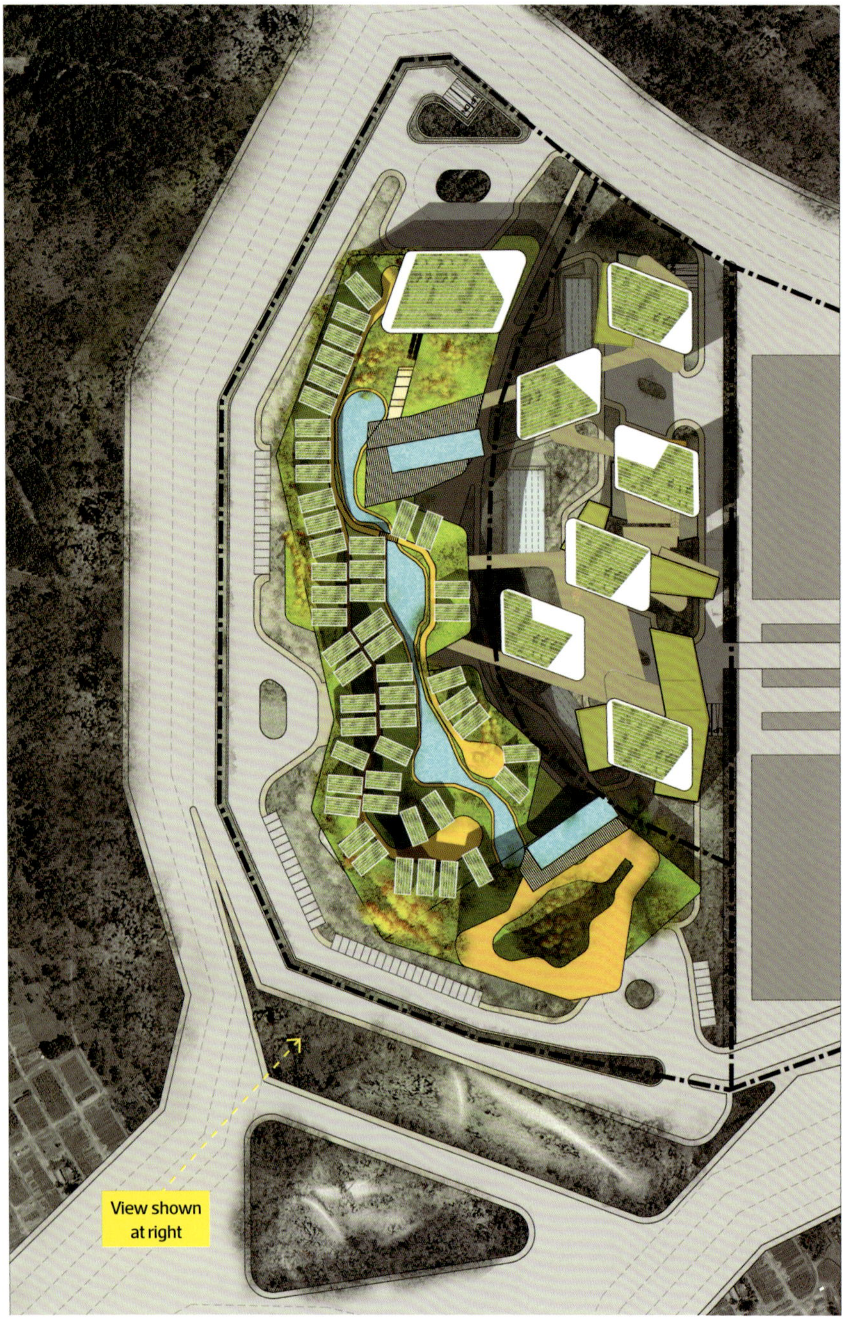

ABOVE
Roof plan of 'PG City'

RIGHT
Ecological nexus and connection from ground plane to the upper horizontal surfaces, facades and roof

Green terrace
Continuous water feature
from roof to ground
Rooftop garden
Buildings in the Park
PGCM

Green Ecoinfrastructure

DESIGN IDEA

Green ecoinfrastructure is essentially an interconnected network of natural areas and open spaces within a site that links to networks outside it. It enables conservation of natural features and characteristics within the site, maintenance of connectivity and an ecological nexus between habitats and retention of the ecosystem's integrity and functions. Further, it serves to sustain clean air and water, to create a greater habitat for sharing resources among species and to provide channels for species movement and interaction, as well as a wide array of other development opportunities for flora and fauna. This green infrastructure occupies the site, providing an ecological framework and nexus across its entirety and retaining links to surrounding greenbelts and habitats. Within this nexus are other green functions, such as local agro-food production.

BELOW
Concept sketch

BOTTOM
Habitats and green connectivity

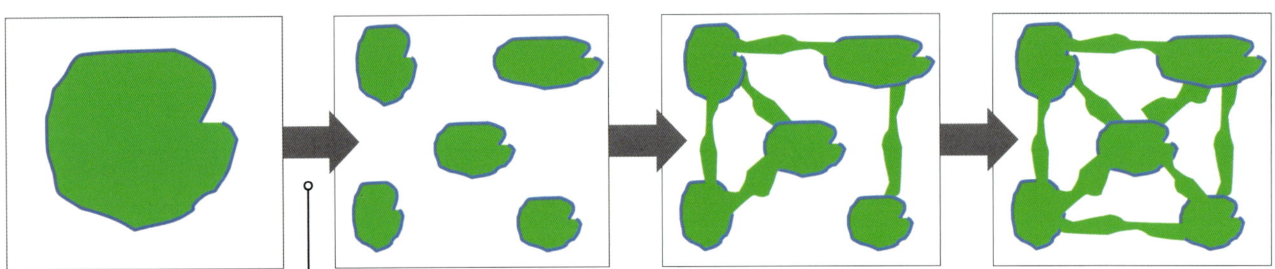

SPIRE EDGE, MANESAR, INDIA

Spire Edge is an office tower standing as an iconic landmark on a new IT park located in Manesar, Gurgaon, India. This tower has a site area of 4,765 square metres and a plot ratio of 1:4.7. The tower is a 21-storey building accommodating offices, an auditorium, a gallery and other facilities. The key design feature of the iconic tower is continuous green ecoinfrastructure at the north façade ascending up the tower via green ramps from the basement, infusing with ecological and social terraces and gardens before coming back down the rear façade via a series of ramps situated around a meeting room. The greenery is brought up to the roof garden by a series of vertical landscaping systems: vegetated green walls, green planter ramps with a pedestrian walkway and a series of sky terraces. The south façade of the building also has a green ramp that brings pedestrians and vegetation from the ground all the way up to a lush roof garden located at the top of the iconic tower that connects to the north façade's green ecoinfrastructure.

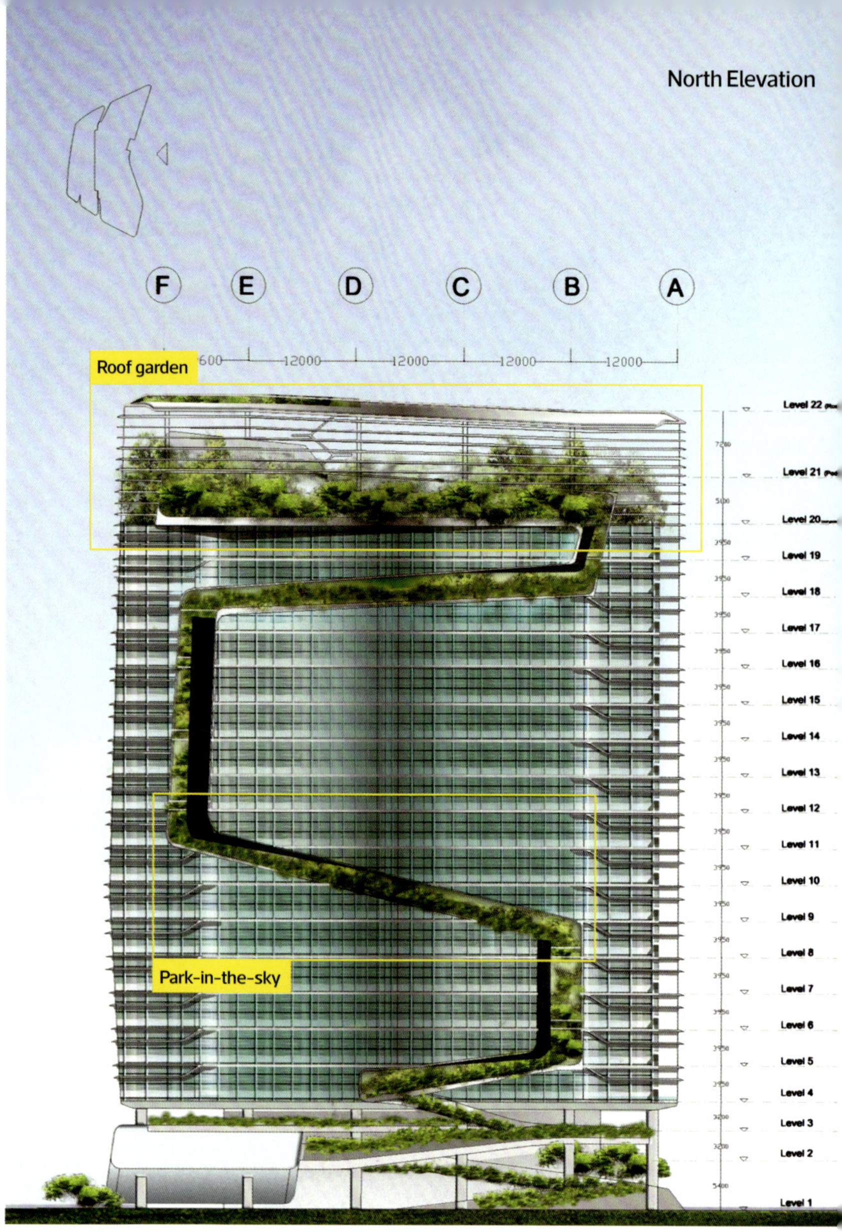

FUNCTIONS & INTENTIONS

Urbanisation, especially over the last several decades worldwide, has led to the denaturing of urban environments in many of our cities and suburbs. Urban construction displaces the ecology of the land by deleting and simplifying its ecological systems and replacing the natural environment with synthetic, artificial, inorganic structures such as buildings, basements, roads, impervious surfaces, paving, drains, bridges, transportation tracks and systems and technological products. We might contend that should this denuding and resurfacing of the land continue unabated, the surfaces of the earth suitable for human habitation will eventually be significantly covered with hardscapes and impervious material. We need to reverse this increasingly artificial synthesizing of our existent natural environment.

The clearing of the natural environment for urban development and the removal of entire ecosystems lead to the loss of fauna, flora, biodiversity and vital ecological processes and all of their existent biotic life, which provide essential and crucial ecological services for humans, including ecological water-related services that contribute to human society's health, livelihood and well-being.

For our densely urbanized areas where natural systems have been removed, we need to reverse this denaturing by extensively restoring, rehabilitating and safeguarding existent urban environments with new greenery. Urban greening involves, particularly in public realms such as streets, squares and plazas, via the creation of new large and small 'pocket' parks,

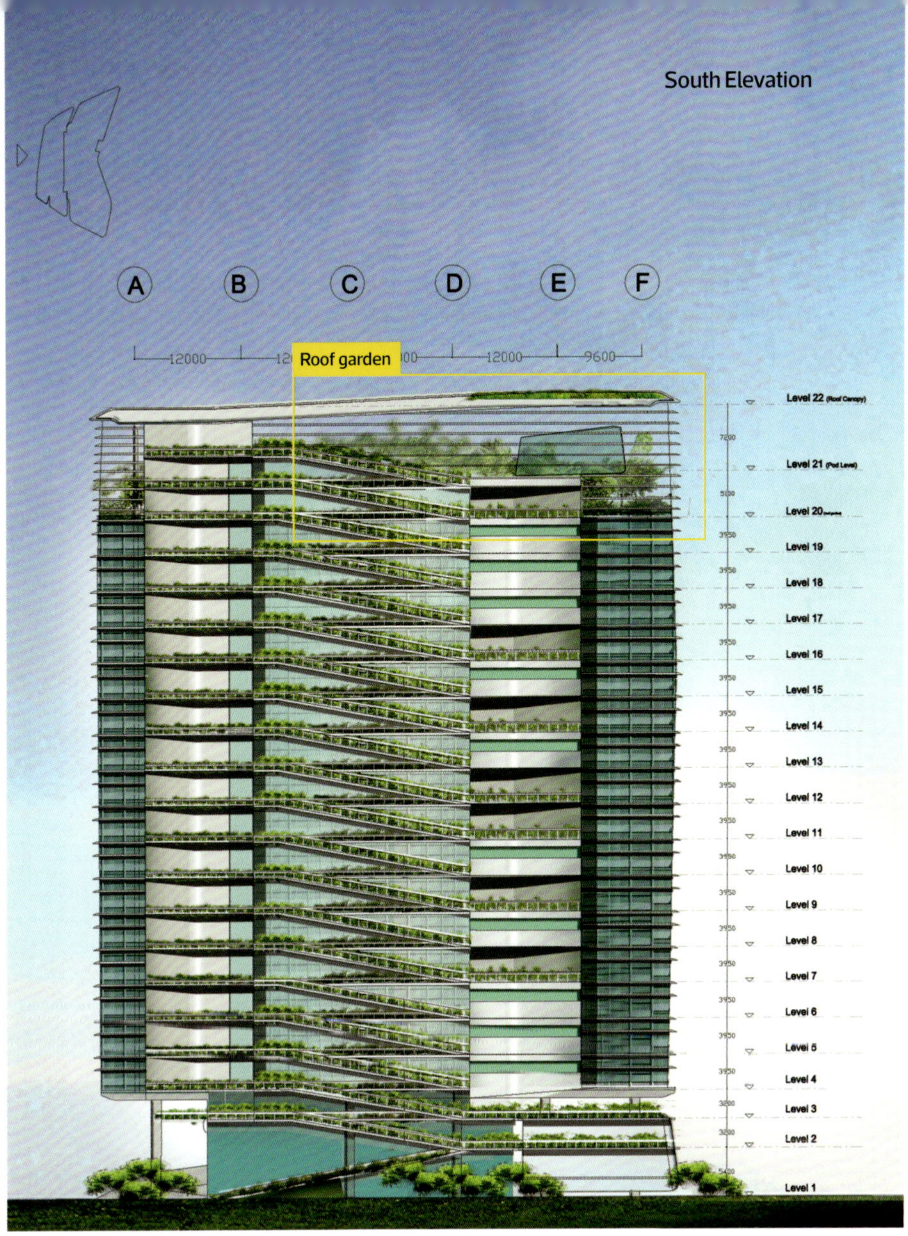

greening of the edges of natural features within the city such as waterways and the addition of multifunctional green ecoinfrastructures that string together and link new and existent parks and green areas; where these infrastructures are interrupted, whether by roads, highways, drains or railways, the intersections are to be addressed with 'ecobridges' and 'ecoundercrofts' to altogether create larger interconnected green realms and corridors. Such greening endeavours contribute to the adaptation and reduction of the effects of global climate change.

Designing for a sustainable, biodiverse urban environment in our cities has to be the most compelling issue facing the planning and design of cities and urban areas today. Our cities are growing increasingly dense, and outside cities we find large tracts of rural land (particularly in the developing world) being callously cleared for urban expansion and road networks, which are burgeoning and becoming more congested and polluted. These, along with other environmental issues, must concern not just our design profession but the entire building industry as a whole. Greening is, of course, not the sole focus of design. In architectural design, we need to address a multitude of factors, where the green criterion is only one of many. However, where economics has the upper hand, green design remains a tenuous imperative. However, from nature's point of view it is the most important and vital, as the sustainment of the health of our planet is in question.

In architectural design, key factors are function, aesthetic, liveability and standards. The first criterion that architectural design must address is function, in which a work of architecture must function effectively. By this we mean that our design must perform excellently with regard to its intended purposes, for example, in terms of circulation (internally and externally), the disposition of its spaces and activities, being environmentally compliant and comfortable, fulfilling the client or promoter's requirements (addressing symbolic functions, meeting enclosural functions, enabling effective marketing, enhancing investment value, etc.) and fitting contextually in the landscape or urbanscape. No matter how green the architecture or the city may be, if it does not function well or is simply dysfunctional, then it is useless. The second criterion architecture must meet is aesthetic; it has to be aesthetically fulfilling, and although this is arguably subjective we need to design with

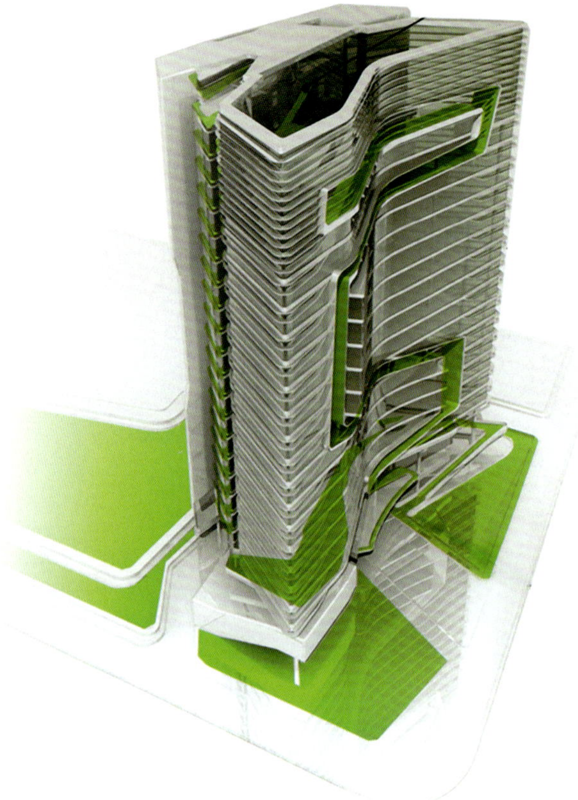

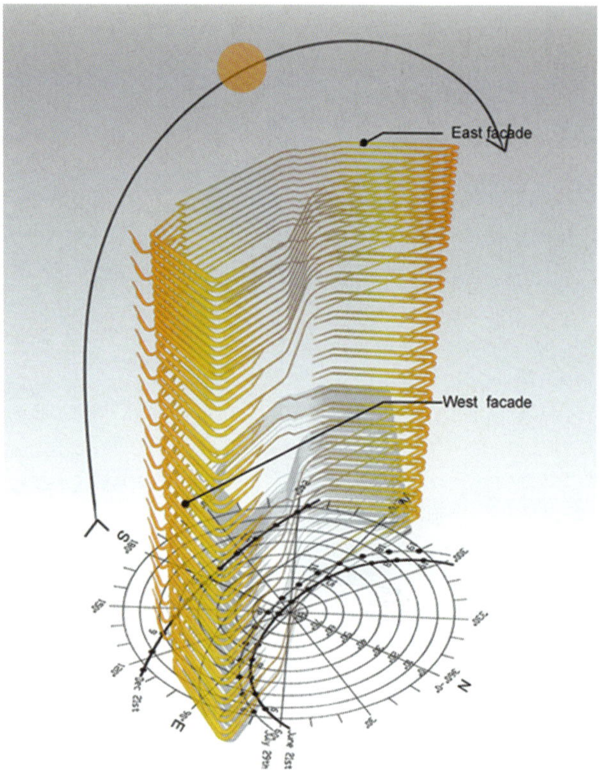

an artist's eye, endeavouring to make the architecture as beautiful as possible. In terms of green design, the aesthetics of the green building or green masterplan are yet to be universally defined. Many buildings that contend to be green are just ugly. The third criterion that architecture must address is liveability; it must make the people who use the building (its users, dwellers and the public) immensely happy and pleased. A green building must uplift and enhance the physical and emotional well-being of those who use it. This is, after all, the fundamental purpose and power of architecture – engendering a positive impact on people's emotions and behaviour. Finally, the fourth criterion that architecture must meet is compliance with usual standards and, in such an instance, being authentically green is one of the standards to be met. Other standards include the need for architecture to remain under budget, to be of high quality (without waste and unnecessary articulation) and to meet local approving authority requirements.

Green design can be regarded as designing to harmoniously biointegrate our built environment with the landscape, water, air and ecology of the land, the natural environment in totality. It is the present dislocation of our human-built environment and activities with the natural environment that is the cause of environmental impairment. Restoring the ecology of our urban environment is much more complex than just planting more. It is not just the physical juxtaposition of inorganic systems and planting. Biointegration must be systemic, seamless and environmentally benign so that in aggregate the environment becomes a living system, functioning as a constructed ecosystem that is well-integrated with nature and its functions, processes and flows, as opposed to remaining an inert system cheek by jowl with the landscape hinterland, still emitting polluting and contaminating discharges. Environmental integration in a benign and seamless way with nature is the key defining function of ecoarchitecture and the ecocity. To function as an integral part of nature, our built environment must no longer be disparate sets of built objects in the landscape separated from nature, but must function like an ecosystem and mimic the attributes, structure and processes of ecosystems and be, in effect, active constituents of nature.

Our current built environment is mostly non-biodegradable and exists within a technosphere in our society,

LEFT
Green link concept

RIGHT
Sunshading strategy

physically disparate from the natural environment. What we have at the moment is a built environment that is a 'through-put' system, in which it takes inorganic, non-biodegradable materials from the planet that are fabricated, transported, used and then thrown away. However, our planet, being a closed system, has no 'away' for us to dispose our used items to. Our used stuff ends up somewhere in the planet, whether in landfills or waterways or incinerated into the atmosphere. Nature has no way to waste; everything in the ecosystem is recycled, and the waste of one organism becomes the food of another. Waste is a human invention. It is this physical dichotomy of the natural with the synthetic, its current non-biointegration with and its disruption of the natural processes and flows in the biosphere, that is the cause of global environmental devastation and climate change. We need to regard all of those used items from our built environment no longer as objects with no value that are to be discarded, but as having reusable and recyclable value, able to be made useful again within our technosphere. These synthetic constituents, hardware and functions of our built environment need to be systemically integrated with the natural landscape's constituents. Our built environment is analogous to biotic constituents in the ecosystem, and for it to function as a constructed ecosystem, it should not be entirely inorganic and synthetic but must structurally have a complementary and appropriate balance of natural, organic constituents, resulting in a holistic system. This, then, is the goal of greening our cities.

Our cities are responsible for integrating our society's economic, industrial, social and ecological activities. To tackle the challenges of climate change and environmental degradation while maintaining social cohesion in a period of rapid global development, we need to create healthy ecologically and socially sustainable urban environments. An approach to designing these could use an indeterminate framework that is defined here as the biointegration of four strands of ecoinfrastructure, colour-coded here as green, blue, grey and red. These are termed ecoinfrastructures because each infrastructure is focused on achieving sustainable objectives that differ from conventional unsustainable infrastructures such as high-energy systems, high water profligacy and inflexible and non-recyclable material usage.

The ecoinfrastructures are:

- The green ecoinfrastructure is the key strand, created along the ecology of the locality. This needs to be an ecological nexus, a continuously linked green infrastructure stretching from the built environment's forms across the landscape to the natural hinterland.
- The blue ecoinfrastructure is essentially the net water system, seeking to close the water-cycle loop in as much as possible through the reuse and recycling of greywater, the natural treatment of black water, rainwater harvesting, sustainable drainage and management of surface-water run-off. Together, the blue and green ecoinfrastructures form the key organisational framework for ecomasterplanning and greening the wider context of the city.
- The grey ecoinfrastructure strand comprises all urban ecoengineering systems necessary for the support and functioning of any human urban development for our contemporary life and its economies. This includes energy systems such as NZEB (Net Zero Energy Built Environment), transportation networks, telecommunication and IT systems and street lighting. The ecoengineering infrastructure must be clean technology, achieving a zero-energy, zero-waste and carbon-neutral built environment without using excessive technologies and thereby having low 'embodied energy'.
- The red ecoinfrastructure strand is our human society, our activities and our accoutrements, including built forms, enclosures, public realms and recreation spaces, pedestrian networks, our society's administrative and legislative systems (governmental, social, economic, industrial, legal, etc.) and our food production and agricultural systems. Achieving successful biointegration of our human society and its activities with the other infrastructural strands demands significant changes to our lifestyles and their systems, including our industrial and economic systems. This would mean a non-wasteful, less profligate, non-consumerist society once our basic requirements for existence have been achieved. Changes include non-wastage of water and materials as well as the closing of all solid, liquid and aerial emission loops. It involves the conservation of non-renewable energy and material resources. It requires changes to the way we move, especially travel by private vehicles, changes to the food that we eat, changes to our industrial production and distribution systems, and requires changing our economies so that they are not based on constantly

FACING PAGE
Green patch shape, edge habitats and interaction

increasing demands, consumption and wastefulness.

Our ecoarchitecture and ecomasterplanning designs must interweave and biointegrate these four ecoinfrastructures (grey, blue, green and red) holistically into a single system, connecting our built environment and its inhabitants seamlessly and benignly with nature. This then defines our strategy for designing ecoarchitecture and the ecocity, as well as the remaking and greening of existent cities and architecture.

Our designing starts, then, with first creating an ecological nexus of continuously connected green strands across the landscape to the natural hinterland, functioning to enhance biodiversity, rectify earlier human-caused fragmentation of existing ecosystems and landscapes and provide ecosystem services where they have been earlier deleted. The ideal ecomasterplan is an interconnected ecosystem, one where wildlife species can traverse across the entire landscape and where habitats remain undisturbed by impervious surfaces, roadways, drains and buildings.

Greening our cities means mimicking the biological structures of ecosystems so that our abiotic constituents are adequately balanced with a crucial extent of biotic constituents. The greater the intensity of our urban environment and its synthetic urban mass, the denser the extent of balancing needed by appropriate biotic constituents.

This addition of biotic content to a designed built form or existing cityscapes should not be just the simplistic addition of more greenery or the extensive planting of trees, shrubs and groundcover, but must be directed and guided by an ecological analysis of the region and locality and the establishment of existing and potential habitat areas, leading to the selection of appropriate native and endemic species of faunal life that need to be brought back to the locality, whether for feeding, breeding or refuge, and the selection of appropriate flora species that will attract these fauna. These species lists then become biodiversity targets to be achieved by designing appropriate landscape planting conditions that will enable the survival of the fauna and floral over the entire year (and its seasons where applicable, depending on the locality's climatic zone). By achieving these biodiversity targets, the entire built environment becomes, in effect, an active, living system, as opposed to a conventional system where the built environment serves as simply a passive receptacle for landscape planting and species selection is often based on ornamental criteria.

The benefit of green ecoinfrastructures to a city's inhabitants is the enabling of a softer and more biophilic environment that enhances their well-being. Biophilia refers to the connections that humans subconsciously seek with the rest of life, where natural love for life helps sustain life. The benefit is a healthier urban environment where vegetation is used to improve external and internal air quality, resulting in improved productivity in working environments. Presently, 3 million people worldwide die prematurely from poor air quality (compared to 1 million deaths from car accidents). China and India have the highest health costs due to air pollution, 12% and 8% of their GDP respectively.

Most of the megacities in the developing world are operating at only 90% productivity due to poor air quality. The planting that we would introduce in ecoinfrastructures could create a healthier microclimate for the city's inhabitants. When plants transpire water vapour from their leaves, they pull air down around their roots; this supplies their root microbes with oxygen. The root microbes also convert other substances in the air, such as toxic chemicals, into food and energy. In the event of the presence of chemical contaminants, microbes such as bacteria can rapidly adapt by producing new colonies that are resistant to the chemicals. As a result, they become more effective at converting toxic chemicals into food the longer they are exposed to those chemicals. It is also important to be aware that the efficiency of plants as filtering devices increases as the concentration of chemicals in the air increases – for example, the removal rate of a chemical is much higher when exposed to 7 parts per million (ppm) than 2 ppm.

The densification of planting in our cities will reduce the urban heat-island effect, especially in localities with hot climates or during hot seasons, thereby lowering the city's ambient temperature. Vegetation improves urban microclimates and outdoor thermal comfort in urban spaces in hot climates. The main benefits of planting are reduced solar radiation and lowered air temperature due to shading and evapotranspiration (c. +/-2°C). These cooling effects increase with the number of plants – studies have shown that an increased amount of urban greening

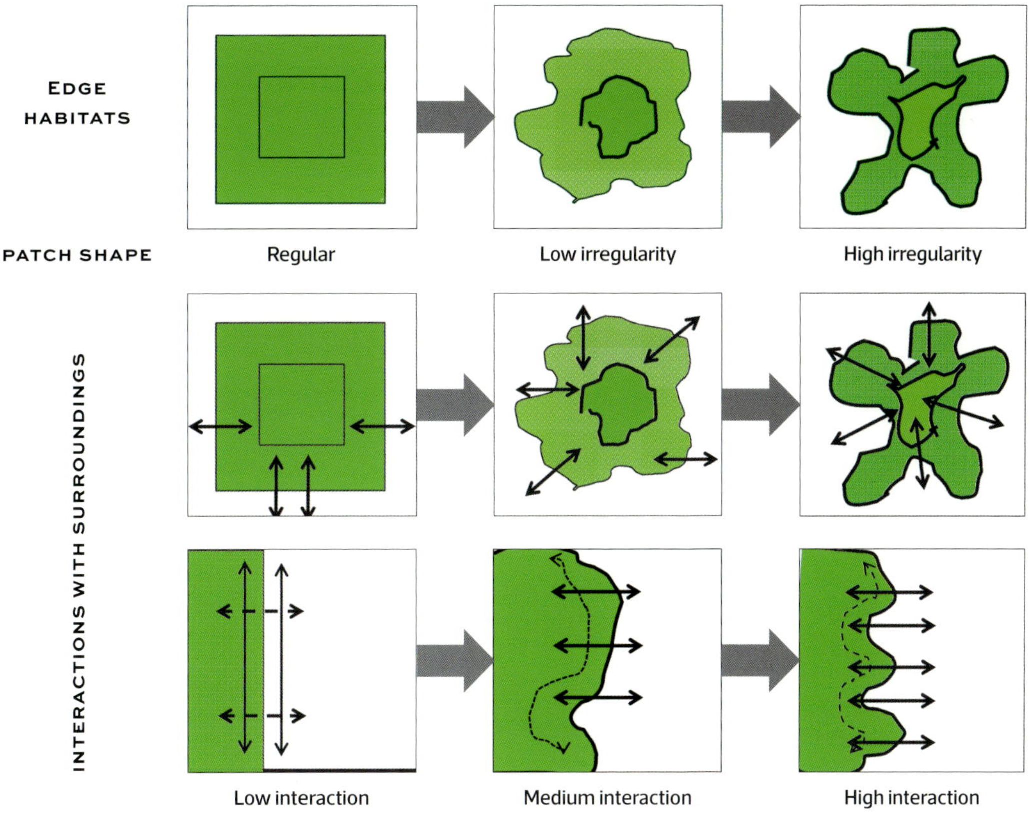

(e.g., trees covering 30% of the ground plane and 100% of green roofs) could approximate the comfortable conditions of a natural forest.

Greening, besides lowering air temperature and essentially improving the thermal comfort conditions of pedestrians, also reduces the energy required to cool buildings. Studies have shown that the Physiologically Equivalent Temperature (PET) decreases with an increase in leaf area, at least up to a Leaf Area Index (LAI) of 5 m^2. Extensively greening a city at specific key localities enhances species biodiversity, avoiding ecological simplification and bringing back species to the city that had previously been intensively urbanized or eradicated. Urban landscaping can serve to conserve, enhance and create new wildlife habitats within the city. Green ecoinfrastructure can repair the ecology of landscapes with increased ecological nexuses, especially landscapes that have been fragmented by human activities and previously constructed urban infrastructures. If we are able to achieve a series of green ecoinfrastructural nexuses across all our cities, throughout our new built developments and over existing urban and rural landscapes, we would have created an increasingly stable ecological realm dedicated to the enhancement of biodiversity. This connectivity is crucial for ecoinfrastructure, as it enables a greater pool of linked natural resources to be shared by the flora and fauna as well as greater species interaction and mobility, leading to greater ecological biodiversity and stability across the cityscape.

Green ecoinfrastructure as a system of linkages should also connect isolated green areas to public parks and other extensive green spaces. This greenway system encompasses extensions and connections of riversides, roads, streets and parks to vertical planting in the city's built forms. This ecoinfrastructure as a 'greenway park connector' then provides the primary key armature for integrating other ecoinfrastructures to achieve successful green design.

In the greening of our cities, and in enabling them to function as 'constructed ecosystems', the other functions and attributes of ecosystems also need to be mimicked. These include reusing and recycling materials within the built environment or technosphere, utilizing net zero waste systems, redirecting energy usage to renewable sources through the NZEB (Net Zero Energy Built Environment), reducing water throughput via closed water systems, reducing carbon emissions through carbon-neutral systems, reducing construction left-overs, and redirecting the built environment's operational solid outputs and end-of-use materials to landfills.

Described here, then, is a strategy for greening our existent dense built environments and cities to become ecoarchitecture and ecocities.

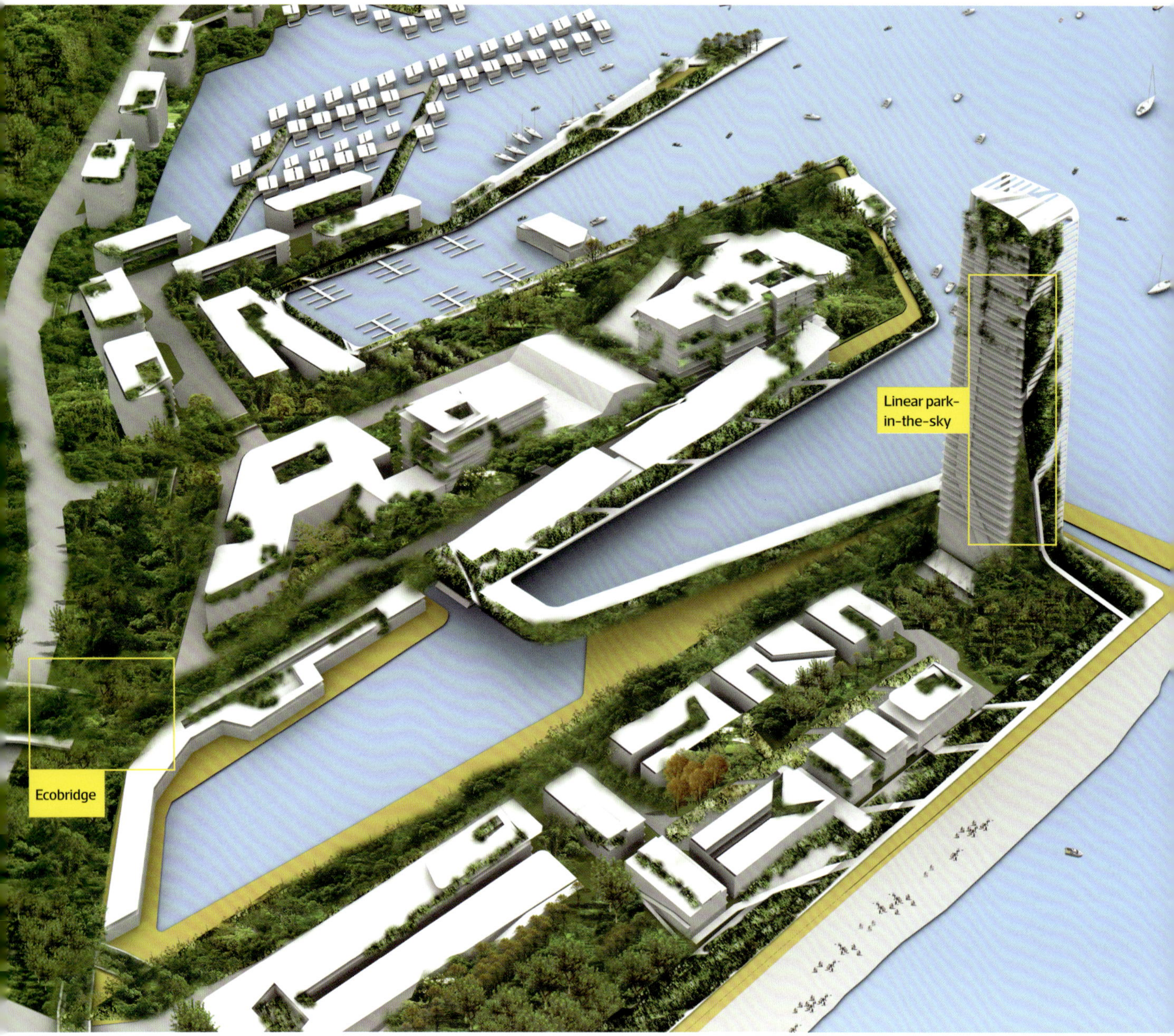

MACAU WATERFRONT, MACAU, CHINA

Known as Project Icon, the Macau Waterfront masterplan envisions the reclamation of three slender fingers of land in Hac Sa Bay as an opportunity to reimagine the possibilities of the urban waterfront as a source of both public pleasure and ecological integration. A major part of the design strategy of this development is its ecological corridor. It is a part of a network of vegetation that forms a central spine down the length of the entire site and physically links the existing ecology of the area's pristine forests to that of proposed reclaimed land. Through a series of green bridges, the ecological corridor allows uninterrupted migration of flora and fauna over roads and into the newly designed parks and green spaces of Project Icon, encouraging species diversity and thereby contributing to a more stable ecosystem. The vegetative sprawl continues from the horizontal plane to the vertical face of the buildings. The ecological corridor also forms a greenbelt that links waterfront activities with commercial, retail, residential, cultural and recreational community spaces.

FACING PAGE
Masterplan laid out as a series of 'fingers'

RIGHT
The continuous ecological corridor spanning the masterplan

SOMA, BANGALORE, INDIA

SOMA is an iconic project designed to harmonize with Vashtu Shastra principles, successfully introducing an ecological corridor that weaves across the 86.75 acres of Rajarajeshwari Nagar. Located in the hot, humid tropics of Bangalore, this site features agricultural land that has become fallow and is to be converted into developed land to accommodate urban growth.

Abutting the land is a forested green reserve that runs all the way down the site's west boundary. This boundary edge forms the springboard for the new green infrastructure, which stretches east across the entire site with connected strands and empty voids in-between, like a linear strip of sticky dough that has been pulled sideways. This green pattern takes the form of new wildlife corridors that straddle the land as a continuous ecological nexus.

ABOVE
SOMA Land Use Plan

FACING PAGE
Continuous ecological nexus

Continuous green ramps
Ecobridge
Green park
Ecobridge

Jahnkassim P.S. & Abkr, Yousif, (2015) The Ganendra Art House – Airflow Performance of a Wind Chimney in the Tropics. Building and Environment, Elsevier, (in progress).

Hart, Sara, (2011) Ecoarchitecture : The work of Ken Yeang. John Wiley & Sons, Ltd. (UK)

Richards Ivor, (2011) T. R. Hamzah & Yeang : Ecology of the Sky, The Images Publishing Group Pty Ltd, Australia

Yeang, Ken (2009) Ken Yeang : Eco Masterplanning. John Wiley & Sons, Ltd. (UK)

Leon Van Schaik, (2009) Vertical Ecoinfrastructure : The Images Publishing Group Pty Ltd, Australia

Chan Chee Hong, (2005) Designing For Thermal Comfort for Housing in Tropical Climate. Undergraduate Dissertation (Civil Engineering) Universiti Teknologi Malaysia.

S.Ahmed, S.Abduli and A. Zain-Ahmad (2005), The Ventilation Performance of a Solar-Powered Attic Fan in Malaysia Climate. Proceedings of the Conference of Sustainable Building in South East. April 11-13.2005, p.470-476

D.Harimi, M.Harimi, V.J.Kurian, N.Bulong, I.Zakaria and I.Gungat. (2005) Evaluation of Thermal Performance of Concerete Tile Under Tropical Climate Condition. Proceedings of Conference of Sustainable Building in South East. April 11-13. p. 447-453

Francois Garde, Leatitia Adelard, H.Boyer and C.Rat. (2004), The Implementation and experimental survey of passive design specifications used in new low-cost housing under tropical climates, Energy and buildings. 2004, 36(4): p.353-366

Jahnkassim, PS (2004), The bioclimatic skyscraper – A critical analysis of the theories and designs of Ken Yeang, Unpublished PhD thesis, University of Brighton

Leon Van Schaik, (2003) Ecocells: Landscapes & Masterplans by Hamzah & Yeang. Wiley-Academy, a division of John Wiley & Sons Ltd. (UK)

Bay, Joo Hwa Phillip, (2001) Three Tropical design paradigms. in Tzonis, Alexander, Le faivre, Lliane (eds.), Tropical Architecture – Critical Regionalism in the Age of globalisation, Wiley Academy.

Zulkifli Ismail, (2001) Post occupancy studies of Roof-Roof House. Final year thesis. B.Arch Universiti Teknologi Malaysia

Frampton, Kenneth, (2001) Studies in Tectonic Culture, MIT Press, Cambridge, U.S.

Potvin, Andre, (2000) Assessing the microclimate of urban transitional spaces. Proceedings of Architecture, City and Environment, Proceedings of PLEA 2000, University of Cambridge, July, 2000, p.581-586

A Green Vitruvius, (1999) Principles and practice of sustainable architectural design : James and James Science Publishers. London

Tzi, Ling LI, (1999) Inside the bioclimatic skyscraper: A critical analysis. Masters dissertation, National University of Singapore, September

Powell, Robert, (1999) Rethinking the Skyscraper - The complete architecture of Ken Yeang, Thames and Hudson, UK.

Yeang, Ken, (1998) The Malaysian city of the future: some physical planning and urban design ideas. Architecture Malaysia, March/April, 1998. Malaysian Institute of Architect's Journal, Kuala Lumpur, p. 70-75.

Hui Seng Kin, (1998) Natural Ventilation of Low-Cost Dwellings in the Hot Humid Tropics Malaysia. Thesis Sarjana Alam Bina, Universiti Teknologi Malaysia.

Yeang, Ken, (1997) The Skyscraper - Bioclimatically considered: A Design Primer, Academy Group, UK.

Blyth, Alistair, (1995) Towards Sustainable design. Architect's Journal 3 August, 1995.

Yeang, Ken (1994) 'Bioclimatic Skyscrapers' in 'Architecture for a New Nation', by Alan Balfour op. cit. p. 8, UK.

Yeang, Ken, (1994) Bioclimatic Skyscrapers. Artemis Publishers, UK.

Zulkifli Yusoff, (1993) Kajian Prestasi Termal Terhadap Konsep Penyaring Linkungan Rumah Bumbung Bumbung Ken Yeang. 5th year thesis. Jabatan Senibina, Universiti Teknologi Malaysia

Yeang, Ken, (1992) Designing the Tropical Skyscraper MIMAR. No. 42, March, 1992. Concept Media.

Kheng Soon, Tay, (1990) The architectural aesthetic of tropicality. In Powell, Robert (ed.) , Line, Edge and Shade: The search for a design language in Tropical Asia: Tay Kheng Soon and Arkitek Tenggara, Singapore : Page One Publishing, Singapore

Yeang, Ken, (1989) Urban Design Ideas for the Tropical City. Proceedings of the Seminar Perancangan: Satu Mekanisme Pengurusan Perubahan Persekitaran, 14-15 January 1989, Fakulti Alam Bina, University Teknologi Malaysia, Malaysia.

Ang, B.W., (1989) ASEAN energy demand: current trends and future outlook. Energy. 1989, vol. 14, no. 12, p. 785 -795.

Steemers, Koen, (1989) The performance of external shading devices - Proceedings of the 2nd European conference on Architecture, 4-8 December 1989, Paris, France.

Yeang, Ken, (1987) Tropical Urban Regionalism: Building in a South-East Asian city, MIMAR Publications, Singapore

Yeang, Ken, (1986) Landuse, Climate and Architectural Form. In Design for High-intensity Development: Proceedings of the International Conference on Urban Design, The Aga Khan Programme for Islamic Architecture, USA, p. 75-80

Yeang, Ken, (1985) The Tropical Verandah City. Longman Publishers, Malaysia

Yeang, Ken, (1984) Notes for a critical vernacular in contemporary Malaysian architecture. UIA International Architect, no. 6, 1984. London, p.16-17.

Brandt Commission, (1983) Common Crisis North-south Cooperation for world recovery. Pan Books, London

Yeang, Ken (1982) A theoretical framework for ecological considerations in the design and planning of the built environment. PhD thesis, University of Cambridge.

Yeang, Ken (1981) Notes on regional influences Affecting Design. Proceedings of Seminar ke Arah Identiti Kebangsaan dalam Senibina, 20-23 January. 1981, Kuala Lumpur, Malaysia.

Yeang, Ken, (1981) Regional influences affecting design, Majalah Akitek, no.1, March, 1981. p. 46-48.

Olgyay, Victor, (1963.) Design with Climate: Bioclimatic Approach to Architectural Regionalism. Princeton Architectural Press, UK.

PROJECT INDEX (A–Z)

ACKNOWLEDGEMENTS

I am delighted to acknowledge all those who have freely contributed their help to the publication of this book; in particular to my Co-Authors, Assistant Professor Shireen Jahnkassim and Humaedah Rosly for their relentless commitment and their unflinchingly long hours given to the delivery of the book.

Secondly, I would like to extend my gratitude to Robert Powell for his essay and to our book's design team, (Andy Chong Soon Onn, Kian Soon Jean, Norashikin Hidayah Mohd Nasir, Caleb Ong Yan Weng, Muhammad Izzuddin B. Azhar, Michael Goodwin and Vijai Kumar) for their work on the artwork for the book. My gratitude also goes to my business partner, Tengku Robert Hamzah for providing the environment for the production of this book.

The publication of this book started as an exhibition of our firm's works at the Universiti Putra Malaysia (UPM) and I am delighted to acknowledge those who have contributed towards the mounting of the exhibition; in particular to the Head of the Architecture Department, Prof. Meor Mohammad Fared, Wan Sofiah Dato Haji Wan Ishak with Sumarni Ismail for their effort in coordinating the exhibition, Nasir Baharuddin in curating our exhibition at the Galeri Serdang, and UPM's dedicated staff.

Finally, I would also thank ORO Editions's team; in particular to Gordon Goff, Vikas Kailankaje, Jake Anderson, Evan Morris and Ryan Buresh for their contribution in the book's publication and overseeing its final design. My gratitude also goes to all our former staff who have contributed to the projects in this book.

—Ken Yeang (Kuala Lumpur, 2015)

The authors would like to thank and acknowledge the contribution of Dr Yousif Abkr of University of Nottingham Malaysia on the CFD simulation studies for Ganendra Art House and evaporative cooling studies for the chapter on 'Evaporative Water Cloud Device'. We would also like to thank Prof Dean Hawkes, former Professor at Cardiff University, Prof David Robson of Brighton University, Dr Kenneth Ip of Brighton University and Prof Abdul Razak Sapian of IIUM.

All figures and graphs relating to Mesiniaga, UMNO tower and IBM tower are cited from the simulation studies and research done by Shireen Jahnkassim, 'The Bioclimatic Skyscraper' unpublished Phd thesis, University of Brighton 2004.

— Shireen JahnKassim

IMAGE CREDITS

APPLIED
RESEARCH
+DESIGN
PUBLISHING

Published by Applied Research and Design Publishing.
Gordon Goff: Publisher

www.appliedresearchanddesign.com
info@appliedresearchanddesign.com

10 9 8 7 6 5 4 3 2 1 First Edition

Library of Congress data available upon request.

ISBN: 978-1-940743-15-8

Color Separations and Printing: ORO Group Ltd.
Printed in China.

International Distribution: www.appliedresearchanddesign.com/distribution

AR+D Publishing makes a continuous effort to minimize the overall carbon footprint of its publications. As part of this goal, AR+D Publishing, in association with Global ReLeaf, arranges to plant trees to replace those used in the manufacturing of the paper produced for its books. Global ReLeaf is an international campaign run by American Forests, one of the world's oldest nonprofit conservation organizations. Global ReLeaf is American Forests' education and action program that helps individuals, organizations, agencies, and corporations improve the local and global environment by planting and caring for trees.

AMERICAN FORESTS
Protecting & Restoring Forests